TO BUILD THE CITY OF GOD

Living as Catholics in a Secular Age

Brian M. McCall

TO BUILD THE CITY OF GOD

Living as Catholics in a Secular Age

Foreword by

CHRISTOPHER A. FERRARA

Angelico Press

First published
by Angelico Press, 2014

For information, address:
Angelico Press
4709 Briar Knoll Dr.
Kettering, OH 45429
angelicopress.com

978-1-62138-073-3

Cover image: Detail from Jan van Eyck:
The Ghent altarpiece: *Adoration of the Lamb*, 1432
Cover design: Michael Schrauzer

Acknowledgments

Earlier versions of many parts of the chapters contained herein first appeared as articles in *The Remnant Newspaper*, *Catholic Family News*, and *Latin Mass Magazine*. I am grateful to these publications for first publishing this work. Other parts of the book are based on lectures I gave at the Roman Forum in Gardone, Italy, and at the Angelus Press Conference in Kansas City. I am grateful to the Roman Forum and Dr. John Rao and Angelus Press for having invited me to give these lectures and for helping to develop my thoughts on these matters.

⊕

To the only legacy I will leave behind that really matters, and that I will leave to live in the City of God, my children: Cormack James Patrick, Mary Catherine Joan, Thomas Emmanuel Pius Benedict George, Joseph Hillarie Edmund Bede Anthony, Michael Robert Hugh Wilfred, and Mare Bernadette Katherine Therese

CONTENTS

Foreword

CHRISTOPHER A. FERRARA

CONTEMPORARY political discourse is as uninteresting as it is unavailing: an endless debate between parties who all agree that ours is a secular age in which Christianity has been privatized and that it must remain so. Having agreed on that sociopolitical status quo, the disputants are essentially contending over exactly how, and how quickly, our once Christian civilization should be lowered into its grave. Liberals, of course, explicitly insist upon the secular status quo, but so do conservatives and libertarians implicitly, despite all their appeals to "moral values" (without prescinding from what the majority wills respecting divorce, contraception, abortion, pornography or any other vice), the common good (understood only as the sum total of the free pursuit of private goods, whatever they might be), and even Christian ethics (but only at the level of "private" morality).

Consequently, the conservative's polemic against the governments that oppress us never strays beyond the boundaries of permissible political thought, within which his every utterance of protest serves only to confirm his prison. The conservative looks upon the very bars of his cell—government by "consent of the governed," meaning majority will—as the only means of escape. Even the most radical libertarian, with his talk of secession, "nullification" and the "stateless society," merely rattles the bars of his own cell, proposing to throw open the doors while remaining inside the four walls of the prison of post-Christian secularity within which he expects the "spontaneous order" of "anarcho-capitalism" to flourish and the State to wither away as in the dreams of Marxists. But what he really proposes is a prison riot that will be put down by force, just as modern "republican governments" were established by force in bloody rebellions against altar and throne. The Civil War is perhaps history's most dramatic example of how secessionists from a government born in revolutionary violence—the United States—engaged in revolutionary violence themselves in order to establish and maintain a virtual replica of that government—the Confederate States—until they lost a contest of wills that claimed more than 700,000 hapless lives on both sides.

Both the conservative and the libertarian fail to recognize that by every historical measure they are liberals of the sort that emerged with the "moderate" Enlightenment and its overthrow of what was once Christendom. The conservative appeals to a "tradition" born in a revolt against Christendom, while the libertarian views himself as a daringly independent thinker who has discarded "the 3 x 5 card of approved opinion,"[1] when in fact his own liberal prescriptions for liberal ills are found on a 4 x 6 card of approved opinion from which such forbidden ideas as the need to restore the Christian commonwealth under the law of the Gospel have been stricken in keeping with the dictates of political correctness. Neither the contemporary conservative nor the libertarian sees that he is an obedient child of revolution, dutifully appealing to revolutionary principles against the intractable ills of a revolutionary age.

In discussing contemporary man's failure to understand the origin of the civilizational crisis in which we find ourselves, Christopher Dawson observed in 1952 that "behind the modern demagogue and dictator there stands the ghost of some forgotten metaphysician."[2] This is a more literary way of expressing Richard Weaver's famous dictum, four years earlier, that "ideas have consequences."[3] Contemporary conservatives and libertarians alike would view with utter incomprehension Weaver's lamentation of the final consequences of such things as "the victory of Occam over Aquinas."[4] But the revolutions of the 18th century giving rise to our *novus ordo*

1. Thomas Woods, "3 x 5 Card of Approved Opinion Strikes Catholic Blog," January 22, 2013, http://tomwoods.com/blog/3x5-card-of-approved-opinion-strikes-catholic-blog/.

2. Christopher Dawson, *Understanding Europe* (Garden City, NY: Image Books, 1960), 174.

3. Richard Weaver, *Ideas Have Consequences* (Chicago: University of Chicago Press, 1984 [1948]).

4. Ibid., 150.

seclorum would not have been possible without a prior revolution in philosophy from roughly 1637 to 1738: the period between the publication of Descartes' *Discourse on the Method* (1637) and Hume's *A Treatise of Human Nature* (1738). Between those two works on the shelf of modern philosophy are, of course, those of Hobbes, Spinoza, Locke, Bayle, Voltaire, and assorted other divines of the so-called Enlightenment. The one aim uniting them all, long since achieved, was announced triumphantly by Spinoza in his *Theologico-Political Treatise* (1670): that theology be "once for all separated from philosophy."[5] In the 19th century no one understood the catastrophe represented by this separation better than the great Catholic counter-revolutionary Don Juan Donoso Cortes: "Theology, being the science of God, is the ocean which contains all the sciences, as God is the ocean in which all things are contained."[6] With philosophy's separation from theology, reason suffered the fate of a fish out of water; and with the death of what the Church calls "right reason" the unaided reason of the Enlightenment *philosophes* ushered in that triumph of the will whose monument is the modern state system.

Now we live in what the French political philosopher Pierre Manent has aptly described as "the age of separations"[7] in which every human endeavor has confidently declared its separation from the revealed truths of theology: the State from the Church, politics from religion, economics from the Gospel, the empirical sciences from Christian ethics, education from Christian formation, and so forth. The holistic vision of the Christian centuries in which all elements of human society were ordered to the highest good—eternal beatitude—has been replaced by a vast collection of social departments, each with its own "autonomous" function contributing to the overall deterioration of a body politic that no longer has a principle of homeostasis, a State that no longer has a soul. With no spir-

5. Spinoza, *Theologico-Political Treatise*, title to Chapter XIV.

6. Don Juan Donoso Cortes, *Essay on Catholicism, Authority and Order* (Joseph F. Wagner: New York, 1925), p. 1.

7. Pierre Manent, *The City of Man* (Princeton: Princeton University Press, 1998), 82.

itual center to hold them all together, things have fallen apart. Likening our situation to that of the Roman Empire at the moment of its fall, Pope Benedict XVI sounded nothing less than the death knell of our civilization: "moral consensus is collapsing, consensus without which juridical and political structures cannot function. Consequently, the forces mobilized for the defense of such structures seem doomed to failure. . . . *The very future of the world is at stake.*"[8]

In this book, the rising Catholic scholar Brian McCall has assembled a collection of essays written around a central theme: the absolute urgency of reestablishing the primacy of theological truth, especially the truths of moral theology, in the political, economic, and domestic orders of society. What is required for this immense task is what has always been required, but was cast aside by Western man during the age of democratic revolution: the social teaching of the Catholic Church, which presents a radical critique of the political, economic, social, and moral errors of our time, arising from Western man's rejection of what the Church calls "the Social Kingship" of Christ.

These pages, accordingly, contain a little feast of thought not to be found on either the 3 x 6 or the 4 x 6 card of approved opinion. Among many forbidden thoughts to be found here:

• that government is not a mere revocable "compact" between ruler and subject based on the "consent of the governed" and majority rule, but rather a human exercise of authority that ultimately derives from God and is thus subject to the duties and limitations imposed by His law (ensuring the true liberty of the subject against majoritarian tyranny);

• that the State ought once again to be morally united with the Church (without prejudice to the respective competencies of the two powers);

• that "the market process" does not invariably produce justice, but more often than not produces institutionalized injustice (no

8. Benedict XVI, Christmas Greeting to the Roman Curia, December 20, 2010.

argument for socialism, but rather for private property and the pursuit of gain moderated by Christian morality, especially the Gospel's injunctions against usury, overreaching in business, and the peddling of vice and corruption);

• that the very survival of society depends upon the hierarchical ordering of the family united by Holy Matrimony with the husband at its head, the wife in due (but certainly not abject) submission to his authority, and the children subject to the authority of their parents.

There is even a defense of monarchy, which will elicit instinctive howls of derision from those who fail to see that such "Chief Executives" as the President of the United States are nothing but elective monarchs whose absurdly vast powers, including the power to destroy the whole world, are unbound by any of the limits to which the mere Christian king was subject.

McCall's approach is not only an *ad extra* presentation of Catholic social teaching in a hostile secular age. He also addresses a problem *ad intra*: the rejection of that teaching by *Catholics*, including "Catholic libertarians" and sitting Catholic members of the Supreme Court. This development reflects what the great Dietrich von Hildebrand observed in 1973, shortly after the Second Vatican Council: "the poison of our epoch is slowly seeping into the Church herself, and many have failed to see the apocalyptic decline of our time."[9] Here McCall confronts a problem identified as early as 1922 in a landmark encyclical by Pope Pius XI, *Ubi Arcano Dei* (1922)—the problem of "social modernism" in the Church:

> Many believe in or claim that they believe in and hold fast to Catholic doctrine on such questions as social authority, the right of owning private property, on the relations between capital and labor, on the rights of the laboring man, on the relations between Church and State, religion and country, on the relations between the different social classes, on international relations, on the rights of the Holy See and the prerogatives of the Roman Pontiff and the Episcopate, on the social rights of Jesus Christ, Who is the Creator,

9. Dietrich von Hildebrand, *The Devastated Vineyard* (Chicago: Franciscan Herald Press, 1973), 75.

> Redeemer, and Lord not only of individuals but of nations. In spite of these protestations, they speak, write, and, what is more, act as if it were not necessary any longer to follow, or that they did not remain still in full force, the teachings and solemn pronouncements which may be found in so many documents of the Holy See, and particularly in those written by Leo XIII, Pius X, and Benedict XV.
>
> There is a species of moral, legal, and social modernism which We condemn, no less decidedly than We condemn theological modernism.[10]

In sum, what McCall defends in these essays, with admirable clarity and intellectual courage, is the Church's defiant *No* to the claims of political modernity, whose movers and shakers hail the triumphs of Liberty ever more loudly as "human society is tottering to its fall, because it has no longer a secure and solid foundation," to quote another of Pius XI's prophetic encyclicals.[11] In that encyclical, *Quas Primas*, Pius expounded to the world's jeers the Social Kingship doctrine whose implications Professor McCall here explores. That today the jeers come from social modernists within the Church as well as her overt enemies without is a sign of the times that bears out Pope Benedict's warning about the future of our world, and thus the great burden Catholics like Brian McCall must shoulder in defense of truths the itching ears of their own Catholic contemporaries no longer wish to hear. Professor McCall's burden may be the burden of Dumah,[12] but the night watchman knows that morning will come and that he must proclaim the morning against the night.

10. Pius XI, *Ubi Arcano Dei* (1922), nn. 60–61.
11. Pius XI, *Quas Primas* (1925), n. 18.
12. Cf. Isaias 21:11–12.

Introduction

MARCUS TULLIUS CICERO and St. Augustine are two of the most significant authors of the ancient Roman world. The former, a pagan, appears at the beginning of the Roman imperial era, with its transition from the ancient republic to the empire. The latter, a Father of the Church, appeared at the end of the Roman imperial era when the old pagan empire was being transformed into chaos by passing through the disorder of barbarism and darkness. These two great men of the Western tradition surveyed the landscape of the Roman Empire and identified the issues facing ancient Rome at the beginning and end of its imperial age.

Cicero, a politician hailing from the nobility of Rome, penned two significant works on the nature of civil society: *On the Commonwealth* and *On the Laws.* In these related works, Cicero explores the philosophical, juridical, and political foundations of civil society and its government. Cicero defined a commonwealth as "the concern of a people, but a people is not any group of men assembled in any way, but an assemblage of some size associated with one another through agreement on law and community of interest."[1] This definition includes three critical elements: (1) a collection of people of some minimal number, (2) an agreement on law, and (3) a common interest. The phrase translated as "agreement on law" is the rich Latin phrase *consensu juris. Juris* comes from the Latin *jus*, a rich polyvalent term possessing a penumbra of meanings beyond the simple English word "law."[2] The range of meanings *jus* embodies includes "law, justice, right, rights, procedures of justice, just

1. Marcus Tullius Cicero, "On the Commonwealth," in *On the Commonwealth and On the Laws*, ed. James E.G. Zetzel (Cambridge, MA: Cambridge Univ. Press, 1999), 18.

2. See Kenneth Pennington, "Lex Naturalis and Ius Naturale," *The Jurist* 68 (2008): 569, 573.

behavior, court, regulations, power, authority."[3] *Jus* also has the "connotation of 'justice'—that is, the broader principles of equity or morality which a legal system is supposed to embody." This rich word is distinguished from the Latin word *lex*, also rendered in English as "law," but with a more specific meaning than *jus*. It refers merely to written rules adopted by a constitutionally approved legislative authority. Thus, when Cicero requires for the existence of a true commonwealth a consensus on *jus*, he is referring to a much more entrenched consensus than a mere agreement on specific laws of a polity. The term *jus* implies a deeper consensus on justice itself. Such a consensus embodies an agreement on the very nature and purpose of law and its relation to right, equity, and justice.

For Cicero this fundamental consensus on *jus* is established not by the mere opinions of men coinciding: "[W]e are born for justice and . . . justice is established *not by opinion but by nature*."[4] This consensus is not something that shifts with the opinions of men but is constituted by nature. The consensus is a given, not a product of human consensus building. Cicero is not so naïve as to think that every person will always agree with the natural consensus on justice. "That is impossible," he says.[5] First principles need to be "well considered and carefully examined" not because all the populace will accept them "but so that they [first principles] will have the approval of those who believe that all right and honorable things are desirable on their own account, and that either nothing at all should be considered good unless it is praiseworthy in itself or at least that nothing should be considered a great good except what can truly be praised on its own account."[6] In other words, a consensus of men does not make first principles good, but rather the intrinsic goodness of first principles should produce a consensus about them.

Cicero admits there will be some plurality of opinions on the nature of the core principles of law and justice. Yet, notwithstanding

3. Cicero, "Text and translation," in *On the Commonwealth and On the Laws*, xxxvi, xl.

4. Cicero, "On the Laws," 115.

5. Ibid., 118.

6. Ibid., 118–19.

some disagreement, to remain a commonwealth, there must be an approval of first principles as desirable "on their own account" and not because of an agreement of opinion.[7] Political authority must go about on the basis of this consensus "making commonwealths sound, establishing justice and making all people healthy."[8] Without such a sharing of core principles of justice, a commonwealth of laws is not possible.

Our American commonwealth, in many ways consciously modeled on the ancient Roman republic, moves ever farther along a path of rejecting the wisdom of Cicero. In place of a deep consensus on *jus*, our society seeks a deep consensus on liberty, and specifically a liberty that prevents a deep consensus on *jus*. We live in what Dr. Thaddeus Kozinski has called "deep pluralism," a system where intractable disputes over first principles and world views is seen as a positive good and a firm foundation of civil and political life.[9] If Cicero's definition is correct, then an American commonwealth rooted in deep pluralism cannot survive as a commonwealth. Perhaps then the crisis of civil society we are experiencing is the death throes of our commonwealth much as St. Augustine witnessed the death throes of the Roman Empire, which could not survive as a juxtaposition of pagan and Christian first principles. This concern will guide our examination of the crisis in civil society witnessed at the dawn of the third millennium. This liberty, which has asserted itself as a replacement for perennial principles of truth, goodness, and beauty, manifests itself in political, social, and economic life. Thus we will survey the crisis in all these spheres. Economics appears to have become *the* shared interest of the American multitude, replacing religion. We will deal with the reverberations of liberty in the realm of economics. As we examine the myriad political, social, and economic concerns and crises of our time, we will explore the ancient and universal principles which explain the causes of and offer a way out of these crises.

7. See ibid.

8. Ibid.

9. Thaddeus J. Kozinski, *The Political Problem of Religious Pluralism: And Why Philosophers Can't Solve It* (New York: Lexington Books, 2010).

To survey the crises of the commonwealth we must understand the outlines of its architecture. Saint Thomas, writing in the Aristotelian tradition, explains the composition of the commonwealth, or perfect community. Communities can be either perfect[10] or imperfect.[11] A perfect community possesses both the perfect or most complete end as well as the complete means of attaining such an end.[12] In a word, the perfect community is completely self-sufficient.[13] A community which aims at a complete common good rather than a limited particular good and thus incorporates the goods of all lesser communities is this perfect community.[14] The nation or commonwealth[15] is a perfect community because it pursues the ultimate end—human happiness—and is self-sufficient in the means to attain that end.[16] The perfect community is comprised

10. In this context, "perfect" is used in a precise sense to mean complete or fulfilled and not necessarily good or virtuous. See Wladyslaw Tatarkiewicz, "Paradoxes of Perfection," *Dialectics & Humanism* 1 (1980): 77, 78 (contrasting the Aristotelian notion of perfection as "complete," "finished," or "flawless" with a paradoxical view of perfection as "ceaseless improvement").

11. Francisco Suarez, *Selection from Three Works*, ed. James Brown, vol. 2 (Cambridge: Clarendon Press, 1944), 86.

12. See ibid., 86–87; St. Thomas Aquinas, "De Regno," in *Aquinas: Selected Political Writings*, ed. A. P. d'Entrèves, trans. J.G. Dawson (1948), pt. I, bk. 1, ch. 2. http://dhspriory.org/thomas/DeRegno.htm; Nicholas Aroney, "Subsidiarity, Federalism, and the Best Constitution: Aquinas on City, Province, and Empire," *Law and Philosophy* 26 (2007): 161–228, 174–77.

13. Suárez, *Selection*, 86.

14. Aristotle, *Politics*, in *Commentary on Aristotle's Politics*, trans. Richard J. Regan (Indianapolis: Hackett Pub. Co., 2007), 4 ("And the association that is supreme and includes all other associations is the absolutely supreme good").

15. The name of this perfect community varies from age to age and author to author. Aristotle referred to the *polis* or "city-state." Aroney, "Subsidiarity," 170. Aquinas varyingly refers to the perfect community as the *civitas* (city), *regnum* (kingdom), and *provincia* (province); ibid., no. 34. Suárez uses the term *civitas* when referring to Aristotle's perfect community. See Suárez, *Selection*, 37. The translators use the word "state" for *civitas* in this passage. Ibid., 86. In the modern context, I have chosen the word "commonwealth" or "nation" as most approximating the concept of the *polis* in Aristotle's time because it lacks the negative modern connotations of the word "state."

16. Aristotle, *Politics*, 5 ("And the perfect association . . . is the political community, now complete, having a self-sufficient end. . . . Therefore, the political community was instituted for the sake of protecting life and exists to promote the good

of a variety of different imperfect communities, such as families, households, villages, etc.[17] Each of these associations shares a particular common end, but each is only to some extent self-sufficient.[18] The family's purpose is to provide the basic nourishments of life for one household and the begetting of children.[19] The village[20] aims at the necessities for a particular trade or profession. Families and other imperfect communities are insufficient either to provide all that is needed for human life or to attain all necessary knowledge.[21] The perfect community, city, or province has the aim of achieving all the necessities of human life and defense against external danger.[22] Each imperfect community aims for an aspect of the complete good but does not encompass all of that complete good, the good life, or human happiness; they are parts of a

life"); "[Aristotle] shows that the good to which the political community is directed is the supreme human good." Saint Thomas Aquinas, *Commentary on Aristotle's Politics*, trans. Richard J. Regan (Indianapolis: Hackett Pub. Co., 2007), 7. "[I]t follows that a communal society is the more perfect to the extent that it is sufficient in providing for life's necessities." Aquinas, "De Regno," pt. I, bk. I, ch. I.

17. See Aristotle, *Politics*, 5 (showing how the union of men and women combine to form households, and households combine to form villages, and villages unite to form the political community); see also ibid., 2 (stating that "since there are indeed different grades and orders of these associations, the ultimate association is the political community directed to the things self-sufficient for human life"). Aristotle continues by proposing "the true relation of other associations to the political community.... First, he explains the association of one person to another. Second, he explains the association of the household, which includes different associations of persons. Third, he explains the association of the village, which includes many households." Saint Thomas Aquinas, *Commentary*, 4; Aquinas, "De Regno," 9 (containing the same list of family, household, and city).

18. See Aquinas, "De Regno," 9.

19. Ibid.

20. The term *vicus*, translated "village," has an economic overtone more than the modern word "neighborhood" or "village," as can be seen when Aquinas says that a village is self-sufficient with respect to "a particular trade or calling." Ibid. Elsewhere, Aquinas refers to the fact that in many medieval towns, streets or sections of a town were divided on the basis of occupation, as evidenced when he says "in one [*vicus*] smiths practice their craft, in another of which weavers practice theirs." Aquinas, *Commentary*, 15.

21. Suárez, *Selection*, 365, relying on Aristotle's argument of sufficiency in *Politics*.

22. Aquinas, "De Regno," 9.

whole.[23] The end of a perfect community is called the common good because it corresponds to the good or end of the common nature of the component parts of the heterogeneous whole rather than to the aggregate of individual ends or goods.[24] Thus any examination of the state of the commonwealth must consider it both as a whole and its component parts, the most fundamental unit of which is the family, or as Aristotle would call it, the household. For this reason the state of economics is critically important, since the original meaning of the term is household management. Economics is the study of the connection between the family unit and the larger commonwealth.

Saint Augustine recognized that Cicero only saw part of the reality of life in this world, at least since the Incarnation. Within, yet distinct and separate from, the City of Man—the commonwealth—grows the City of God. The Church is at one and the same time a separate commonwealth of a portion of men—those who have been adopted through baptism—but also coterminous with the commonwealth. Although the City of God and the commonwealth pursue different ends, since they possess joint jurisdiction over the same subjects, who live in both realms, their fate is inter-related. "[I]n this present world [the two cities are] commingled, and as it were entangled together."[25] The old pagan Roman Empire could not survive in a state of conflict with the City of God. Saint Augustine observed the final days of its life. A new civilization was being born in its place, a civilization which sought to integrate the City of God and the commonwealth in opposition to the City of Man at war with the City of God. The goal of Christendom was to found the consensus on *jus* on a synthesis of the truths of natural philosophy known through the

23. Aquinas, *Commentary*, 7 (stating that "an association is a whole, and wholes are ordered so that one that includes another is superior. . . . And the association that includes other associations is likewise superior. But the political community clearly includes all other associations, since households and villages are included in the political community").

24. Henri Grenier, *Thomistic Philosophy: Vol. 4, Moral Philosophy* (Charlottetown, Prince Edward Island: St. Dunstan's University, 1950), 358.

25. St. Augustine, *City of God*, Bk. XI, ch. 1. http://www.newadvent.org/fathers/1201.htm.

Greco-Roman tradition and the principles of Christianity.[26] Like Augustine we stand on the crumbling ruins of this civilization. Its founding consensus built on the harmony of the commonwealth and the Church could not survive an invasion by the City of Man begun in the Renaissance and the Reformation. Wielding the sword of false liberty, or license, the forces of the City of Man infiltrated and started the dismantling of the great synthesis. The crises we see all around and within us—in the family, education, culture, the economy, and politics—are consequences of this breach of the city walls. Like Augustine's *City of God*, this book seeks to survey and diagnose the progress of this decomposition throughout the economy, politics, and society, as well as point the way to what could emerge as a new commonwealth based on the consensus on *jus*.

The method I employ throughout the book is to begin most chapters by exploring the most general and basic principles of politics, economics, and society, and then in subsequent chapters turn to the implications of rejecting these principles in particular circumstances. I am no Cicero nor am I a St. Augustine. I do not pretend to have written a comprehensive treatment of Catholic political, social, economic, and religious thought. I merely try to apply the wisdom of Tradition to our times. All I can do is paraphrase the dying comments of St. Thomas Aquinas and declare that anything written well in this book is not mine but merely borrowed from our intellectual ancestors. Anything mistaken or poorly written is my own.

26. For a detailed account of the story of the building of this synthesis, see John Rao, *Black Legends and the Light of the World: War of the Words and the Incarnate Word* (St. Paul, MN: Remnant Press, 2011).

1

The Natural Relationship of Church and State Within the Kingdom of Christ

Based on the Encyclical *Immortale Dei* of Pope Leo XIII and *Quas Primas* of Pius XI

> *"It is because the reign of Our Lord is no longer the center of attention and of activity for those who are our praepositi, that they lose the sense of God and of the Catholic priesthood, and that we can no longer follow them."* —ARCHBISHOP LEFEBVRE, *Spiritual Journey*

THESE PROFOUND WORDS come from the final testament of his Excellency Abp. Marcel Lefebvre in which he succinctly and keenly diagnoses the crisis in the Church through which we continue to perilously navigate. Although written in the context of the crisis in the Church, I believe these words can equally be applied to the crisis in civil society, a crisis which reverberates through every level of the commonwealth—politics, culture, the economy, and the family. That there is a crisis seems most obvious. Our economy and our government are spiraling out of control. Everywhere we meet dissatisfaction. Reading the general news and the last several national elections will reveal much cynicism and dissatisfaction with the state of our government, economy, and culture. All throughout the world, be it in Libya, Pakistan, Egypt, Iraq, Greece, or Palestine, and now Wall Street, we see massive unrest. What is the ultimate cause? "[T]he reign of Our Lord is no longer the center of attention and of activity." The explicit or implicit denial of Christ's Kingdom is the cause.

The most important implication of Christ's Kingdom is the obligation to profess the true religion and render divine worship to Christ, an obligation muted by *Dignitatis Humanae*. This section will look merely at the political/legal organization of civil society in its natural sphere of operation—for Christ is King not only over the ecclesiastical but also civil society. His Holiness Pope Leo XIII called for the Christian constitution of nations in his encyclical *Immortale Dei*. This requires even more than professing the true religion; it requires the entire constitution of a country to be directed by the principles of Christ's Kingdom.

The Problem with Modern Liberal Government

As he surveyed the state of civil society around him, Leo XIII saw a society in ruins due to what he called a "hackneyed reproach of old."[1] The devil really has nothing new to offer. It is the same false bargain: elevate man to the place of Christ the King. Leo explains this hackneyed approach further:

> Many, indeed, are they who have tried to work out a plan of civil society based on doctrines other than those approved by the Catholic Church. Nay, in these latter days a novel conception of law has begun here and there to gain increase and influence, the outcome, as it is maintained, of an age arrived at full stature, and the result of progressive liberty.[2]

The source of the problem is the rejection of the Church's traditional doctrine on the constitution of civil society. Contrary to the error of liberalism, the Church as the repository of the Truth concerning Man, his nature, and his end does possesses definitive knowledge about the implications of these truths for the organization of civil societies.

The rejection of this truth results in government claiming to be its own source of power, sometimes expressed as power deriving from the people governed, which in practice means the same thing. The so-called divine right of kings falsely asserted in the seventeenth

1. Leo XIII, *Immortale Dei* (Vatican City: Libreria Editrice Vaticana, 1885), no. 2.
2. Ibid.

century and America's manifest destiny to "make the world safe for democracy" both in different ways derive from the rejection of the proper understanding of the nature of the world. Both errors in different ways distort the correct notion of authority descending from God to legitimate rulers of communities. Whether we acknowledge it or not, all authority comes from God, but any particular use of that authority may not come from God depending on how well it corresponds to the divine plan for the universe.[3]

The tyrannical power of an ever-growing state apparatus that we meet in bureaucratic offices, voluminous and penal tax codes, airport security lines, and politically correct "hate crimes" is a result of the unnatural separation of the government of civil society from the Church. We live today with the ruins created by Thomas Jefferson's "wall of separation," which is only a way to escape the Kingship of Christ by walling it off behind this iron curtain.

Just as the true conception of civil society is based on truths about Creation, the false conception of modern liberal society is based on its own false "creation" myths, the mythical state of nature, and the fabricated social contract. This last is the most unusual contract in the history of law. Nobody actually consented to it. There is no record of its contents. There is no way to terminate or abrogate or amend it. Unbelievably, in contrast liberals call the truth of creation a myth! Since liberal society was created in a mythical state of nature by a mythical contract, it has no real foundation and hence no constraints. Since it is simply willed into existence by the rebellion of man against the divine plan for the universe, it logically results in legal positivism, or in the words of the English poet Alexander Pope, "whatever is, is Right."[4] Man is a law unto himself.

The false and oppressive government that reigns today was begotten by false political ideas begotten by a false philosophy (especially a false ontology and metaphysics), which itself was begotten by a false religion. As Leo XIII explains:

3. See Denis Fahey, *The Mystical Body of Christ in the Modern World*, 3rd ed. (Palmdale, CA: Christian Book Club of America, 1994), 14.

4. *An Essay on Man.*

> But that harmful and deplorable passion for innovation which was aroused in the sixteenth century threw first of all into confusionnthe Christian religion, and next, by natural sequence, invaded the precincts of philosophy, whence it spread amongst all classes of society. From this source, as from a fountain-head, burst forth all those later tenets of unbridled license which, in the midst of the terrible upheavals of the last century, were wildly conceived and boldly proclaimed as the principles and foundation of that new conception of law which was not merely previously unknown, but was at variance on many points with not only the Christian, but even the natural law.[5]

As St. Augustine observes in *The City of God* (Bk 19, chap. 25), a city cannot possess true virtue without the true religion. Protestantism turned religion into an individual affair. The autonomous believer had a direct, individual relationship with Christ—acceptance of Christ as personal Lord and Savior. In the ecclesiastical realm this reduced *the* Church to an invisible collection of all these personal churches (each individual and Christ). This philosophy had repercussions in the political sphere. Society was transformed from an association of men united in agreement about what constitutes justice[6] into a mere collection of autonomous free-thinking individuals and an all-powerful State. Just as the personal relationship with Christ needed to be liberated from the authority of the Church, so the individual could dominate the relationship, and so too the state had to be freed from the authority of the Church in order that it could dominate the individual. This wall of separation between spiritual and temporal considerations runs right down the middle of our country and right down the middle of man's nature. His spiritual and temporal aspects are divided by the same wall dividing Church and State. This is exactly the result desired by the philosophy preached by Luther: "Assuredly a prince can be a Christian, but it is not as a Christian that he should govern. As a ruler he is not

5. Leo XIII, *Immortale Dei*, no. 23.

6. Cicero, "On the Commonwealth," I, 39 ("A commonwealth is a constitution of the entire people. The people, however, is not every association of men, however congregated, but the association of the entire number, bound together by the compact of justice, and the communication of utility").

called a Christian, but a prince. The man is Christian but his function does not concern his religion."[7]

The first "Catholic" president of the United States, John F. Kennedy, showed that he learned his Protestant "catechism" well when he merely paraphrased these words in his famous speech in Houston in 1960:

> I believe in an America where the separation of church and state is absolute, where no Catholic prelate would tell the president (should he be Catholic) how to act . . . , where no church or church school is granted any public funds or political preference. . . . Whatever issue may come before me as president—on birth control, divorce, censorship, gambling or any other subject—I will make my decision in accordance with these views, in accordance with what my conscience tells me to be the national interest, and without regard to outside religious pressures or dictates.[8]

The result of this bad religion and bad philosophy, says Leo XIII, is that "the safety of [civil society] is exceedingly imperiled by evil teachings and bad passions."[9] These evil teachings have only spread their errors more since Kennedy's unholy vow was uttered.

The Solution: Catholic Truth

As with the crisis in the Church, the solution to this grave disorder in civil society is the acceptance, once again, of Catholic Truth about the nature of the universe, man, and civil society. The problem is a crisis of ideas at the highest level. False theories of Church and state are based on false theories about man and creation, the state of nature, and the social contract. We thus must go back to the most basic principles of how the world is organized. Christ's Kingdom encompasses all of creation. Like any earthly kingdom, his is a Kingdom ordered by laws written into the very fabric of creation. We will look briefly at how these laws, eternal, natural, divine, and

7. Quoted in Fahey, *The Mystical Body of Christ in the Modern World*, 15.

8. John F. Kennedy, Address to the Greater Houston Ministerial Association, September 12, 1960, Houston, TX. http://www.americanrhetoric.com/speeches/jfkhoustonministers.html.

9. Leo XIII, *Immortale Dei*, no. 49.

human relate to one another and the implications for temporal rulers of civil society.

We know that God is a perfectly ordered Being. He is not the product of random mutation as the evolutionists falsely claim. Since creation is a reflection of God, it too is ordered and hierarchical. God established creation as an ordered kingdom based on a hierarchy of laws. At the summit of this hierarchy is the eternal law, which is nothing other than the divine plan for the universe that establishes the idea or type of every created being.[10] The eternal law fixes the nature of every created being and establishes its particular end or purpose of being. The end of each creature reveals its nature. Man's end comprises two parts. His natural end is that great concept discovered by the use of reason by the ancient philosophers, natural happiness or human flourishing (*Eudaimonia*). Yet the eternal law also endows man with a supernatural end: beatitude or the state of knowing God as he is. These two ends are not of equal value. The supernatural, by definition being on a higher level, is superior to the natural end of human happiness. Thus, the ends of man fixed by the eternal law make man what he is. Only in attaining his true ends can man be what the eternal law requires him to be.

As Leo XIII explains, the fact of this end has implications for the purpose and nature of civil society:

> For one and all are we destined by our birth and adoption to enjoy, when this frail and fleeting life is ended, a supreme and final good in heaven, and to the attainment of this every endeavour should be directed. Since, then, upon this depends the full and perfect happiness of mankind, the securing of this end should be of all imaginable interests the most urgent. Hence, civil society, established for the common welfare, should not only safeguard the well-being of the community, but have also at heart the interests of its individual members, in such mode as not in any way to hinder,

10. St. Thomas Aquinas, *Summa Theologica*, 2nd ed., trans. Fathers of the English Dominican Province (London: Burns, Oates & Washburne, 1920), I–II, Q. 93, art. 1. http://www.newadvent.org/summa/.

but in every manner to render as easy as may be, the possession of that highest and unchangeable good for which all should seek.[11]

Yet this metaphysical truth must be translated into more particular rules of action. It is one thing to know one's end or goal but another to know the actions necessary to attain it. I might know that I must travel to Kansas City to address a conference, but this knowledge is useless unless I have a means—a map, a car, a plane ticket—that can actually get me there.

God has provided the means for every creature to attain its created end. Since the end of different creatures differs, the means differ. God moves all creatures to their end by means appropriate to their nature. For irrational creatures such as animals, their end is attained by instinct, a faculty appropriate to their created nature. But man is a rational creature. God moves man to his end by the use of reason. This means of movement is called the natural law—rational norms of moral action that man is capable of knowing and using to direct all his actions. Saint Thomas calls the natural law nothing other than the participation of man in the eternal law, by which he means that man participates in the eternal law by using his reason to choose the good and avoid the evil and thus attain the end established for man by the eternal law.[12] Lucidus in his submission to the teaching of the Second Council of Arles in 473 calls the Natural Law "the first grace of God" (*per primam Dei gratiam*) and affirmed along with Romans 2:15 that the natural law is "written on every human heart." The natural law is a gift of God, the first grace, to provide man the means to attain his end fixed by the eternal law.

The natural law operates in man by making known to the intellect basic principles of good action: do good, avoid evil, human life should be preserved, human beings should pro-create and educate children, knowledge should be cultivated, and man should live in society (*in societate vivere*).[13] From these principles man can make determinations of good actions in the varying contingent situations in which he finds himself. The principles of the natural law can be

11. Leo XIII, *Immortale Dei*, no. 6.
12. Aquinas, *Summa*, I–II, Q. 91, art. 2.
13. Ibid., I–II, Q. 94, art. 2.

deduced from considering the essence of man. The principles are part of what makes man what he is. Knowledge of them is therefore within the capabilities of all men; they are written on his heart.

Right reason can then determine proper action in light of these deduced principles. By knowingly choosing actions that correspond to the principles of natural law, man participates in the eternal law and can attain his end.

But the rational nature of man does not guarantee successful participation. In fact, failure occurs. The source of failure is the Fall, which affected our ability to use natural law to reach both our natural and supernatural ends. In addition to original sin, individual sin creates patterns of bad behavior which further weaken our ability to reason rightly. In addition to the natural inclinations of natural law written on the heart, man also must contend with urges and appetites and acquired inclinations not ordered to his end. The natural inclinations can be confused with these other feelings or desires. In addition to natural inclination, man also has instincts (in the sense of the sole faculty operative in other animals) and inclinations acquired by habit.[14] Irrational animals cannot be confused about the instincts they have; rational man can.

In the *Summa Theologica*, Aquinas argues that it is impossible for people to attain even their natural end by means of the natural law as a result of this wounding of nature after the Fall.[15] Saint Thomas teaches that all the powers of the soul have been rendered "destitute of their proper order . . . which destitution is called a wounding of nature."[16] In one of his last works, he goes so far as to claim that the natural law has been destroyed (*destructa erat*) in us by the Fall.[17] The wounding manifests itself in different ways. The degree

14. See J. Budziszewski, *The Line through the Heart* (Chicago: ISI Books, 2009), 61–77 (discussing how unnatural inclinations can be acquired and become co-natural).

15. Aquinas, *Summa*, I–II, Q. 109, art. 2 ("But in the state of corrupt nature, man falls short of what he could do by his nature, so that he is unable to fulfill it by his own natural powers").

16. Ibid., I–II., Q. 85, art. 3.

17. Prologue, *The Two Precepts of Charity*, in *Opera Omnia*, ed. Roberto Busa, SJ (Stuttgart: Frommann-Holzboog, 1980), 26 (author's translation).

of difficulty or ease in actually arriving at a correct knowledge of the precepts of the natural law depends on the level of principles at issue. The more general and basic the proposition, the more accessible it is to the human intellect after the Fall. The more remote and particular, the more opportunity exists for errors.[18] Saint Thomas explains "the more we descend into detail," the more uncertainty exists as to conclusions.[19] Thus, the general principles of natural law are universally valid for all men and theoretically knowable by all men, but depending on the level of detail not universally known by all men.[20] Saint Thomas uses the example of the Gauls whom Caesar reported knew it was wrong to steal but thought it was not wrong to steal from foreigners.

The effects of original sin, exacerbated by individual sin, result in our attempt to reason using natural law under a handicap. Since reason is impaired and passions are disordered, we can buttress the use of deductive reason by forming good habits in light of the advice and opinion of the wise. Yet even the wise labor under the same impediments to reason. Thus, the advice of the wise is only as good as the extent to which they have overcome these impediments. Recognizing our plight after the destruction of the natural law in us, Aquinas argues that God saw the need for a legal solution, a different law to counterbalance the law of sin (*fomes peccati*). Immediately after making his startling statement that the law of nature has been destroyed in us, Aquinas continues: "It was necessary for man to be redirected to the works of virtue and turned away from vice, that the law of the Scriptures was necessary."[21] The law of the Scriptures (*lex scripturae*) is the first part of a two-part division of the divine law. Aquinas emphasizes that the divine law is obligatory and necessary for knowing what is good, what the natural law obligates us to do. He uses the word *oportebat* to indicate that it was necessary for the law of the Scriptures to be promulgated for men to attain

18. Aquinas, *Summa*, I–II, Q. 94, art. 4.

19. Ibid.

20. Ibid.

21. Prologue, *The Two Precepts* (author's translation of *oportebat quod homo reduceretur ad operavirtutis, et retraheretur a vitiis: ad quae necessaria erat lex Scripturae*).

virtue. Divine Law is not optional or gratuitous, but necessary for the rational participation in the eternal law, or the natural law. Aquinas drives this point home when he argues that

> [I]t is obvious that all people are not able to persevere in knowledge and therefore a brief summary of the law was given by Christ so that it might be able to be known by all and nobody would be able to be excused of the observation of it [the law] through ignorance.[22]

Aquinas's emphasis on the necessity of the divine law, briefly given by Christ for all people, is striking. He is emphasizing that we cannot persevere[23] in knowing what is right without this additional law. Later, he repeats that human action cannot be "good or right" unless it is harmonized with delight in the divine rules.[24] He repeats that the divine "Law ought to be a rule of all human actions."[25] Both of these passages invoke the very definition of law itself as a rule of human action. This reference to the definition of law indicates that he is speaking of divine law as a real law, and not just speaking metaphorically.

Aquinas maintains that the precepts of divine law encompass all that the natural law obligates us to do, the whole law. "He who observes the Divine command and law, fulfills the whole law."[26] The phrase "the whole law" (*totem legem*) appears to be a reference to the eternal law. Since the eternal law is the entire rule and measure of the universe, it contains the whole of the law, including natural law, which is nothing but a participation in it. Yet the "Divine Law partic-

22. Ibid., (author's translation of *Sed manifestum est quod non omnes possunt scientiae insudare; et propterea a Christo data est lex brevis, ut ab omnibus posset sciri, et nullus propter ignorantiam possit ab eius observantia excusari*).

23. Ibid. The use of the verb *insudare* to express this notion demonstrates the arduous nature of persevering in knowledge of what is right. The verb means to sweat or perspire in doing something.

24. Ibid., (author's translation of *Ad hoc autem quod actus humani boni reddantur, oportet quod regulae divinae dilectionis concordat*).

25. Ibid., (author's translation of *Sed sciendum, quod haec lex debet esse regula omnium actuum humanorum*).

26. Ibid., (author's translation of *Sed considerandum, quod qui mandatum et legem divinae dilectionis servat, totam legem implet*).

ipates in the eternal law more perfectly" than the natural law, since the divine law is not mediated through weakened human reason.[27]

The divine law contains rules of action to assist man in finding his way not only to his supernatural end but even to his natural end. Some precepts of divine law relate to the worship and knowledge of God. Others clarify for the now darkened mind of man the principles of natural law which before the Fall would have provided a clear guide of action. The Ten Commandments and the other moral precepts of revelation are examples of these. Since the Fall, man cannot reach even his natural goal and build a good and just society on earth without the assistance of the divine law.

One of the major criticisms of those of us who advocate the necessity to conform our society to the natural law (with regard to the regulation of marriage, for example) is that great injustices have been perpetrated throughout history: slavery, genocide, war, oppression. Thus, they argue, there is no natural law written on the hearts of men. The reply to this criticism is that the natural law is written there, but our minds weakened by the effects of the Fall cannot clearly read and apply it without recourse to the aid of divine law. Thus, any project that attempts to argue for use of the natural law without recourse to the divine law (as even the "Catholic" new natural law school does) is doomed to failure.

I will share a personal example. In law school, I engaged one of my atheist professors in a debate about abortion. This professor considered himself to be using natural law reasoning. He falsely deduced that abortion was morally licit as a conclusion flowing from the premise of the principle of the natural liberty of all men, a principle acknowledged by Catholic natural law scholars such as Gratian. Yet within Gratian's hierarchy of principles, this rule is subject to being harmonized with the preservation of innocent human life. I can think of no better example of failed human reason making false deductions from natural law precepts when the guidance of the divine law is ignored. The only corrective to this common failure is

27. See John Rziha, *Perfecting Human Actions: St. Thomas Aquinas On Human Participation in Eternal Law* (Washington, DC: Catholic University of America Press, 2009), 271 (citing Aquinas, *Summa*, I–II, Q. 99, art. 2, Reply to Objection 2).

recourse to the divine law preserved by the Church. The Church is the guardian of the divine law, which is necessary to correct our failures in making false deductions of natural law principles. Refusal to seek such recourse leads to dire consequences. As Leo XIII explains:

> To exclude the Church, founded by God Himself, from life, from laws, from the education of youth, from domestic society is a grave and fatal error. A State from which religion is banished can never be well regulated; and already perhaps more than is desirable is known of the nature and tendency of the so-called civil philosophy of life and morals. The Church of Christ is the true and sole teacher of virtue and guardian of morals. She it is who preserves in their purity the principles from which duties flow, and, by setting forth most urgent reasons for virtuous life, bids us not only to turn away from wicked deeds, but even to curb all movements of the mind that are opposed to reason, even though they be not carried out in action.[28]

Now that we have delved into the understanding of man's struggles to live up to his nature, we can come to address the final layer of Christ's Kingdom but the first in our order of knowledge: human laws and the necessary relationship between them and the Church.

Man does not accomplish this participation in eternal law alone. One of the precepts of the natural law is that man is meant to live in society, or as St. Thomas, following Aristotle, asserts, "man is naturally a civic and social animal."[29] Thus, to understand human law we must examine it in context. To do this we must understand the nature of a community.

Aristotle defined a community as a "human association . . . instituted for the sake of obtaining some good."[30] Communities are different from "a mere multitude of men" in that a political community is "bound together by a particular agreement, looking toward a particular end, and existing under a particular head."[31] From this definition two elements emerge: (1) an agreed common

28. Leo XIII, *Immortale Dei*, no. 32.
29. Aquinas, *Summa*, I–II, Q. 72, art. 4.
30. Aristotle, *Politics*, bk. I, ch. 1.
31. Suárez, *Selections*, vol. 2, 86.

end or purpose and (2) an authority structure to make particular decisions relevant to attaining that end. Political communities can be either perfect[32] or imperfect.[33] A perfect community possesses both the perfect or most complete end as well as the necessary means of attaining such an end.[34] In a word, the perfect community is completely self-sufficient.[35] A community which aims at a complete good and thus incorporates the goods of all lesser communities is this perfect community.[36] Two perfect communities exist since there are two complete ends of man, natural and supernatural. The nation or commonwealth is a perfect community because its end is human natural happiness.[37] The Church is the second perfect society because its end is the supernatural end of man. In contrast, imperfect communities pursue either an incomplete end or are not self-sufficient to attain their end. Examples of imperfect communities would be families, businesses, parishes, or community associations.

The second element of the definition, a community under a common authority, explains the role of government within the perfect community. Its role is to make human laws or particular determinations that assist man, in his fallen state, in living rightly (in harmony with eternal, natural, and divine law) and thus attaining his

32. Here, "perfect" is used to a precise sense to mean complete or fulfilled and not necessarily good or virtuous. See Wladyslaw Tatarkiewicz, "Paradoxes of Perfection," *Dialectics and Humanism* 7 (1980): 78 (contrasting the Aristotelian notion of perfection as "complete," "finished," or "flawless" with a paradoxical view of perfection as "ceaseless improvement").

33. Suárez, *Selection*, vol. 2, 86.

34. See ibid., 86–87; Aquinas, "De Regno," bk. I, ch. 2; Aroney, "Subsidiarity," 174–77.

35. Suárez, *Selection*, 86.

36. Aristotle, *Politics*, I, 1, 2 ("And the association which is supreme and includes all other associations is the absolutely supreme good").

37. Ibid., I, 1, 17 ("And the perfect association . . . is the political community, now complete having a self-sufficient end. . . . Therefore the political community was instituted for the sake of protecting life and exists to promote the good life"); Aquinas, *Commentary*, comment 2 ("he [Aristotle] shows that the good to which the political community is directed is the supreme human good"); Aquinas, "De Regno," bk. I, ch. 2 ("[I]t follows that a society will be the more perfect the more it is sufficient until itself to procure the necessities of life").

natural and supernatural ends. Human laws then are meant to be particular determinations of the natural law to make it easier for men to order their actions rightly to promote justice and peace, or put another way, virtuous life in community. Justice is "the right relations of the members of the society" and peace indicates "the 'tranquility of order,' the proper ordering of society to God as its last end."[38] Human laws are thus not a law unto themselves but rather the final stage in making concrete and particular the laws of Christ's Kingdom, the eternal, natural, *and* divine laws. I will give a modern example to illustrate this limited role of human lawmaking. The natural law requires that men act in society so as not to unnecessarily and unreasonably endanger the lives of others. To drive on random sides of the road would endanger the safety of others. Thus, the natural law requires that all drive in an orderly way on the same side to reduce the risk of collision. Whether that should be the right or the left side is not determined by natural law. There is no inherently moral side of the road. The choice is the responsibility of human authorities over the community to determine which, the right or the left, should be used. Once this determination is made, however, the natural law obliges us to comply with the human law since it is a rational determination of the natural law. Saint Thomas uses another example.[39] The natural law requires that evildoers who harm the justice and peace of a community should be punished. Yet the natural law does not specify in which way particular crimes should be punished. Human lawmakers are charged with the obligation to participate in Christ's rule by determining the particular punishments for particular crimes. They are not free, however, to determine that crimes should be rewarded rather than punished or to punish morally good actions. Such examples emphasize the limited but important role of human lawmaking in contrast to the delusions of grandeur of modern liberal positivism.

Thus, civil society must be governed subject to this hierarchy of laws. Human laws rewarding (funding) abortion or bestowing

38. Christopher Blum, "What is the Common Good?" *The Downside Review* 120 (2002): 86.

39. Aquinas, *Summa*, I–II, Q. 95, art. 2.

benefits of marriage on two people incapable of contracting it or purporting to dissolve valid marriages are not determinations of natural law consistent with the principles of divine law. Such "illegal laws"[40] are beyond the authority of the human lawmakers delegated with the obligation to determine "legal laws" by the ultimate governor of the universe, Christ the King. Put another way, human laws are binding on men only to the extent that they are derived from the eternal law (through the mediation of the natural and divine laws). As St. Thomas says, "Laws framed by man are either just or unjust. If they be just, they have the power of binding in conscience, from the eternal law whence they are derived."[41] The authority of human government thus rests on its participation in the eternal law, or put another way, the participation in the Kingdom of Christ of which the eternal law is the constitution. Only by governing civil society in harmony with these higher laws can man attain even his natural end—happiness in community—to say nothing of his supernatural end. Pope Leo XIII explains that in a society constituted on these Christian truths, "divine and human things are equitably shared; the rights of citizens assured to them, and fenced round by divine, by natural, and by human law; the duties incumbent on each one being wisely marked out, and their fulfillment fittingly insured." Here lies the true safeguard against human tyranny—not in fictitious social contracts made by mere men but in the refuge of the ordered Kingdom of Christ and his laws.

Human history has shown that not all human societies have been so well constituted. We have already seen that individual men can and do err in deducing and applying principles of natural law when they refuse the aid God has provided to compensate for the wounds of sin. Rulers of civil society make law under the same difficulties. Just as individual men need to use the divine law to assist in forming their judgments, so do rulers of civil society. Saint Thomas specifically contemplates that human rulers can formulate human laws that contravene the natural law. In such a case the purported laws are not really laws at all. He says, "Consequently every human law

40. See ibid., I–II, Q. 96, art. 4 (in which Aquinas uses the term "legal laws").
41. See ibid.

has just so much of the nature of law, as it is derived from the law of nature. But if in any point it deflects from the law of nature, it is no longer a law but a perversion of law."[42] Further, human laws that require men to violate the divine law, such as worshiping idols, must be disobeyed.[43]

The Church is the custodian and guardian of the natural law and the divine law. Thus, the Church's perennial teaching on the content and interpretations of these higher laws are indispensable in the work of making human law to govern civil society. The Church is primarily concerned with the supernatural end of man and governs her perfect society primarily in light of this end. She leaves to civil rulers the detailed determinations of human laws relating to the perfect society concerned with the natural end of man (such as our traffic regulation). In light of her role of teacher and guide with respect to natural and divine law, however, the civil authorities are obligated to have recourse to her to assure that particular human laws are really derived from, and not in contravention of, these higher laws.

For example, the civil government may be considering enacting legislation regulating the effects of marriage. They must consult the precepts of natural and divine law to know what is the nature and end of marriage: the lifelong union of one man and one woman for the purpose of begetting and rearing children and for the mutual support of the spouses. Detailed rules about the nature and transfer of marital property, etc., must be written in conformity with this higher law. If the civil authority were to enact a law contrary to these, such as New York did by conferring the legal benefits of marriage on two men or two women, then the Church may intervene to correct the civil authorities by pointing to the higher law.

Further, since the supernatural and natural ends of man are distinct but not unrelated, the Church may intervene in civil government when the human laws have the effect of frustrating the supernatural end of man even if purporting to further an aspect of his natural end. Thus, a human law attempting to provide for the

42. Ibid., I–II, Q. 95, art. 2.
43. Ibid., I–II, Q. 96, art. 4.

more efficient provision of material goods for the community might require factories to operate seven days a week. Even though this law purports to deal with the natural end of man,[44] it interferes with his ability to fulfill his supernatural duties to honor the Lord's Day. The Church may again intervene to protect the supernatural interests of man.

Put another way, the jurisdictions of civil government and the Church are distinct, just as the natural and supernatural ends of man are distinct. Yet they are not independent; they overlap. Both the government of the Church and civil society take place under the natural and divine laws, and both within their sphere are participations in the eternal law. Pope Leo XIII explains:

> In matters, however, of mixed jurisdiction, it is in the highest degree consonant to nature, as also to the designs of God, that so far from one of the powers separating itself from the other, or still less coming into conflict with it, complete harmony, such as is suited to the end for which each power exists, should be preserved between them.[45]

The Church and the civil authorities are meant to work together in such mixed areas, the Church providing the certainty of knowledge with respect to the principles of natural and divine law, the civil government applying them through particular human law. The Church also monitors human lawmaking as a guardian of the supernatural perfect society, ensuring that the natural end of man is pursued in a way that furthers, rather than hinders, Man's supernatural end.

The eminent English jurist, John of Salisbury, developed the image of the body politic to describe this relationship between the civil and ecclesiastical societies. The Church is the soul of the body politic, and civil society is the body. Just as the soul directs the specific actions of the body, so too the Church is meant to guide the direction of the body under its head, the governors.

44. In reality, such a law does not further but in fact harms man's natural end. The tyrannical government of the French Revolution attempted to abolish the seven-day week and instituted a rest day every ten days instead. The natural effects on man and beast alike were disastrous.

45. Leo XIII, *Immortale Dei*, no. 35.

Leo XIII invokes this image of John of Salisbury when he describes the harmonious relation of Church and State:

> The Almighty, therefore, has given the charge of the human race to two powers, the ecclesiastical and the civil, the one being set over divine, and the other over human, things. Each in its kind is supreme, each has fixed limits within which it is contained. . . . But, inasmuch as each of these two powers has authority over the same subjects, and as it might come to pass that one and the same thing—related differently, but still remaining one and the same thing—might belong to the jurisdiction and determination of both, therefore God, who foresees all things, and who is the author of these two powers, has marked out the course of each in right correlation to the other. . . . There must, accordingly, exist between these two powers a certain orderly connection, which may be compared to the union of the soul and body in man.[46]

To separate Church and state as did the philosophical heirs of Luther, such as President Kennedy did, is to separate the soul from the body. This, as we know, is the very definition of death. The wall of separation between the Church and the State is an attempt to free human law from the natural and divine laws and ultimately to break free of the eternal law. Its effect is to kill the body politic. The crisis and calamities we witness in our society are the observable proofs of this death, just as stench and decomposition are signs of physical death. Such a dire result is why Bd. Pius IX condemned so vigorously the error that "the Church ought to be separated from the state and the state from the Church."[47] Sadly, the idealized integral humanism embraced by the Second Vatican Council and most churchmen since has jettisoned this condemnation and instead called across the wall of separation to Luther, Jefferson, and Kennedy to proclaim that they could build a virtuous, just, and peaceful society from behind their wall using the dead corpse of a de-souled body, their own human laws. They no longer needed the Church to guide men to even their natural end. Ignoring the effects

46. Ibid., no. 13.

47. Pius IX, *Syllabus of Errors* (Vatican City: Libreria Editrice Vaticana, 1864), no. 55.

of the Fall, men could build a just and peaceful society cut off from the soul, the guardian and interpreter of the higher laws. As to their supernatural end, the Church could look to that behind its own wall of separation all by itself enjoying the new "religious freedom" from within its gilded cage.

Economics in the Social Reign of Christ the King

This physical death of the body politic obviously manifests itself at levels of the organism. The economic communities comprising the commonwealth will clearly be affected by a break with the head, Christ the King. Pope Pius XI in his landmark encyclical *Quas Primas* reaffirmed the necessity of Christ's rule over every component community as well as the entire commonwealth: "It would be a grave error, on the other hand, to say that Christ has no authority whatever in civil affairs, since, by virtue of the absolute empire *over all creatures* committed to him by the Father, all things are in his power."[48]

This quotation summarizes the doctrine of the Social Reign of Christ the King. It is absolute in its formulation: "all creatures" are subject to Christ. Yet in what way does Christ's dominion relate to all creatures? The application of the doctrine to the political and public life of governments and nations is obviously an important topic, which is discussed in Chapter 6 of this book. Its application to the economic business sphere is something that often receives less attention. Some might even assert that the doctrine bears no relation to business dealings. We will explore in the remainder of this chapter whether and to what extent this doctrine of the Church applies to the economic ordering of society.

Our method will be to examine the text of the encyclical for indications of its applications. We will then look at the immediate context of *Quas Primas*, and in particular the first encyclical of Pius XI, *Ubi Arcano*. We will then broaden the context to the philosophical and theological history of this question. Finally, we will turn to a few practical issues in the corporate and commercial world and apply what we have learned.

48. Pius XI, *Quas Primas* (Vatican City: Libreria Editrice Vaticana, 1925), no. 17 (emphasis added).

So, first turning to *Quas Primas* itself, we have seen that Pius XI makes it clear that Christ's kingship extends to all creatures. Pius XI emphasizes that this subjugation extends throughout the entire hierarchy of society. He does so by referring to the summit and the basic unit of society: "Nor is there any difference in this matter between the individual and the family or the state; for all men, whether collectively or individually, are under the dominion of Christ. In him is the salvation of the individual, in him is the salvation of society."[49] By referring to the state, the individual, and the family, his Holiness encompasses all of the intermediate levels and associations of society. This would include corporations, partnerships, trade unions, and other business organizations. No one and no group is excluded.

One may attempt, however, to limit this application to all people only in the public sphere. Economics and business involve, one might assert, private orderings and therefore are not affected directly by the public acknowledgement of Christ. Just as Pius XI condemns the proposition that Christ's kingship has no place in public life, he likewise does so with respect to private affairs: "When once men recognize, *both in private and in public life*, that Christ is King, society will at last receive the great blessings of real liberty, well ordered discipline, peace and harmony."[50] Christ's reign affects every aspect of our lives as Pius XI says: "if this power embraces all men, it must be clear that *not one of our faculties* is exempt from his empire."[51] Not only do the demands of Christ's Kingdom extend over private and public aspects of our lives but they extend over all human activities and abilities, or faculties. Clearly buying, selling, trading, borrowing are human actions and thus fruits of our faculty to think, communicate, and act. Thus, just as Christ's law and kingship cannot be excluded from the public functioning of governments and the making of laws affecting education and marriage, so too it cannot be dismissed from business affairs, whether of individuals or collective associations.

49. Ibid., no. 18.
50. Ibid., no. 19 (emphasis added).
51. Ibid., no. 33 (emphasis added).

Quas Primas itself acknowledges that the malady, to which the feast of Christ the King is being instituted as a remedy, involves economic matters. His Holiness laments "that insatiable greed which is so often hidden under a pretense of public spirit and patriotism, and gives rise to so many private quarrels; a blind and immoderate selfishness, making men seek nothing but their own comfort and advantage and measure everything by these."[52] Pius XI refers to the two pillars of Christ's Reign as it applies to economics: charity and justice. "It [Christ's Kingdom] demands of its subjects a spirit of detachment from riches and earthly things, and a spirit of gentleness [charity]. They must hunger and thirst after justice...."[53]

Thus, we have seen that the general description of Christ's reign contemplates an all-encompassing change in society, political as well as economic. Yet Pius XI does not explicate in detail the issues he alludes to. This is primarily because *Quas Primas* emerges from a long line of Catholic, and specifically papal, teaching explaining these issues. Pius XI himself on two occasions in *Quas Primas* refers to his first encyclical, *Ubi Arcano*, and explains that *Quas Primas* is a continuation of this diagnosis of modern errors begun in *Ubi Arcano*. Let us turn then to *Ubi Arcano*.

This first encyclical of Pius XI was written in 1922 when much of the West was in the denial of the Roaring 20s. "The Great War had put an end to war and brought peace," people told themselves as they Charlestoned away the nights. The Church, however, sees the Truth (the correspondence of the mind to reality), and the Truth was that the world was on the brink of more strife and discord. World War II and all the intense and bloody conflicts that follow to our very day showed the truth of *Ubi Arcano*'s prediction of future discord; the world was sick and needed medicine. In *Ubi Arcano*, Pius XI diagnoses the problems which are preventing true peace; it is, as he made explicit in *Quas Primas*, the rejection of Christ's Kingship in private as well as in public life. The Encyclical is a sharp and clear diagnosis of the causes of discord and violence among men. For our purposes, however, we will limit our examination to

52. Ibid., no. 24.
53. Ibid., no. 15.

the part of the diagnosis dealing with economic matters. From the outset, Pius XI indicates his diagnosis encompasses both politics and economics when he states that rivalries that give root to war lie in the "manipulations of politics" and the "fluctuations of finance."

> In the first place, we must take cognizance of the war between the classes, a chronic and mortal disease of present day society, which like a cancer is eating away the vital forces of the social fabric, labor, industry, the arts, commerce, agriculture—everything in fact which contributes to public and private welfare and to national prosperity. This conflict seems to resist every solution and grows worse because those who are never satisfied with the amount of their wealth contend with those who hold on most tenaciously to the riches which they have already acquired, while in both classes there is common the desire to rule the other and to assume control of the others' possessions.[54]

This strife over the maximization of individual economic self-interest is the root of all disorder. What fuels this disease?

> Many are intent on exploiting their neighbors solely for the purpose of enjoying more fully and on a larger scale the goods of this world. But they err grievously who have turned to the acquisition of material and temporal possessions and are forgetful of eternal and spiritual things, to the possession of which Jesus, Our Redeemer, by means of the Church, His living interpreter, calls mankind.[55]

Society's end has become disoriented. Economic acquisition has taken priority over eternal and spiritual things. What are these spiritual things? Again, charity and justice are the answer. The unbalanced attention to material issues is contrary to the charity of Christ's Kingdom where eternal salvation is of primary not secondary concern. "It is in the very nature of material objects that an inordinate desire for them becomes the root of every evil, of every discord, and in particular, of a lowering of the moral sense."[56] An inordinate desire for increasing material things makes charity cold

54. Pius XI, *Ubi Arcano* (Vatican City: Libreria Editrice Vaticana, 1922), no. 12.
55. Ibid., no. 21.
56. Ibid., no. 22.

and drives unjust decisions. Pius XI teaches that "it is never lawful nor even wise, to dissociate morality from the affairs of practical life, that, in the last analysis, it is justice which exalteth a nation: but sin maketh nations miserable" (Prov. 14:34).[57] Thus, morality is not something separate from economics and commercial dealings; the Church is not confined to commanding infallible precepts with respect to sexuality and other private "personal" issues. She teaches as the viceroy of Christ the King what moral principles need to inform economic regulation and transactions. Note: It is moral principles, not economic principles, which must govern. "It is Jesus Christ who has revealed to the world the existence of spiritual values and has obtained for them their due appreciation. He has said, 'For what doth it profit a man, if he gain the whole world, and suffer the loss of his own soul?'" (Matt. 16:26).[58] This statement is qualified lest we interpret it in a Jansenist fashion. "This does not mean that the peace of Christ, which is the only true peace, expects of us that we give up all worldly possessions. On the contrary, every earthly good is promised in so any words by Christ to those who seek his peace: "Seek ye *first* the kingdom of God, and his justice, and all these things shall be added unto you" (Matt 6:33; Luke 12:31).[59] The Church is not unconcerned with economic prosperity and meeting the needs of and providing some earthly comfort to men, but these things must be sought *after* seeking the kingdom of God and his justice.

To summarize, Pius XI teaches through *Ubi Arcano* and *Quas Primas* that true peace can only come through the acknowledgement of Christ's Kingdom already present in the world. This kingdom embraces all people, organizations, and faculties. It covers commerce and finance. Some of the ways economic systems in existence in the world of Pius XI and today fail to acknowledge Christ's kingship include placing an inordinate desire on material things and economic prosperity. What constitutes an inordinate desire? It is when our *primary* purpose in creating, executing, and judging eco-

57. Ibid., no 25.
58. Ibid., no. 36.
59. Emphasis added.

nomic laws and behavior is economic prosperity rather than seeking *first* the kingdom of God and his justice. To repeat, this does not mean the efficiency or economic effects of law and policy are irrelevant, but they must be of secondary, not primary, importance.

Before turning to the practical application of these principles to the making and judging of commercial law and the structuring of our economic activity, we should step back again to the larger context. As the Angelic Doctor would recommend, we can begin with *the* Philosopher, Aristotle. Aristotle teaches that economics and its learning are subject to politics, which is that art that directs society to its end, the good.[60] He says, "we see even the most highly esteemed of capacities to fall under this [referring to politics], e.g., strategy, economics, rhetoric."[61] Economics is thus a subordinate discipline. The Catholic philosophical improvement on Aristotle is that even politics, as that which tells what we ought to do, is subordinate to moral theology. John O'Hara summarizes the Catholic approach to economics thus: "The best usage of the present time is to make political economy [or the science of making wealth] an ethical science, that is, to make it include a discussion of what *ought* to be in the economic word as well as what *is*. This has all along been the practice of Catholic writers. Some of them even go so far as to make political economy a branch of ethics and not an independent science."[62]

It is in this philosophical milieu that we can see the papal assertion of the Church's right and *competence* to teach definitively on the making of economic laws. Thus, Leo XIII can state in *Rerum Novarum*: "We approach the subject with confidence, and in the exercise of the rights which manifestly appertain to Us, for no practical solution of this question will be found apart from the intervention of religion and of the Church."[63] Likewise Pius XI states in

60. Aristotle, "Politica," *The Basic Works of Aristotle*, ed. Richard McKeon, trans. Benjamin Jowett (New York: Random House, 1941), 1127.

61. Aristotle, "Ethica Nicomachea," *The Basic Works of Aristotle*, 936.

62. "Political Economy," Catholic Encyclopedia. http://www.newadvent.com/cathen/12213b.htm.

63. Leo XIII, *Rerum Novarum* (Vatican City: Libreria Editrice Vaticana, 1891), no. 24.

Quadragesimo Anno,

> [T]here resides in Us the right and duty to pronounce with supreme authority upon social and economic matters. Certainly the Church was not given the commission to guide men to an only fleeting and perishable happiness but to that which is eternal. Indeed the Church holds that it is unlawful for her to mix without cause in these temporal concerns; however, she can in no wise renounce the duty God entrusted to her to interpose her authority . . . in all things that are connected with the moral law. For as to these, the deposit of truth that God committed to Us and the grave duty of disseminating and interpreting the whole moral law, and of urging it in season and out of season, bring under and subject to Our supreme jurisdiction not only social order but economic activities themselves.[64]

Thus, although the Church does not assert authority over the study of economic facts (predicting the likely practical consequences of using wealth or productive assets in a particular way), she, in the name of Christ the King and as guardian of the natural law, asserts divine authority over judging the morality or immorality of willing or permitting these consequences. We can see from this proposition that the doctrine of the Social Reign of Christ the King precludes an approach to corporate and commercial issues that judges laws and actions on the sole, or at least primary, basis of economic results: What decision produces the most efficient or value-maximizing result? Although a Catholic approach can take into account this data, it cannot form the basis for the moral judgment of whether that result, even if value maximizing, is right or wrong.

Pius XI in accord with Leo XIII and their predecessors, held that no area of our lives, individually or collectively, can be separate from the Social Reign of Christ the King. This includes our business dealings. The Church has the right and competence to critique our economic order when it seeks first wealth and efficiency in priority to Christ's charity and justice.

What more specifically then are these principles that must take

64. Pius XI, *Quadragesimo Anno* (Vatican City: Libreria Editrice Vaticana, 1931), no. 41.

priority over efficiency and wealth maximization? The first was mentioned in Part I: seek you *first* the kingdom of God and his justice. The end of man is eternal salvation. All economic laws must be judged first and foremost on whether they tend to increase the likelihood of souls attaining this goal and if they conform to the justice of God. Justice must be understood in its complete sense, not merely commutative justice but distributive as well. Commutative justice refers to a fairness of dealing between individuals; distributive justice refers to the fairness of the distributions of the common goods of a society among its members. Distributive justice does not mean an equal sharing among members of society (i.e., communism) but rather a distribution that, although uneven (in that it reflects the natural hierarchy created by God), does not exclude anyone from the basic necessities of eternal salvation and human life in the interim. Just as a forced equal sharing of goods is against nature, which includes a natural hierarchy of stations in life, it is likewise unnatural for one individual or group to aggregate all or nearly all the goods of a society to themselves to the exclusion of others. The root of a distribution that violates distributive justice is, as Pius XI indicated, an "inordinate" desire for wealth. An inordinate desire is one not directed to its proper end. Pius XI says a man cannot desire for himself an increase in wealth "which he does not need to sustain life fittingly and with dignity" or to be used in fulfilling "a very grave precept to practice almsgiving, beneficence, and munificence" as "the Sacred Scriptures and the Fathers of the Church constantly declare in the most explicit language. . . ."[65] Thus, the fact that a particular decision produces a more efficient result is neither good nor bad; it is a fact that must be evaluated in terms of its effect on salvation and its accordance with commutative and distributive justice. As noted above, a just acquisition of wealth is not an egalitarian one; the amount depends on the "station in life" of the individual involved. A prince is justified in having more wealth, as it is necessary to fulfill his station in life. Also notice that charity is not an "option," a deed above and beyond the requirements; it is an obligation not of justice but an obligation nonetheless.

65. Ibid., no. 50.

It may be appropriate to pause at this point and focus on a possible source of concern. The above analysis, one may argue, does not comport with the Church's defense of private property. Restricting the way people use economic resources they own (as morality would suggest) violates private ownership of those resources. True, the Church has always defended the private ownership of property, and Pius XI strongly condemned the confiscations of private property by communist regimes. For example Leo XIII states: "For, every man has by nature the right to possess property as his own."[66] Yet ownership does not involve freedom to use that property as one sees fit without reference to the moral law. As Pius XI teaches in *Quadragesimo Anno*: "[T]here must be first laid down as foundation a principle established by Leo XIII: The right of property is distinct from its use."[67] He is likely referring to Leo XIII when he wrote in *Rerum Novarum*: "it is one thing to have a right to the possession of money and another to have a right to use money as one wills."[68] Even John Paul II reaffirms his predecessors in this respect in *Centesimus Annus*: "While the Pope proclaimed the right to private ownership he affirmed with equal clarity that the use of goods while marked by freedom is subordinated to their original common destination as created goods, as well as to the will of Jesus Christ as expressed in the Gospel."[69] Again, efficiency or maximization cannot be the end of commercial activity as this is not the ultimate destination of material things.

Let us summarize what we have seen thus far. The proclamation of Christ as King of the entire world must affect all people and all aspects of their lives. It is only in this sense that we can completely appreciate the weight and necessity of the Church's teaching in economic matters and documents such as *Rerum Novarum* and *Quadragesimo Anno*. Economics is not a neutral science separable from moral theology. No law or decision can be evaluated without con-

66. Leo XIII, *Rerum Novarum*, no. 6.

67. Pius XI, *Quadragesimo Anno*, no. 47.

68. Leo XIII, *Rerum Novarum*, no. 22.

69. John Paul II, *Centesimus Annus* (Vatican City: Libreria Editrice Vaticana, 1991), no. 30.

sidering the salvation of souls and God's justice (commutative and distributive) as the primary approach.

Let us briefly introduce some examples of this approach to the commercial sphere. This is meant to be illustrative and introductory, as we cannot in the time here allotted thoroughly consider each. Subsequent chapters will take up some topics in more depth, so this chapter can serve as an introduction.

Let us begin with the governing of corporations. Our capitalist society tends to focus debate on to whom directors of companies owe duties: to shareholders only or to some other constituencies, creditors, employees, etc. Most agree the substance of the duty is the same: maximize the economic benefit of the group to whom you owe the duty. In fact, most people would say the duty of a corporate director is to make the most money possible for the shareholders. The approach we have been examining does not begin with the question of "to whom is the duty owed?" but rather "what must the director have as his purpose in making decisions for the company he manages?" Thus, the paradigm of corporate decisions is not value maximization with a debate over who benefits from the maximization. Rather, will the decision further the kingdom of Christ and comport with his justice? Once directors recognize their primary fiduciary duty lies here and not to the special economic interests of one or more groups, the true nature of corporate responsibility is recognized. As Our Lord indicated to Pontius Pilate during his sacred Passion, the nature of his Kingdom involves the delegation of power through the varied hierarchies of authority. "Jesus answered: Thou shouldst not have any power against me, unless it were given thee from above" (John 19:11). Managers of businesses hold positions of authority. In acknowledging the overarching structure of Christ's Kingdom they must recognize their authority is inextricably linked to the authority of Christ, whence their authority derives. Just as the prince or government of a country must conform decisions to the law of Christ, so too must those in authority in business. This means evaluating both the justice of their decisions and the effect on the salvation of those within the community they govern, the corporation. Thus it is not a question of whose value or interest is maximized, but which decisions are both just and tend towards salvation of those affected. Within these constraints, economic efficiency may be pursued.

Again let us take an example. A board of directors is deciding to set the hours of operation for its factory and the length of shifts. Economic evidence is presented that a 24/7 operation with two twelve-hour shifts would reduce costs and produce more profits for shareholders and even improve net pay for employees. Traditional analysis would then ask if the directors need to take into account the "interests" of the labor force in this decision. Yet the Catholic question would be different. Would this arrangement advance or retard the observation of the precepts of Christ?. Our first simple observation is that a seven-day operation does not comply with the divine command to honor the Sabbath both by fulfilling religious duties, i.e., hearing Mass and abstaining from servile work. Next, such a schedule is not compatible with the obligations (note not the interests) of the workers towards the other communities of which they are integral members, most importantly the family. This decision, regardless of its efficiency, is therefore clear. The directors must subordinate profits to the moral requirements affected by the decision.

Turning to anti-trust laws, this field is often judged in terms of economic efficiency. A particular business should be prohibited from combining with another company because it creates an economic inefficiency: the ability to extract monopolistic rents, which distorts the market. Thus, acquisitions are judged solely in terms of their *effect* on the economic market not in terms of their effect on people involved (be they employees or investors) and not in terms of distributive justice. The approach is not "will this proposed private ordering of productive property concentrate productive property to such an extent as to violate distributive justice?" Will the economies of scale of a Wal-Mart, although potentially economically efficient and even price reducing, violate the principle of subsidiarity? The reign of Christ is concerned with a just distribution of productive property. Leo XIII explains in *Rerum Novarum*: "To this must be added that the hiring of labor and the conduct of trade are concentrated in the hands of comparatively few; so that a small number of very rich men have been able to lay upon the teeming masses of the laboring poor a yoke little better than that of slavery itself."[70] The effects of conglomeration on a just distribution of productive property need to be taken into account even if a business combination would be more efficient and profitable.

Let us turn to the current rationale for consumer protection laws. There are generally two approaches to this topic: either it should be abolished as a distortion of "free" market forces, or justified only inasmuch as it maximizes efficiency by compensating for imperfections in the "free" market. Christ's reign looks first to the justice of transactions and their effects on people. Is this product harmful spiritually? Even if someone is willing to pay a certain amount when given all information about what he is buying, this does not justify giving legal protection to the transaction. Usury laws, for example, can be evaluated in a new light. Even if willing to pay a rate of interest because the individual values the good consumed with the loan more than future income, a person may be prohibited from entering into such a loan if it is contrary to justice or harmful to salvation.

I certainly am not attempting to provide answers to all of these questions at this point, but am arguing for a particular methodology for doing so. It is one that requires each answer to be rooted in the first principles established previously. Leo XIII and Pius XI recognized that just as the doctrine of Christ the King, which required governments to publicly recognize the right of Christ and his Church over and through their public laws, was radically opposed to the secularists, so too it is radically opposed to the very methodology and vocabulary of our free-market economic system that values cheap prices and big profits at all costs. We will only find the correct answers to questions of corporate governance, commercial regulation, etc., when we start asking the right questions. Asking the right questions requires reordering our priorities and principles to acknowledge the fundamental and universal rule of Christ as expressed through the teaching office of his Church. We need the Church to teach clearly and authoritatively again, like Leo XIII and Pius XI, that how we make money matters. Christ needs to rule not only in every capitol building, school, and home, but in every factory and corporate board room. We need to restore "all" things in

70. Leo XIII, *Rerum Novarum*, no. 3.

Christ. This all includes the way our economy and commercial affairs are structured. Only in the reign of Christ will we find the peace (and prosperity) of Christ.

Conclusion

In contrast to Luther, Jefferson, and John F. Kennedy's vision of a human ruler of nations, hiding behind his wall of separation, St. Thomas Aquinas describes a truly Christian, therefore truly human, ruler:

> Therefore, since the beatitude of heaven is the end of that virtuous life which we live at present, it pertains to the king's office to promote the good life of the multitude in such a way as to make it suitable for the attainment of heavenly happiness, that is to say, he should command those things which lead to the happiness of Heaven and, as far as possible, forbid the contrary. What conduces to true beatitude and what hinders it are learned from the law of God, the teaching of which belongs to the office of the priest. . . .[71]

Reaffirming St. Thomas's teaching of the Christian ruler needing to be instructed by the Church so as to make right judgments in ruling the nation, Leo XIII summarizes his argument thus: "Such, then, as We have briefly pointed out, is the Christian organization of civil society; not rashly or fancifully shaped out, but deduced from the highest and truest principles, confirmed by natural reason itself."[72]

Only by returning to these principles can the ills of our out-of-control government be solved. John Dickinson in his introduction to the classic Catholic treatment of political philosophy, *The Statesman's Book of John of Salisbury*, describes the former Catholic worldview thus:

> It has become a historical commonplace that mediaeval thought was dominated by the conception of a body of law existing independently of the authority of any government and to which all positive law must conform and to which government no less than individuals owed obedience. Rulers were thought of as bound by a higher law . . . which accordingly made it possible to apply to their acts another criterion of legality or illegality. In the words of the

71. Aquinas, "De Regno," bk. 1, ch. 16.
72. Leo XIII, *Immortale Dei*, no. 16.

> *Policraticus* "between a tyrant and the true prince there is this single or chief difference: that the latter obeys the law and rules the people by its dictates. A tyrant is one who oppresses the people by rulership based upon force while he who rules in accordance with the laws is a prince." "There are certain precepts of the law which have a perpetual necessity having the force of law among all nations.... And not only do I withdraw from the hands of rulers the power of dispensing with the law, but in my opinion those laws which carry a perpetual injunction are not subject at all to their pleasure."[73]

What he describes is the Kingdom of Christ.

We must not be discouraged by the signs of morbid decay of our country. Like Lazarus, it may only rest in the tomb and can be resurrected once again to be a flourishing body politic by tearing down the wall of separation and allowing the soul to re-enter the body. It has happened once; Leo XIII believed it could happen again:

> Christian Europe has subdued barbarous nations, and changed them from a savage to a civilized condition, from superstition to true worship. It victoriously rolled back the tide of Mohammedan conquest; retained the headship of civilization; stood forth in the front rank as the leader and teacher of all, in every branch of national culture; bestowed on the world the gift of true and many-sided liberty; and most wisely founded very numerous institutions for the solace of human suffering. And if we inquire how it was able to bring about so altered a condition of things, the answer is, beyond all question, in large measure, through religion, under whose auspices so many great undertakings were set on foot, through whose aid they were brought to completion.[74]

73. John Dickinson, *The Statesman's Book of John of Salisbury* (New York: A.A. Knopf, 1927), xxviii (internal citations omitted).

74. Father Dennis Fahey echoed this same assessment half a century after Leo XIII: "The truth was recognized that all men were members of Christ, actual or potential, and that society as such was bound to favour membership of Christ.... Social life, in which Politics and Economics would be put into watertight compartments and sectioned off from the life of members of Christ was completely alien to the minds of that day. Western Europe as a whole then recognized the authority of the Vicar of Christ the King and his right to say what was moral or immoral in Politics and Economics." Dennis Fahey, *Money Manipulation and Social Order* (Palmdale, CA: Christian Book Club of America, 1944), 77.

The death of this flourishing body politic lies at the feet of both Church and State. The state built the wall of separation; the post-conciliar Church willingly accepts the imprisonment of the soul and even celebrates it rather than calling, as President Reagan did across the Berlin Wall, "Take down that wall!" How does our country regain such a thriving body politic? The answer is the same as that Abp. Lefebvre gave to restore the Church. "The reign of Our Lord" must again become "the center of attention and of activity" of both our civil and ecclesiastical rulers. In place of the wall of separation, his Kingdom with its hierarchy of laws must stand in the center of the relationship between Church and State.

2

Marriage and Family: The Foundation of Political and Economic Society

As we observed in the Introduction, the commonwealth as the perfect society is built out of the unification of a multitude of imperfect societies. The foundation of the commonwealth is the most basic and fundamental of those societies—the family—or as Aristotle called it, the household. Economics is the science, or knowledge, of household management. Politics is the art of directing the individual ends of various households to the common good of the political community. All begins with the family, which is founded by marriage. As Pius XI prophetically observed, the enemies of the Church and the Christian commonwealth know that they must dismember the family for their assault to succeed.[1] Thus, one cannot understand the collapse of the modern commonwealth without understanding the nature of its foundational cell and the viruses that trouble it in our era. This chapter delves into the essence of the family established by the natural law and considers the family's communication with the larger community, which is to be ruled by modesty and propriety. Specifically, the topics of modesty of dress and behavior, the use of technological means of communication, and the education of children to enter into the arena of economics and political life constitute the key practical battlegrounds where the battle for the Natural Law vision of the family is being waged.

1. Pius XI, *Divini Redemptoris* (Vatican City: Liberia Editrice Vaticana, 1937), no. 11.

Marriage—It's Natural: Natural Law Arguments in Defense of Marriage

One of the most divisive and important issues in the opening of this century is the issue of marriage. From some states' attempts to claim the obvious and define marriage in law to others' attempts to invent a new definition of it, to those trying to make "marriages" by other names—civil unions—the nature of marriage and its survival in our society has been in the forefront of public debate, rising all the way to the US Supreme Court.[2] Although the nature of marriage has been divinely revealed and its dignity has been raised for Catholics to a sacrament, marriage is a real state that exists under the Natural Law. For those who refuse to listen to divine revelation on—false—principle, it is useful to make arguments in support of the divinely ordained nature of this institution based in natural reason. It is imperative to do so at this time in particular, as the organs of power in our society are bent on denying that marriage is the lifelong union of one man and one woman for the purpose of begetting, rearing, and, as discussed in more detail later in this chapter, educating children. We have a president and media Gestapo who propagate the falsehood that marriage is whatever we, or rather they, declare it to be.[3] Interestingly, in a public debate in November 2012 I participated in over California's Proposition 8, my challenger began his remarks by stating that he believed the state had no business defining what constituted a marriage. He concluded therefore that the law should let anything be accepted as a marriage that is claimed to be such by individuals, regardless of its form. I began my reply by saying that he was absolutely correct in his premise that the

2. In June 2013, the US Supreme Court declared the Defense of Marriage Act, which required the federal government to recognize only the union of a man and a woman as a marriage, unconstitutional. The Court also refused to reverse a lower court ruling invalidating California's Proposition 8, which prohibited so-called same-sex "marriages" in that state. See *United States v. Windsor*, 570 U.S. 12 (2013) and *Hollingsworth v. Perry*, 133 S.Ct. 2652 (2013).

3. As goes the family so goes the entire society. As we shall see in the later discussion of economics, such radical individualism and liberalism will be at the root of economic errors. If one can define for oneself what is a marriage, what prevents one from defining for oneself what is economically just?

state had no business defining marriage. His inference was, however, incorrect. The reason the state has no business defining marriage is that no person has the competence to do so. The State, and any individual, for that matter, is likewise incompetent to define or redefine what is water, fire, or the sun. Marriage is what it is, as these other substances are. People have the ability to think about and understand to a greater or lesser extent what comprises the preexisting essence of marriage. The state only has the ability to craft laws with respect to the implications flowing from this reality to the extent necessary for the common good. The institution itself is not in any way subject to the volition of individuals or the state to determine its nature.

So if marriage is not whatever we want it to be, how do we know that it is the lifelong society of one man and one woman for the purpose of begetting, rearing, and educating children? There are two sources of our knowledge: the natural law and the divine law. In this chapter we will consider the natural law reasoning which proves this definition. We will examine the natural law, not because it says anything different from divine law or is superior to it; on the contrary, as they both have their origin in the same source, the eternal law, the divine reason, they are completely in accord with one another. Our reason is that we must be familiar with these arguments to defend the truth in a nation whose leaders willfully refuse to listen to arguments from the divine law. Our ultimate object must be the total willing conversion of society to Christ and his Church so that all joyfully and willingly accept the divine law and desire to act accordingly. In the interim, prior to that time which we must work toward in tandem, if our society conforms its mores, institutions, and laws to the natural law, the common good will be better served. Again, we should not abandon the efforts towards conversion; yet we should seek to improve the current situation by reference to arguments made on the natural level, the only level of discourse open to those in whom grace is not yet operative. As St. Thomas would say, since grace perfects nature, the more people conform to nature, the more disposed they are to accept grace.

With this explanation for the need of articulating natural law arguments about what constitutes marriage, let us turn to the substance. Natural law thinking employs a methodology of deriving principles of moral action ("ought statements") from what we can discern about the way things are since we ought to act in accordance with the way things are. One approach to reasoning from the nature of things to the law obligated by such nature looks at the purpose or function of things to deduce proper action on the basis of asking whether the proposed action accords with or detracts from that purpose. We examine the essence or nature of things to discern their purpose or end. Good actions are ones in harmony with those ends, and evil actions are opposed to those ends.

We can thus make arguments about what marriage is (and derivatively what society should recognize as such in its institutions) by examining the function or purpose of the act distinguishing this state of marriage from others. The thing that separates marital relationships from other relationships is the use of a particular act, appropriately enough referred to for centuries as the "marital act." Now what is the function or purpose of this act? Simple observation demonstrates that this act has the function of bringing into existence other creatures like those making use of it. The function of the act, that which it naturally produces, is procreation. This logical inference is no different from concluding that the function of inhaling is to breathe oxygen and remain alive.

Some try to argue that it is possible to use the marital act for other purposes. Yet the fact that a thing oriented for a purpose is capable of being misused for another purpose does not disprove the fact of its natural inclination. One can use the ability to inhale to breathe in deadly poison, but doing so is not using the act in accordance with its natural function. Modern technological knowledge about the operation of the biological aspects of the marital act has only confirmed what people have always known. For the act to be oriented towards this function of procreation, a male and a female must be the participants. The resort to use of the marital act (or more accurately a part of it) by two persons of the same gender is inherently not ordered to this purpose. The purpose is in no way capable of being attained in this manner.

So far we have proven only that a man and a woman together making use of the marital act are necessary to orient it towards its natural function. We have not yet demonstrated the further conclusion that for humans (as distinguished from other animals) the act involves a long-term stable relationship between the partners. To do so we need to consider human beings not in relation to what they have in common with animals but the aspect of their nature that distinguishes them.

First, we can note that unlike many animals, human beings are born incapable of satisfying even the most basic needs for survival. They require an extended period of complete care by mature humans to even survive. Just on a physical level, people are born social animals (creatures that depend on being present in a society). This indicates another purpose associated with the act of procreation. It must be undertaken in a situation in which a society exists, the presence of people capable of fulfilling this long-term need for care. Thus, the end of the act can be further described as procreation and care (or rearing) of offspring.

Yet some other animals also require similar periods of physical care. Man is further distinguished from all animals by his unique characteristic of having the use of reason and volition. It is also evident that these powers are present but not capable of being used at all initially. They need to mature. Human history also demonstrates that they are capable of being used well or poorly. As St. Thomas explains, we need to be trained in the use of these faculties and in the subjection of the lower faculties (the passions, for example) to them. If modern psychology has proven anything, it has demonstrated the great complexity inherent in this process of training of the reason and the will. Training in the use of these complex, interrelated faculties requires more than mere physical care. It requires education and discipline. These processes extend over several decades (almost one decade before the faculties are even able to be used—the age of reason) and another decade to acquire the discipline of how to use them well. Again, as modern psychology has demonstrated, the details of each person's path to making proper use of these faculties is highly unique. It interacts with the nuances of each individual's personality type and other factors. Thus, those directing this process must be able to acquire the relevant breadth of experience of the contingent factors present for each new child over the course of time. The aspect of the end of the marital act, which we have called the education and training of children, requires a fixed, stable society, i.e., a society that is not dissoluble and whose members are not coming and going. Again, man is a social animal. He needs stable social interaction to develop and make use of his faculties. Where people can come and go from a place at will, they are not in a society; they are merely sharing for the moment living space. The reason and will need to be made to work in harmony with man's social nature. This learning is acquired by observing and experiencing others living in society. One living in an environment that is not a society of two adults that can serve as the model for societal interaction is unable to be educated in the use of his social nature. The particular implications of this observation for the process of managing (in the fullest sense of this term) this household society and its relations with the outside world will be explored in the next section of this chapter.

Human experience confirms the conclusion that people need to be reared in the society of a marriage. One need not look to Catholics (or even natural law proponents) for evidence that children who grow up in incomplete or non-existent familial societies have greater difficulties in mastering the use of reason and their wills.

Another aspect of the social nature of man confirms the need for a man and a woman to form this society. As Aristotle and St. Thomas explain, society is born out of the incomplete nature of individuals. This does not mean that human beings are incomplete physical forms (like a dog with a missing leg). Rather, they are incapable of fulfilling all of their needs themselves (in the broadest, not just material, sense). Society results from the completion of each member through interaction with the others. A society is formed among those in need of what others have. Thus, neighborhoods form, in part, because some families produce food, others clothes, others shoes, and they need to live together to complement and fulfill one another's material needs.

Now, men and women complement or complete each other. We have already seen this on the physical level. Neither a man nor woman contains within himself or herself what is necessary to beget a child. Each one brings something to complete the process. It is also true on other levels. Men and women's physical, intellectual, emotional, and spiritual compositions differ and therefore complement each other. Therefore, a society of merely one type is incomplete, lacking the balance of complementary abilities. This is why societies of one gender need to transcend the mere natural level: a supernatural grace, religious vows, is needed to make such an unnatural society possible. Grace supplies for the want of nature in such supernatural societies.

The state of marriage is a natural society. (I recognize that Christ transformed this natural state among the members of the Church into a supernatural sacramental state; yet grace does not eradicate nature but merely builds on it.) Thus, for this society to be a society it requires members that complete one another. This society needs to be more than long lasting; it needs to be comprised of members that complement rather than mirror one another.

To summarize, the ends or purpose of the marital act are the begetting, rearing, and education in a society of children. These ends require the use of the act by a man and a woman who have formed a stable, enduring, and complementary society.

Now, some may object to these arguments by suggesting that the end of the act can be defined not as we have, but as the attainment of pleasure. We can observe that the act results in this sensation, so whenever it does so, it is fulfilling its purpose. The problem with this argument is that pleasure is not a useful guide for practical decision making about means to proper ends. The experience of pleasure is a by-product of attainment of a proper end (or put another way, of doing good), but it can also accompany other situations. For example, one may experience a sensation of pleasure in inhaling burning tobacco smoke. Yet this sensation of pleasure does not correlate with a conclusion that smoking tobacco furthers the good or end of bodily health and preservation of life. This type of reasoning is analogous to the following argument: I need to go to Egypt. I know that if I am in Egypt, I will feel hot. I board a plane that lands in Panama. I experience the sensation of being hot. I would wrongly conclude that I have reached my end destination, Egypt. Pleasure may then be an aspect of a properly oriented act (or, as Aristotle and St. Thomas would say, in attaining a state of happiness), but it is not identical to it. Pleasure therefore cannot be an end (or good) in itself, as it is merely an attribute associated with ends.

This trap of misconceiving pleasure as a guide to right behavior is not the exclusive property of those holding an incorrect understanding of marriage. Even some Catholics, such as Christopher West, have succumbed to this fallacy by making pleasure (albeit one they attempt unsuccessfully to keep properly restrained within marriage) the center of the argument.[4]

This following of pleasure to find the definition of marriage has led to confusion and the ineffective fight against the insanity of same-sex "marriage." A majority of Catholics support the legalization of same-sex "marriages."[5] It was a Supreme Court with a Catholic majority that invalidated the Defense of Marriage Act. While only two of the six Catholic justices voted to strike down DOMA, the four in the dissenting opinion relied not on natural law principles to justify their decision, but on democratic principles, thereby still upholding the right of the People to define marriage as they wish. How is this possible? The Church has been betrayed by Catholic justices in the majority and the dissent of this decision because, in the words of St. John Fisher, "the fort has been betrayed even of those who should have defended it." The Second Vatican Council is really the ultimate party to blame for this court decision and for Catholics' confusion over the essence of marriage. The Council adopted the false idea that reality can become whatever a majority, no matter how nefariously procured, declares it to be.

As documented in scholarly detail by Roberto de Mattei in *The*

4. See e.g., Christopher West, *Theology of the Body Explained: A Commentary on John Paul II's Man and Woman He Created Them* (Pauline Books & Media 2007). For commentary on the problematic way in which Christopher West discusses the marital debt, see "Christopher West's ideas on sexuality ignore 'tremendous dangers,' Alice von Hildebrand says," *Catholic News Agency*, May 12, 2009, available at http://www.catholicnewsagency.com/news/christopher_wests_ideas_on_sexuality_ignore_tremendous_dangers_alice_von_hildebrand_says/.

5. Robert P. Jones, "After DOMA, the fading future of religious opposition to same-sex marriage," Washington Post, June 27, 2013. http://www.washingtonpost.com/blogs/on-faith/wp/2013/06/27/after-doma-the-fading-future-of-religious-opposition-to-same-sex-marriage/.

Second Vatican Council: An Unwritten Story, the Council unfolded on the premise that a majority of bishops in council could change the reality of Catholic teaching. That which centuries of Tradition and pope after pope had declared wrong was all of a sudden declared right. The notion of the collective government of the Church rather than the monarchial government of the Church is merely a rehashing of the errors and failures of Conciliarism in the late Middle Ages.[6] The participation of Catholics in ecumenical hoot-a-nannies was condemned by pope after pope. The propositions that the Church and state should be separated and that people had a right to publicly practice false religions had been solemnly condemned. Yet the French Revolution in the Church, as the Council was described by Cdl. Suenens, tried to sweep all this reality away and proclaim a new reality of collegiality, ecumenism, and religious liberty. Now by a wave of the *mihi placet* (it pleases me), post-conciliar popes declare this obvious contradiction to be continuity.

Specifically relevant to the understanding of marriage and the Supreme Court's denial of reality is the reversal of the Tradition's definition of the ends of marriage. As the Church's philosophy of teleology holds that what things are is a function of their end, a change in the definition of the ends of something involves a change of the definition of what it is. Here, the "what" is the reality of marriage as the union of a man and woman for the end of procreation and rearing of children. The Church had always and everywhere taught that the primary end of marriage is the procreation and rearing of children. The secondary end is the mutual support of the spouses, and the third end the quieting of the desires of concupiscence. The second and third end relate to emotional and physical pleasure. The emotional support of the spouses and the quieting of the appetites are pleasures that accompany the fulfillment of the primary end of the marital act. The sensation of pleasure is not the guide but rather the accompaniment of the primary end. The innovators sought at the Council to overturn this hierarchical definition and topple the primary end from its position of primacy. Their goal was either to invert the order of ends, placing pleasure as the highest

6. See Rao, *Black Legends*, 239–43, 263–64.

and procreation the secondary end, or institute an incommensurability of the ends of marriage, thus holding them all of equal value, a novel philosophy that would be developed by John Finnis and Germain Grisez after the Council to defend the novelty of the Council.[7] As Dr. Roberto de Mattei writes, "Unfortunately the family morality formulated in the chapter 'The dignity of matrimony and of the family' in *Gaudium et spes* would incorporate the suggestions of the innovators, rather than those of the defenders of traditional morality."[8] The prophetic criticism of the ideas of the innovators made by Cdl. Ruffini has come to fulfillment in the acceptance of same-sex "marriage" by Catholics, including Supreme Court justices:

> It seems that the concept of matrimony as we have understood it until now, dogmatically and morally, has to change, at least in practice. But is it possible that the Church was mistaken until now, and that adaptation to today's society forces us to declare that what was always held to be immoral is [now] in keeping with morality?[9]

Cardinal Ruffini was at the time specifically referring to another type of unnatural union than that at issue in the Supreme Court—that of the contraception of marital acts—but his observation equally applies to the issue decided by the Court. Once procreation is no longer the primary end of the act, and the emotional and physical pleasures are elevated to its equal or superior, then denying the fulfillment of these two ends for those who want to do so with someone of the same sex is, in the language of Justice Kennedy (a Catholic), a denial of their dignity. Since same-sex actors attempt to fulfill the newly elevated ends of marriage, they must be recognized as married even though their act is not ordered to the primary end of marriage—procreation. By disturbing this hierarchy of ends,

7. See e.g., John Finnis, *Natural Law and Natural Rights* (Oxford: Oxford University Press, 2011), 92–95, 410. For a more detailed discussion of Finnis's rejection of a hierarchy of ends or goods, see Brian M. McCall, "The Architecture of Law: Building Law on a Solid Foundation, the Eternal and Natural Law," 10 *Vera Lex* 47 (2009).

8. Roberto de Mattei, *The Second Vatican Council: An Unwritten Story*, trans. Michael J. Miller (Fitzwilliam, New Hampshire: Loreto Publications, 2012), 396–97.

9. Quoted by Mattei, *The Second Vatican Council*, 394.

which subordinates pleasure to the primary end, *Gaudium et spes* cleared the way for a definition of marriage based on pleasure. The decision of the Catholics in the Supreme Court decision to invalidate the Defense of Marriage Act was made not in Washington, DC, but in St. Peter's in this chapter of *Gaudium et Spes*, a document even Pope Benedict XVI worried was imbued with the errors of Pelagianism.

The ineffective dissent of the Catholics in this Court decision was also decided in St. Peter's through the entire course of the Council, which proceeded as if majorities of votes could change reality or truth. The dissenting opinions of the Catholic justices would have upheld the Defense of Marriage Act using liberal principles. They would uphold the law not because it is a restatement of the immutable natural law but because it is the will of the people. Whether the government should bestow the rights and benefits of marriage on non-marriages is not an issue of truth and justice but merely a choice to be left to the "political branches." Justice Scalia dissented simply to uphold the right of the people to decide whether or not to deny reality and violate the principle of non-contradiction and declare that which is not a marriage to be a marriage. He wrote: "We might have covered ourselves with honor today, by promising all sides of this debate that it was theirs to settle and that we would respect their resolution. We might have let the People decide."[10] All hail and bow down to the "divine" revelation of the god of the People. The people had spoken in the Defense of Marriage Act, and therefore according to Scalia the cause is closed. A federal law declaring these unnatural acts to be marriages would be perfectly legal according to Justice Scalia's argument as long as the People vote in favor of it. Truth is relative and changes with majorities. Justice Alito lines up with Justice Scalia to defend the lunacy of the People to declare their own reality: "I hope that the Court will ultimately permit the people of each State to decide this question for themselves."[11] If a majority of votes at a Council of the Church can

10. *United States v. Windsor*, 570 U.S. 12 (2013), Scalia, J., dissenting. http://www.supremecourt.gov/opinions/12pdf/12-307_6j37.pdf.

11. Ibid., Alito, J., dissenting.

declare that which has always been wrong to be right, then the will of the People must be respected to do the same. For Scalia and Alito and those joining parts of their dissents, the error of the majority is not their denial of the reality of marriage but their intervention to cut short the political debate over whether we should launch off into the deep of contradiction of nature.

Sadly these Catholic jurists on the majority and the dissent who are clearly not in "full communion" with reality or Catholic doctrine should be pitied more than criticized. They are sheep who were led to the guillotine slaughter by their revolutionary shepherds in 1789 in the Church. They are simply in "full communion" with the implications of Vatican II. Truth is not the correspondence of our mind to reality but the bending of reality to what the will of the People decrees. If even the most holy supernatural sacrifice of the Mass can be reshaped to the tastes of modern man, why cannot the natural institution of marriage? If the Mass should be made more pleasurable for the tastes of modern man, why cannot marriage? Such is the fruit of following pleasure rather than reality. Justices Kennedy and Sotomayer simply were more consistent in their use of the contradiction in *Gaudium et spes* than the dissenters, who will live with whatever the outcome of the votes are in a Church Council or in the Congress.

We have proven from the book of natural observations that the nature of the marital act indicates ends that necessitate a complementary and permanent society to be formed between a man and a woman. The emotional and physical pleasures that accompany the formation of this society do not define it but rather follow its formation. Since God is the author of both nature and direct revelation, we know that these conclusions from natural law will concur with revelation. A brief look at the traditional Nuptial Mass will confirm such. Marriage is referred to as an institution ordained for the "propagation of the human race" (first part of the Nuptial Prayer). Note this phrase is not just the birth of more individual humans but the propagation or continuation of the human race (*humani generis*), which requires the training and education in that which makes one human. The Epistle from St. Paul speaks directly of the complementary roles of man and woman that make up the marital society (Eph. 5:22–33). There are several references to the need for permanence, e.g., "May you see your children's children" (Second Post-Communion).

Natural and divine revelation concurs. Their Author designed it this way. Marriage is designed to further the purpose for which it was created. The fact that divine revelation (even from the first book of the Bible) needs to reaffirm this fact demonstrates why we need to be reminded of the conclusions of nature. Men poorly trained in the use of their reason can fail to recognize this truth written in our nature. Yet the law written on the heart cannot be totally erased (even if obscured). The more natural law arguments are made, eventually the heart will see the truth of the way things are. Those in power know this all too well. Unable to defeat the arguments from nature, their only resort is to pass laws that deny reality and then attempt to silence contrary arguments by force of law dressed in the guise of law.

Authority in the Household: With All My Worldly Goods I Thee Endow

Few serious Catholics surveying the state of our society would deny that the Catholic infallible and irreformable teaching on marriage has been under direct attack for some time. The varying legal and social volleys (the legalization of homogender "marriage," no fault divorce, pervasive adultery) make advances due to a weakened belief in the defining characteristics of marriage. In addition to outright attacks on marriage, attacks on core characteristics of marriage destroy our understanding of the institution. The first of these attributes is indissolubility. Once a valid marriage is contracted, it may only be dissolved by the death of one spouse. The reason for this truth is simple. Once married, the two previously separate people become two in one flesh. A body cannot be taken apart absent death. Leo XIII summarizes this principal thus:

> From the Gospel we see clearly that this doctrine was declared and openly confirmed by the divine authority of Jesus Christ. He bore witness to the Jews and to His Apostles that marriage, from its institution, should exist between two only, that is, between one

> man and one woman; that of two they are made, so to say, one flesh; and that the marriage bond is by the will of God so closely and strongly made fast that no man may dissolve it or render it asunder. 'For this cause shall a man leave father and mother, and shall cleave to his wife, and they two shall be in one flesh. Therefore now they are not two, but one flesh. What, therefore, God hath joined together, let no man put asunder.'[12]

The second principal is the divinely ordained hierarchy within the marriage and family. The enemies of marriage set out to destroy this second principle before the first, which attack is their current object. Thus, many Catholics of good will who valiantly defend the first principle of marriage have absorbed the rejection of this second principle. Pius XI warned the faithful over three quarters of a century ago that this was the goal of the communists: to destroy this natural ordering within the family:

> Communism is particularly characterized by the rejection of any link that binds woman to the family and the home, and her emancipation is proclaimed as a basic principle. She is withdrawn from the family and the care of her children, to be thrust instead into public life and collective production under the same conditions as man. The care of home and children then devolves upon the collectivity. Finally, the right of education is denied to parents, for it is conceived as the exclusive prerogative of the community, in whose name and by whose mandate alone parents may exercise this right.[13]

The true principle that has been undermined even among Catholics can be summarized by the statement that the husband is head of the wife and the family. The family is a heterogeneous rather than a homogeneous body. A homogenous body contains parts that possess no life apart from the body. A human body is homogenous as an arm cannot exist in any way separately from the body. A heterogeneous body is composed of parts that have a life that can exist separately from the whole. There is a natural unity that exists in a homogeneous organism. A heterogeneous organism needs a princi-

12. Leo XIII, *Arcanum* (Vatican City: Libreria Editrice Vaticana, 1880), no. 5.
13. Pius XI, *Divini Redemptoris*, no. 11.

ple of order to unify it.[14] This order consists in a balance between individuals pursuing their individual path to their end and the need for that to be done commonly, which is the common good. The principle of order is the power of authority that is entrusted with the task of making decisions for the common good of the body, leaving to individuals the election of means not directly touching the common good. The eternal law, although fixing the ends of creatures, does not fix for man the means to those ends. The eternal law legislates the course of these means only in general by implanting the natural inclinations. The eternal law provides for the cooperation of man in formulating the principles of election of means through working out determinations of the principles of natural law in organized heterogeneous societies.[15] These societies require a head, a principle of order to unify them.

As the marriage union constitutes a new body that is heterogeneous, that body must have different parts, including a head and a heart. The husband is the head. Pope Leo XIII clearly states, "The husband is the chief of the family and the head of the wife. The woman, because she is flesh of his flesh, and bone of his bone, must be subject to her husband and obey him; not, indeed, as a servant, but as a companion, so that her obedience shall be wanting in neither honor nor dignity."[16]

Attacks on marriage proceed by attaching both the indissolubility of marriage and the hierarchical ordering of the family. For example, two persons of the same gender cannot enter into a marriage since neither could fill the role of "head" of such a union (both being of the same gender). Once marriage is seen as a purely equal partnership, why can't both equal partners dissolve it?

Many Catholics spend much time attempting to debate these first principles and such efforts are praiseworthy. Yet traditionalists know all too well from the liturgical debacle of the past fifty years that often our actions (including symbolic actions) can do more to reinforce (or destroy) belief than can rational argument. Thus, all

14. See Grenier, *Thomistic Philosophy*, 289.
15. See Aquinas, *Summa*, I–II, Q. 108, art. 2.
16. Leo XIII, *Arcanum*, no. 11.

the magisterial protestations of the need for belief in the Real Presence achieve little aside contradictory practices, such as Communion given in the hand, the simplified forms of purification of the sacred vessels, lay ministers of Communion, the abolition of preserving the canonical fingers, etc. Details are important; they can maintain or destroy belief. As with practically everything Catholic, we can easily apply this lesson from the liturgy to marriage.

Over the course of centuries, the Holy Ghost has encouraged and guided customs and practices that reinforce the understanding of and belief in the two foundational principles of marriage. Since the husband and wife become one flesh, the custom evolved of taking one name. The retention of separate names implies the retention of separate individuals, not two in one new societal body. The question thus follows: Whose name? As the head of the marriage, the husband's primary duty (and burden) is to represent the family to the outside world, whereas the wife's duty is to properly order the interior life of the home. It is a logical corollary of the headship of husbands that his name should be enlarged to represent the entire family unit. The trend to retain maiden names in marriage undermines the proper understanding of the new one body.

Likewise, until the past century and a half, property was not held individually by each spouse but by the one flesh. Since the husband was the head of that one body, it was held in his name. The squawking of modern feminists notwithstanding, such a practice was not intended to oppress women. With the obligation to hold the marital wealth comes the duty of doing so in the best interests of the whole body, not just the head. Again, this duty is natural as one does not act against the interest of his own flesh (which now includes the wife). The husband may have held property in his own name, but he was not free to use it solely for his own benefit. He bears a solemn obligation to provide for the needs of his wife and their children. The taking on of this responsibility is seen in the custom of the dowry. In recognition of this burden, on marriage the wife's family transfers a portion of their wealth to the husband to aid him in this obligation. This understanding, that the husband although legal owner of the marital property is not the sole beneficiary of such wealth, is clearly seen in the words of the Traditional Rite of

Marriage. While placing the wedding ring on his wife's finger, he says, "With this ring I thee wed; this gold and silver I thee give; with my body I thee worship; and with all my worldly goods I thee endow." Webster defines "endow" as "to furnish with an income; *especially*: to make a grant of money providing for the continuing support or maintenance of."[17] As there is no reciprocal right of the husband or obligation for the wife, the Traditional Rite does not prescribe that these words be said by the wife. As the husband bears the obligation to support the wife, the wife is endowed with the right to be cared for in all her physical needs by the husband. It is to satisfy this duty that the husband owns the property. Seen in its proper context, such a system is actually beneficial for women. They have a right to demand their husband use all worldly goods for their care and benefit.

Following from the above discussion it is obvious why it is the husband's primary obligation to procure the resources the family unit requires. This is why until about the middle of the last century, the work force was comprised mostly of men. This is not to say that women were incapable of performing much of the work men did, but rather that it was the man's primary obligation to provide and the wife's right to be provided for. This is not to say that women were prohibited from work out of necessity (i.e., if her husband became seriously ill and was incapable of providing for them). Again, the liturgy provides an analogy. In ordinary circumstances only the priest should bring the Blessed Sacrament to the sick. Yet we know from the life of St. Tarcisius that in the extraordinary need of the persecutions, lay people and even children were required to fulfill this duty not typically belonging to them. The problem with modern understanding is that the extraordinary exception has become the ordinary norm. Lay ministers hand out Communion while priests sit sipping coffee on the altar.[18] Likewise, wives work while capable husbands stay at home. The extraordinary has

17. Merriam-Webster Online Dictionary. http://www.merriam-webster.com/dictionary/endow.

18. Such an incident was reported to me by an eye witness while we lived in England in the early years of this century.

become normal. As a result of this change in practice, people begin to consider the exception to be the rule.

For the past several decades, more wives have left the home to enter the workforce. In 1950, approximately 35 percent of women were either employed or actively seeking employment. In 2004, this percentage had risen to approximately 60 percent.[19] The effect this has caused is that the real wages of men have declined so much that many more families are unable to survive with only one person working.[20] Even a cursory knowledge of simple economic rules told us this would happen. As the supply of labor increases with more women entering the workforce, the price for labor decreases. Thus, the change to two-worker families has not actually improved the net income of families. This appears to be yet another false promise of the devil come to pass.

Turning from economics to politics, we see that voting prior to the turn of the twentieth century was a public act undertaken by men. Again, contrary to the cries of the suffragettes, the reason was not that women were incapable of making elective decisions, but that as one flesh, man and woman should vote as only one voice not two (and even opposite, thus cancelling each other out). Again, as the headship is placed on the husband, it was the husband who bore the burden of expressing the choice of the one flesh after properly considering the matter (including what his "heart" or wife had to say on the matter).

Thus both in the political and economic realm, the body of a marriage is comprised of different members. The husband as the head looks outward to represent the body to the world, to speak for it in political matters and to bring home the fruits of the labor inflicted on him by Adam's sin. The wife as the heart looks inward to care for and love the body of the family. The Catechism of the Council of Trent says it beautifully: "The wife should love to remain

19. See Bureau of Labor Statistics, "Labor Force Statistics from the Current Population Survey," Civilian Labor Force Participation Rate. http://www.bls.gov/cps/.

20. John Forman, *Making America Work* (Baltimore, MD: The Urban Institute Press, 2006), 28.

at home unless compelled by necessity to go out."[21] Before we take to the streets to argue with the world regarding the nature of marriage, we should pause and look at the daily liturgy and ceremonies of our own marriages. Do they conform to these principals of marriage? Do we act as we believe—that we are really one indissoluble body of which the husband is the head? As with the Real Presence or the nature of the priesthood, if the answer is no (we do not act as we believe), we will eventually change our beliefs to conform to our actions. The remaining sections of this chapter consider further aspects of the family's practical contact with the outside world and how incorrect practices are a manifestation of the incorrect principles identified in this chapter so far.

A Crisis of Authority

As should be evident from the considerations in this chapter thus far, the City of Man has been waging war against the City of God for control of the commonwealth on the battlefield of the family. The City of Man attempts to alter the reality of the essence of the family by redefining the nature of marriage. Such a profound assault on reality is bound to have reverberations. The prior section of this chapter introduced the need for authority in the family. As degenerate moderns attempt to mock marriage by forming families with two heads rather than one heart and one head, it is no wonder that the entire concept of authority in the family is under attack. The current crises throughout our economy and our nation are at their core a crisis of authority. Those possessing authority refuse to exercise it for the common good. Secular and ecclesiastical leaders snivel and push papers around endless committees and conferences as Church and civil society collapse around us. The pope shies away from his infallible authority to combat heresy. Predators abuse children while cardinals hand wring and file bankruptcy to protect their assets.

On the other hand, those who attempt to use their God-given authority for the common good of those in their care are thwarted at every turn. The Reformation was an assault on ecclesiastical

21. *Catechism of the Council of Trent* (Charlotte, NC: TAN Books, 1982), 352.

authority, the French Revolution on the authority of legitimate rulers of nations. The ongoing round of the Revolution is focused on destroying the authority of parents. The family is the most basic and fundamental unit of authority in human society. The totalitarian megalomania of liberalism must eliminate all that opposes its oppression in the name of freedom. With the conquest of Church and monarchy complete, having executed or reduced to harmless bureaucrats these two pillars of authority, all that stands in liberalism's way now is the authority of parents over their children. Authority in the home is under attack.

One day two legal news items crossed my desk providentially. Together they epitomize the practical and theoretical attack on rightful parental authority in our nation. First on the practical level, the US Supreme Court in *Brown v. Entertainment Merchants Association* struck down a California law banning the sale to children of extremely violent video games. The "conservative" Catholic Justice Scalia wrote the majority opinion declaring that businesses have a constitutionally protected right of free speech to sell incredibly violent video games to little children. Scalia's unholy alliance was completed by Justices Kennedy, Ginsberg, Sotomayor, Kagan, Alito, and Roberts (the final two filing their own concurring opinion). Only Justices Thomas and Breyer had the courage to dissent from this violation of the sanctity of the family, the innocence of children.

The "conservative" Justice Scalia struck a victory for the goddess Liberty—the right of video game manufacturers to fill the minds of our children with violent rot and make a hefty profit while doing so without their parents' knowledge or permission. Scalia and his hodgepodge alliance of "conservative" and liberal justices worship at the same altar of the goddess of liberty, proclaiming that the government has no right to restrict or regulate the content of free speech. Error indeed has rights in their jurisprudence—and not only error, but dangerous error, error that corrupts the youth. Scalia, unfurling his "traditionalist" jurisprudence, ruled that there is no "longstanding tradition in this country of specially restricting children's access to depictions of violence."[22] What a shame; if only

22. *Brown v. Entertainment Merchants Association*, 131 S.Ct. 2729 (2011).

the Founding Fathers had had the foresight to put an exception in the Constitution to protect children from violent video games, we could have had a longstanding tradition to do so! Scalia even has the audacity to compare such violently sensuous and morbid games to *Snow White* and *Hansel and Gretel*. To protect the preservation of our traditional fairy tales, we need to indiscriminately provide the same freedom to satanically inspired mass murder games. What more proof do we need that our society has completely lost touch with the objective moral order? With "traditionalist" logic like this, who needs enemies?

Traditionally going all the way back to even pagan Roman law, children were understood as having a particular legal status. Observing human nature, traditionally the law accepted that children possess the power of reason from their creation, but only gradually and with much guidance come to be able to use it rightly. Virtue as an acquired habit of acting can only be achieved under the direction and care of an educator. For this reason did God design the family. Every child is meant to be born under the authority of two parents whose masculine (head) and feminine (heart) qualities combine in a harmonious union of balanced authority. The government is charged with the obligation to make laws to support the exercise of this authority of the parents to assist in the promotion of virtue. A law protecting children from enticing experiences of evil is an example of such support. Traditionally, laws upheld the authority of the *paterfamilias* (the father of the household) to rule and protect the community in his care. Likewise, the dangers of exposure of the youth to senseless and bloodthirsty violence have been recognized since ancient times. Saint Augustine in his *Confessions* (6.8.13) tells the story of his friend Alypius, who is forced to attend the ruthlessly violent gladiatorial games. He intends to keep his eyes shut and not watch the pagan spectacle. Yet he finds the draw of the violent orgy irresistible and eventually opens his eyes. He becomes instantly addicted to the gore of the games and invites more friends to come to future games. Fortunately, he repents of this lapse, but St. Augustine demonstrates a truer understanding of the weakness of fallen human nature than does Justice Scalia in recognizing the corrupting dangers of exposure to such evil.

But Scalia and his six colleagues know that in this great era of Enlightenment, man has transcended his fallen nature. The age of liberty has arrived, and error and evil not only have equal rights but constitutionally protected equal rights of free speech, thanks to the Founding Fathers' not knowing about the future invention of grotesquely violent video games. Our tradition demands that little children be free to buy virtue-destroying entertainment!

The second article I read on the same day was a summary of a forthcoming book[23] by Jeffrey Shulman of the "Catholic" Georgetown University Law Center. His book, the essence of the argument of which has been published in a prior law review article,[24] aims at ending the erroneous legal belief that parents have a right to control the education of their children. No, says Shulman, they only have a duty to educate them, and if they fail to educate them as the state sees fit, the state can take control. His reading of parent/child law reveals "the notion that the only entrusts the parent with educational custody of the child, and does so only as long as the parent meets his or her duty to serve the best interests of the child."[25] Professor Shulman argues that "[t]his harm standard protects religious parenting rights at too great a cost: It sacrifices the best interests of the child in order to bolster parental authority. It is a cost that children should not be asked to bear.[26] Note: God no longer entrusts the rearing and education of the child to his co-operators in creation (the parents who engage in acts suitable for procreation). No, it is the state that giveth and the state that can taketh away—when it deems the parents' plan of education is not in the "best interests of the child." A standard which Professor Shulman argues is too favorable to the parents.

What are these "best interests?" According to Shulman, it is not the acquisition of truth but "intellectual incitement" that will pre-

23. Jeffrey Shulman, *The Constitutional Parent: Rights, Responsibilities, and the Enfranchisement of the Child* (New Haven, CT: Yale University Press, 2014).

24. Jeffrey Shulman, "Who Owns the Soul of the Child?: An Essay on Religious Parenting Rights and the Enfranchisement of the Child," 6 *Charleston Law Review* (2012): 101–163.

25. Ibid., abstract to article, available at http://ssrn.com/abstract=1763854.

26. Ibid., 111.

pare the child "to make free and independent choices."[27] The parents fail if they restrict "the spectrum of knowledge available to the child,"[28] and thereby fail "to prepare the child for obligations beyond those of familial obedience."[29] Like Scalia, Shulman proclaims the philosophy of liberalism. Freedom of choice is the ultimate good. Evil and error and violent video games must have equal rights. Education, according to Shulman, means helping children "to leave their homes and leave behind the ways of their parents. Or, at least, it means giving children the choice to do so."[30] Education is about liberating children from the traditional values of Christianity handed down faithfully from generation to generation through the guidance of the family. But according to Shulman the law of parent child relationships must "protect" children from "this sort of 'protection,' ensuring that children receive a truly public education that can bring its students a much needed respite from the ideological solipsism of the enclosed family."[31] Public education, according to Shulman, "disrupts the intramural transmission of values from parent to child. It threatens to dismantle a familiar world by introducing the child to multiple sources of authority—and to the possibility that a choice must be made among them. Indeed, the open world of the public school should challenge the transmission of any closed set of values."[32] What could possibly be meant by "closed set of values?" Perhaps he means Catholicism, with its closed system of values not open to the diversity of divorce, "free" love made possible by contraception and abortion, and most importantly unnatural homosexual behavior. Yes, if parents are protecting their children from exposure to these fruits of liberalism, the state must free the child to enter the paradise of public education.

Since the days of Rousseau and Dewey, this has been the aim of the public education system: to free children from the authority of

27. Ibid., abstract to article. See also Ibid., 113.
28. Ibid., 136.
29. Ibid., abstract to article.
30. Ibid.
31. Ibid. This argument is elaborated on pages 138 and 142 of the article.
32. Ibid., article abstract. See also Ibid., 139.

their God-given parents so as to expose them to the goddess of liberty. That is why our schools take little innocent souls from their parents to expose them to the new games of the coliseum, distorted and dysfunctional families, Internet and Facebook proficiency, and books about Johnny having two daddies. Shulman argues the power of law must be used to force this freedom on children and the fictional "right" of parents must be abolished in American law, replaced by a duty held at the pleasure of the state, ever ready to snatch away any little ones who are being oppressed with the transmission of traditional values, protecting them from the sewer of a culture in which we live.

The "closed system of values" of Catholicism denounced this error decades ago through the authoritative voice of the Supreme Pontiff, Pius XI when he wrote in the encyclical *Divini Illius Magistri*:

> The family therefore holds directly from the Creator the mission and hence the right to educate the offspring, a right inalienable because inseparably joined to the strict obligation, a right anterior to any right whatever of civil society and of the State, and therefore inviolable on the part of any power on earth. That this right is inviolable St. Thomas proves as follows: The child is naturally something of the father . . . so by natural right the child, before reaching the use of reason, is under the father's care. Hence it would be contrary to natural justice if the child, before the use of reason, were removed from the care of its parents, or if any disposition were made concerning him against the will of the parents. And as this duty on the part of the parents continues up to the time when the child is in a position to provide for itself, this same inviolable parental right of education also endures.[33]

Long gone are the days of such clear thinking. Such is the pervasive victory of liberalism. A law professor at a Catholic university argues against the God-given right and duty of parents to education their children by transmitting the closed system of Catholic truth. A Latin Mass-attending Catholic justice writes the majority opinion upholding the right of businesses to profit by selling virtue-destroying video

33. Pius XI, *Divini Illius Magistri* (Vatican City: Libreria Editrice Vaticana, 1929), no. 32.

games to little children. Where are our higher authorities in the Church to denounce these violations of God's order? Where are the bishops recalling Pius XI's words? They fiddle while parental authority burns in a Washington court house and the theoretical underpinnings of this diabolical attack are proclaimed from Georgetown. God help us—He is the only one who can!

Modest Contact with the World: Women in Pants and Similar Frauds

Having been involved in a number of Traditional Mass communities on both sides of the Atlantic, I have encountered many different points of view, debates, and controversies. There is one topic, however, that universally seems to spark furious debates even among traditionalists who apparently see eye to eye on all issues: women wearing trousers, or, as we say over here on this side of the pond, pants. I have seen a room of people solidly united in their abhorrence of the *Novus Ordo*, the state of "Catholic" schools, rampant heresy in the clergy *etc., etc.*; yet once this topic is raised, the room quickly divided into intractable "camps." The "Long Skirts" were seen by the "Casual Jeans" crowd as puritanical clothes police, and the latter were seen by the former as deluded compromisers with modernity. The Traditional movement must be a counter-cultural crusade not just a special interest group advancing its "preference" for Latin. Otherwise the entire effort is merely an antiquarian club of little social relevance. I doubt anyone would disagree that fashions and clothing are a significant part of culture. Attachment to traditional teachings about the nature, constitution of, and relationships within the family must be more than intellectual. These truths must have practical expression in our lives. Notwithstanding a culture that attempts to claim the way we present ourselves physically has no bearing on who we are or what we believe, Catholics must rise above such thinking. The way we dress and comport ourselves in public represents our world view. Thus, I think it necessary that we air this issue and carefully examine the arguments. To be fair, I will disclose that I am firmly in the "Long Skirt" camp (not that I wear them myself, but none of the women or girls entrusted to the care of the family of which I am the head may, nor desire to, wear pants).

With my cards on the table and knowing the tempests this may rouse, I will lay out two principle arguments for the unacceptability of women wearing trousers. (Yes, not just in Church when Father can see, but always.) Do you think it would be acceptable to say, "I don't speak obscenities in Church but at home," or "I don't gossip in Church but it is acceptable when I am out to dinner"? The arguments are related but distinct. Too often I have heard them conflated, which has not advanced the logic of the argument. The first reason relates to modesty, but the more definitive second reason is the Catholic anthropological understanding of the differences between men and women. Before rehearsing the arguments of reason, we should establish that reason is in harmony with revelation. Saint Paul with respect to the obligation to be modest teaches: "Let your modesty be known to all men. The Lord is nigh" (Phil. 4:5). As to the second argument: "A woman shall not be clothed with man's apparel, neither shall a man use woman's apparel: for he that doeth these things is abominable before God" (Deut. 22:5).

To address the modesty argument we must first understand the background. Modesty is a virtue that is a gift of God given to us to protect the great virtue of purity, which is given to us to protect the awesome creative power God has bestowed on us—the ability to participate in the creation of an immortal soul. God has revealed to us that sacred things are to be veiled and protected. Traditionalists should know this instinctively. The crowning glory of creation, our first parents—the one creature that bears the image of God himself—were veiled in a walled garden atop a mountain. The Law was given to Moses on a mountain veiled by a great cloud. The tablets of this Law written by the hand of God together with the manna that foreshadowed the *Panis Angelicus* to come were ordered by the Lord to be veiled within the Ark of the Covenant, which itself was to be protected in the fortress of the Temple, with its many layered courtyards leading to the Holy of Holies, with its great veil stretched across the entrance. This veil was torn asunder at the crucifixion to signify that this place was no longer sacred. The Blessed Sacrament is kept in a golden ciborium (the new Ark) and in the locked tabernacle (the new Holy of Holies), which contains a veil both behind the doors and over the outside. The chalice and paten that will enthrone the King of Kings when not in use in the act of sacrifice must be veiled. I could multiply the examples, but these will suffice.

The great creative power is likewise sacred. For this reason, God has veiled it within the confines of the sacrament of marriage. And within this fortress, the power is veiled within the wife. Just as the veil of the Holy of Holies was only to be parted by one man among all the chosen people of God, the Great High Priest, so too the creative power veiled within the inner sanctuary of each woman is to be unveiled by one only, and that within the confines of marriage. Yet, as even the veil of the Arc itself required further veiling, matrimony is veiled in the garment of purity or chastity. The sentinel at the door of this virtue (or the cherubim on the outside of the Ark) whose task is to protect purity against intrusion is the practice of modesty in dress, speech, action, and deportment.

Now that we have established the cosmological importance of the guardian of modesty as a principle, we have to turn with more precision to its application. In this we must draw a distinction. Despite the lie proclaimed for decades now that men and women are the same, thousands of years of human history expose the truth. Men and women are different and contain different tendencies towards sin. Men are more easily led to sins against purity through the sense of sight. For this reason, modesty for men chiefly requires custody of the eyes as the guard of purity. Women are more tempted through vanity to attract the eye of men. Despite the denials of the evolutionists, we are the children of our first parents. Eve's sin lay chiefly in offering the forbidden fruit and Adam's in partaking of it. This does not mean that men need be unconcerned with the modesty of their own dress nor women with the custody of their eyes. Men can offer the forbidden fruit and women can be drawn to impurity through their eyes, but this pattern is less typical. As anecdotal confirmation of this fact, consider whether men or women are more often the subject or consumer of pornographic material. Thus knowing each others' weaknesses, we are obliged in charity not to aid the devil in his work of temptation. Men must not encourage women's seductions by offering the gratification of a response, and women must not offer material to unbind the custody of the man's eye.

Since we are focused on the issue of women's dress, we will leave the topic of men's responsibility for another time (which should not be taken as a sign of its unimportance). Since men are drawn to sins of impurity through the eye (which as our Savior tells us can even be committed completely in the heart; Matt 5:27–28), women are obligated to dress in a manner that obscures the contours of their body, to conceal and not to reveal. A veil flows over its subject and hides lines of distinction and contour. This is why the timeless principles that the Church has laid down for women's standards in modesty in dress apply both to the extent the body is to be covered (a top no lower than two fingers' breadth below the pit of the neck, a skirt that is below the knee, sleeves that are at least a quarter length), but also the way the clothing accentuates the female form (fabric that is not transparent nor clings to the body). In light of these principles it is obvious that pants, no matter of what material or cut, tend not to conceal the female form in a veil but rather accentuate it. The sanctuary of the great creative power is not veiled from men's weak eyes as it would be with a skirt or dress (of proper length and cut). As Colleen Hammond has documented in her excellent work *Dressing with Dignity*, advertisers have found through research that when women dress in pants, men's eyes were universally drawn to the precise location of this creative sanctuary.[34] To know that women in pants have this effect on men and to wear them is thus a sin against charity as well as modesty. It is a false dichotomy to ask: Isn't it better that a woman wear loose trousers as opposed to a short mini-skirt? This is a false comparison used to advance a false conclusion. Catholics do not accept that a lesser of two evils becomes a good. Such a question is equivalent to asking whether it is not better to murder someone with a gun than with slow poisoning. Murder of the body, or soul, is wrong in any form. Certainly it is true that loose-flowing pants might be more modest than a tight mini-skirt (which would also be wrong), but the pants would violate the second principle: distinction of gender.

As I indicated at the outset, the two arguments although distinct are related. Women must veil their form to obscure its contours out

34. Colleen Hammond, *Dressing with Dignity* (Charlotte, NC: TAN Books, 2005).

of charity towards men. Yet, in addition to being modest (if of the appropriate length), skirts and dresses are appropriate attire for women because they more fittingly highlight the nature of women as different from men. Women are tabernacles capable of housing and protecting the hidden life of an immortal soul. In this way women are an image of Our Blessed Lady, the most perfect tabernacle that enclosed him whom the entire world cannot contain. Although men can strive to imitate the virtues of Our Lady, their bodies are incapable of mirroring her in this way. A skirt or a dress bear a visual similarity in shape and cut to a tabernacle veil, which trousers do not. For the woman wearing them and the man gazing on them, skirts and dresses serve as a poignant reminder of the sacred dignity of woman as tabernacle of life as distinct from the unique dignity of men. This last sentence strikes at the heart of the fraud perpetrated on our society by liberalism, the fraud that there is no significant difference between men and women. The ultimate insanity of this fraud is the idea that our gender is not bestowed by God but is a mere social convention we can change at our pleasure (going so far as mutilating our own bodies to effect the change). To perpetrate frauds, images of the truth must be destroyed. To force acceptance of the fraudulent idea that gender is changeable, images that highlight inherent differences must be wiped clean. In this sense I find it not to be a coincidence that a culture that strives so hard to desecrate this great Holy of Holies of women through contraception and abortion is also a culture that casts aside the veil-like form of dresses distinctive of women. Just so, the ravaging of the dogma of the Real Presence was accompanied by the violation of the tabernacles by removing them.[35]

Beyond losing this beautiful reminder of women's great dignity,

35. Some people have objected that in some non-Western cultures such as Hungary and India, women wore attire similar to pants and that the Church did not demand abandonment of this style for admission to the Church. On further examination, it becomes clear that the garment at issue was always a distinct female garment never worn by men. Even though it might bear a vague similarity to Western pants, these Slavic and Eastern cultures always maintained distinct male and female garments and thus did not violate the second principle respecting natural distinctions of gender, which operates independently of the principle of modesty.

the wearing of pants for centuries exclusively worn as men's clothes has serious ramifications for the relationships within the family. As Cdl. Siri stated in a notification concerning this issue, "The wearing of men's dress by women affects firstly the woman herself, by changing the feminine psychology proper to women; secondly it affects the woman as wife of her husband, by tending to vitiate relationships between the sexes; thirdly it affects the woman as mother of her children by harming her dignity in her children's eyes."[36] At the root of Cdl. Siri's analysis is a keen observation that women's wearing of pants, proper attire for men, is motivated by a desire to compete with men and even a desire to be a man. "[T]he clothing a person wears, demands, imposes, modifies that person's gestures, attitudes, and behavior such that from merely being worn outside, clothing comes to impose a particular frame of mind inside."[37]

What is the frame of mind that skirts promote? First, the softness of femininity is underscored by the flowing nature of a skirt with its fluid movement as opposed to the utilitarian and angular look of pants. Second, the skirt with its similarity to a veil reminds the woman of her obligation to guard the great creative potential within her. This does not mean that men bear no responsibility to avoid impure violations of this tabernacle. Their obligation is to turn away from the offered fruit. Woman, however, as the bearer of this power must protect it from being exposed to men's thoughts. Third, the modest restraint that should be the hallmark of womanliness is encouraged by a skirt. When wearing a skirt a woman must be more conscious of her movements, more restrained in swift and rough gestures, due to the open nature of the skirt. Thus, skirts encourage modest, feminine gestures and activities as opposed to a more masculine demeanor. It is prideful to assert that "I can wear jeans and resist the erosion of my feminine attitude. I can remain an obedient wife and still wear men's clothes." As Cdl. Siri explains, "True, the effects of wearing unsuitable dress are not all to be seen within a short time. But one must think of what is being slowly and

36. Giuseppe Cardinal Siri, "Notification Concerning Men's Dress Worn by Women," Letter, 1960. http://www.olrl.org/virtues/pants.shtml.

37. Ibid.

insidiously worn down, torn apart, perverted."[38] These delusions are merely new lies of the Father of Lies: "I can eat the forbidden fruit and not die; I can decide what is good and evil." Our fallen human nature cannot act and dress in one way and continue to think and believe another way. Is wearing pants once going to turn a traditionalist wife into a feminist? Obviously, it will not. Yet regularly doing so can cause her to think as if she were a feminist. In the same way, going to one *Novus Ordo* will not usually cause one to become a Modernist; yet one cannot continually attend the *Novus Ordo* and maintain traditional doctrine. To think we are above the psychological nature of our fellow creatures is the pride that will precede our individual fall.

Before concluding this discussion, I will address three common objections I have often met on this subject. First, dressing in a womanly fashion will make us look different from the rest of the world—make us look abnormal. Saint Paul has already addressed this. Our modesty is to be *known* before men. We should be recognized as Christians by our modesty. If we live in a non-Christian world, that means looking and acting somewhat differently. Further, if dressing immodestly leads us and others into sin, Our Lord has already told us what to do with things that lead into sin (poke out our eye; cut off our hand). If we are to do violence to our own bodies to avoid sin, can we resist throwing away our pants? Is it better to "fit in" with the look of the modern woman or "fit in" with heaven?

The second argument is that women cannot fulfill their responsibilities because some activities cannot be done in a skirt. If the pioneer women who tamed the vast wilderness of our country or ploughed the Great Plains could fulfill their duties in full skirts (not to mention hoops and corsets), how can any woman engulfed in the ease of modern gadgets and conveniences say they need to wear pants to perform their duties? I will concede there are certain physical activities that would be near impossible in a skirt (fighting in trench warfare, for example). Yet, if there is something really impossible to do in a skirt, does this not indicate this is an activity inappropriate for a woman to perform? A simple test of modest and

38. Ibid.

feminine behavior can be summarized: if you can't do it modestly and gracefully in a skirt, you shouldn't do it at all.

Third, women have complained they are too cold in skirts. This may be true, but is it due to the skirt? Is it not due rather to the abolition of appropriate undergarments for women? Without going into unnecessary detail, the "fashion" industry has nearly suppressed necessary compliments appropriate (for modesty and temperature) to skirts. Again, as another test of this argument, do we think that our feminine ancestors in the cold winters of New England, Russia, or Norway froze or threw off their skirts for their husband's pants? No, they wore appropriate complimentary clothing in cold weather together with their skirt.

Both revelation and reason agree that women should not be attired in men's clothing but in modest, feminine attire. Pants reveal the lines and contours of the feminine form and the wearing of them is thus difficult to reconcile with principles of modesty and charity towards the known weakness of men. The use of men's clothing changes the psychology of women and men. Women, wives, and mothers lose their sense of distinctiveness, gentility, modesty, and restraint, and men lose their respect for the elevated sacredness of women. A brief review of what has been possible in the wake of women first taking on men's clothes in the 1940s would include widespread violation of the sixth and ninth commandments, contraception, abortion, sacrilegious desecration of the tabernacle of women by sterilization, complete gender confusion in every perversion against nature, women fighting in the military, and universal divorce. Although other causes of these ills exist, they all are only possible on such a scale in a psychological milieu that destroys the distinctiveness of men and women upheld in Christian maidenhood and womanhood veiled from the sinful glare of men. Is it a surprise that people fail to accept the distinction of roles within the family, the head and the heart, when distinction in appearance has vanished?

Men's Obligations of Modesty and Dignity

The prior section of this chapter explained why women in charity have an obligation to dress in a way that conceals rather than reveals their figure. Women who do not dress in a feminine way also degrade their dignity as tabernacles of creation and distort their psychology and damage their relationships with their husbands and children. For this reason St. Paul exhorted women, "In like manner, women also in decent apparel: adorning themselves with modesty and sobriety...." (1 Tim. 2:9).

In developing this argument, I alluded to the duties of men with respect to modesty. They are manifold. For where women bear a responsibility, men as the head of families will always bear a complementary one. For example, wives must be subject to their husbands, but husbands must love their wives to the same extent Christ loves the Church, which means being willing to offer themselves up for their wives (Eph. 5:22–26). God created men to hold a position of authority. With that authority comes responsibility for those over which it is held. Those in authority will be called to answer for themselves and for those placed under their authority. This fact identifies the first obligation of men with respect to modesty. Men are responsible for the modesty (or immodesty) of the women entrusted to them. For every girl or woman who walks the streets in pants, there is a husband or father who will one day have to answer for his failing. Men can fail this duty in two ways: (1) by permitting immodesty and (2) by encouraging it. I have met both types. "I can't do anything about it, my daughter just insists on wearing those tight jeans." Then there are the men whose pride enjoys observing the ogling desire in other men's eyes gaping at the attractiveness of their wife. Both types will have much to answer for on the *dies irae.*

Men are generally the stronger physical gender. They have an obligation to use this strength to protect the modesty of women. This requires not only rescuing women in physical danger. Men also must never permit lewd conversation or undignified gestures to be tolerated towards, or in the presence of, a woman. The honor of women's purity should be defended with the same rigor that we would defend our Church's sanctuary against a sacrilege. Using St. Paul's analogy that men represent Christ and women the Church, men are obligated to defend a sacrilege of the sanctuary of a woman. This means that men need to exhibit the fortitude to rise up in protest against the daily conversations about the physical attributes of some particular woman or the discussion of her private activities. Joining in, or at least standing silently by, when a woman is talked of without the respect due her sacred role may preserve popularity on the job site or around the coffee machine in the office, but it does not win the friendship of him who offered his life for the sanctification of his bride.

If men and women do not complement each other in virtue (obedience and loving responsibility), then they will do so in vice. Thus, it is not a surprise that in the cesspool of our times (inaccurately referred to as a culture), women wear immodest and degrading clothing and men encourage and tolerate it. I have never done a scientific study, but my instinct tells me that it is mostly men who film and produce the billions of dollars of pornography women participate in each year. Without women willing to dress and act indecently and men willing to give an *imprimatur* to them for doing it, the world would look very different. Women may have to answer for how they are attired, but men will have to answer an even greater judgment. From him to whom much is given much is expected!

Men hold a double responsibility due to their position. A man is not only responsible for the immodesty of his wife and children; he also has obligations in his own dress and deportment. As women are bound by modesty to dress consistently with two principles (concealing their physical form and dressing in a matter appropriate to the dignity of their sacral duty), so too men must be guided by these two principles. First, men are obligated not to be seen with their bodies unduly exposed. This means that even if you are mowing the lawn in 98-degree weather, you do not do it without a shirt on. Men also cannot don trousers that display or accentuate the part of their anatomy through which original sin is transmitted to the next generation. As with women the principle is to conceal not reveal.

Beyond this obligation, men must always dress in a way befitting their station of authority. This second principle requires the rejection of the modern obsession with being casual at all times and in all places. This modern trend plays right into a natural sloth to which men are prone. Men tend to be more lax than women in concern for their cleanliness and neatness. Anyone with young sons knows that they must be constantly reminded to keep their hands washed, nails trimmed, shirts tucked in, and hair combed. Men have a serious responsibility and should dress in a way reflecting that sobriety. Obviously, attire needs to be appropriate for particular physical activity. I am not suggesting getting out a tuxedo to repave the driveway. (Although I have to mention I was once impressed when I saw a young Irish man walking the Chartres pilgrimage in a coat and tie. I have to admit I felt a pang of guilt as I entered the presence of Our Lord in Chartres Cathedral and looked at my rough hiking clothing.) It is most important that men dress with a minimum of formality when performing tasks most connected to their role of headship.

After Mass, the other major venue for men's headship role is in the work place. It was for this reason that in ten years of practicing law (several of which spanned the DotCom boom and the "business casual" craze) I never entered the office without a suit and tie. In my new role of professor, my children would think I had been struck with a grave mental illness if I went off to the classroom in anything other than the same. Despite years of being told it doesn't matter how sloppy you look, people do react differently to men dressed neatly and appropriately. In fact, men think about themselves differently. The toil Adam's failure of responsibility bought us is serious; we should therefore dress seriously. Although there will need to be some variation in details due to varying work environments, this principle is not only a requirement of office-bound men. I know of a Catholic father who owns his own business that entails climbing through attics and onto roofs, tasks not conducive to wearing a jacket and tie. Yet he does not take this necessity as a license to climb roofs in torn jeans and old t-shirts plastered with billboard-like slogans. He works in a uniform of long khaki trousers (even on scorching Oklahoma summer days) and blue Oxford long-sleeved shirts. No matter what our work, men need to dress in a dignified way.

As with women, I do not think it a coincidence that a culture that attacks men's headship in the family and encourages men to throw off restraint of their passions also encourages men to throw off the restraint of buttoned-up shirts and ties in exchange for shoddy, oversized, sloppy clothes nobody could see as worthy of respect.

"Casual" clothes may feel more comfortable; that is no excuse for immodesty in women, nor should it be a valid excuse for abandoning a mode of dress appropriate for men.

So men have many responsibilities towards themselves and the women in their charge. Men must dress modestly, neatly, and soberly. Men should not appear at Sunday Mass in sloppy casual clothes. Men need to reclaim their rightful authority—but with that authority comes grave responsibilities. Our Lord has said that the world should know his followers by their love. It should also know them, male and female, by the way they dress. Men and women, let your modesty be known before all.

Shall We Dance?
The Modesty and Order of the Family in Action

Modesty involves more than clothes; it involves words and actions. Modesty in all its forms is meant to reflect proper order. The ordering of the household should show itself in the order of exterior acts. Yet our commonwealth seems to thrive on disorder in acts. The art of dancing presents a telling example of the proper role order should play in our actions.

While attending a rehearsal for a St. Patrick's Day performance of Irish Dance by four of my children, I listened to their teacher correct the young ladies for walking toward their young male partners to start the traditional Céilidh dance, Haymakers' Jig. She corrected, "Ladies, wait where you stand for the gent to come and escort you to the dance." The comment caught my attention because it reflected one of the important benefits of preserving traditional dancing in the education of our children. Although in this chapter I focus on Irish traditional dancing, much of what I wish to share in this column applies to other forms of traditional dance.

Due to the deep cultural corruption of our times, traditional Catholics run a great risk of falling into a Protestant error: Puritanism. Since Protestants espouse a distorted view of grace and nature coupled with an individualistic rather than social understanding of human nature, throughout history they have often reacted to excesses in human behavior by iconoclasm, smashing all things in the name of a stark and bare purity. Remember it was the arch-

Puritan Oliver Cromwell, as well as many early American Puritan colonies, that banned dancing along with Christmas celebrations. One can only imagine Cromwell's fits of apoplexy were he to see a modern "nightclub" rife with behavior reflecting that of brutes rather than rational creatures. Yet, in opposing the lascivious character of modern corruptions of dance, we must be careful to avoid condemning the good and beautiful for the sins of its illegitimate cousin.

One of the reasons we supported the establishment of a weekly Irish dance class at our chapel was to provide a balance to the homeschooling experience. It provided a physical and musical activity for the homeschooled children whose educational experience by necessity is dominated by reading books and following written lesson plan instructions. Yet, after four years, I have come to appreciate a plenitude of other virtues and lessons transmitted through studying traditional dance.

First, dance, like all art, is a vehicle for transmitting cultural history. If that history is Catholic, traditional dances will pass on Catholic history. Irish dance is an example. Readers may be familiar with some of the commonly recognizable aspects of Irish dance: the brightly decorated costumes and the stiff, almost immobile upper body position. These traits result from the history of the persecution of Catholics in Ireland. The dance dresses usually are embroidered with traditional Irish designs. Often these designs are elaborations of ancient Irish imagery used in the times of persecution to pass on the Faith. Since official teaching of the Faith was banned by the English oppressors, the Irish had to resort to pictorial codes to pass on the Faith, such as the Trinity Knot. As to the stiff upper body combined with clenched fists, this posture represented the interior resistance of the Irish Catholics. The Protestant English might control and order the externals of Irish society, but the Irish resisted in their heart. Their feet might move to the English commands, but their wills resisted. One explanation further holds that the English Penal Code (remember the Puritans?) forbade all dancing. The Irish thus restricted movement to below the waist and put split doors on their cottages (so the top could be open and the bottom closed). Passing redcoats would only see stiff upper bodies and not realize the illicit dancing was going on below. The now familiar Irish dance hard shoes (from which American tap shoes developed) are believed to have developed from fishermen from the West who wore heavy clogs tapping their feet to pass on the traditional rhythms when traditional Irish music was banned by the English.

Beyond preserving the cultural history of persecuted Ireland, traditional dancing transmits many important social qualities. First, it teaches that true art derives from a preservation of order. In stark contrast to modern do-it-your-own-way gyrations, traditional dance imposes order on the bodily movements reflecting the control of the body by the soul we strive to regain through grace and the practice of virtue after this integrity was lost by our first parents. Irish dance is divided into steps of eight counts on one foot, and then the mirror steps are repeated on the other foot. Although good dancers appear natural in their light leaps and movements, they are following ordered choreography, some of which, like the set dance St. Patrick's Day, go back hundreds of years. The order of dancing provides a balance between creativity and order, unlike "modern" art's call to just make it up. Experienced dance masters devise variations on existing steps within the rhythm and pattern of existing dances, thus developing a healthy mixture of tradition and creativity. Unlike modern dance, where all you need do is stand up and flail around, traditional dancing requires time and perseverance to learn and master the steps and choreography. One cannot just jump up and try traditional dancing without a period of instruction and practice. Irish dance instruction institutes a hierarchical order of dancers progressing through various levels of dance proficiency by mastering certain steps. This experience teaches an important lesson about the acquisition of all knowledge. We are not little atomized intellects as Descartes or more recent Modernists would have us be, discovering all knowledge by our own unencumbered intellect. We learn from other men. Truth must be passed on. *Tradidi quod accepit.*

Finally, traditional group dances, called Céilidh dances, teach important lessons about the relations between men and women. Similar to English country dancing, the Céilidh dances involve male and female partners dancing a set choreography within a group of dancers. A balance is maintained between the pairing of male and female, but only within the context of a larger social group. There is none of the exclusive pairing off to rock around groping each other, a sight pervasive at modern high school proms. The partners come together throughout the dance for a few steps, separate, dance a few steps with a "side" or alternate partner, and then perform a series of steps as a group. Such dances teach important lessons for young people considering courting. Courting should be accomplished under the prudent watchful eye of a larger community, which allows some time for the courtiers to come to know each other but within the context of the community's movements. Modern courting reflects modern dance, pairing off prematurely into dark corners unsupervised and unstructured. Traditional courtship was taught through traditional courting rituals like Céilidh dances.

Also, as the instructions of my children's teacher demonstrated, the proper relations between boys and girls are taught. The gent walks to his lady, never waiting for her to come to him. He escorts her out to the floor and directs her actions through the dance. His behavior is to be marked by respect and courtesy for the lady. All dances end with a bow of courtesy. The choreography of many dances provides opportunities for the couple to demonstrate their individual dance proficiency with the man and then the lady stepping back through a few measures to allow the other to exhibit a solo step. (Note that ladies go first!) These rules teach the important truth that social relations, including marriage, involve an ordered and hierarchical combining of individual personalities into a harmonious whole, the husband and wife, and then the larger community.

Therefore, I argue, let us respond to the degenerate filth masquerading as a culture not by turning life into a puritanical black-and-white world devoid of beauty and goodness. Let us, rather, teach our children to dance, to love their ancient cultural heritage, and thereby to pass on important truths about courting, marriage, and social life.

Shall we dance?

Educating the Offspring—
Forming the Whole Person

Thus far we have focused on the formation of a household through the state of marriage and its implications in the structure and outward expression of the family. We have seen the primary end of marriage is the procreation and education of the children born of the marriage. We must now turn to the second aspect of this primary purpose: the education of children. We have already noted that man's rational nature requires more than material care for the physical needs of children. As a rational and social animal, man requires formation in the use of rational powers within the context of a social unit. We will consider the nature of this education, which must be more than job training, as well as contemporary errors that eviscerate education of its nobility.

The Church has always taught that parents are entrusted by God with the responsibility to form and educate their children for their return to their Creator. Although parents are not obligated to do all the educating themselves (they can entrust their children to schools so long as those schools give a true and good education), the buck stops with the parents. They bear the responsibility for seeing that a proper education is given to their children. They will have to answer before God that they discharged this duty. Whenever God imposes an obligation on someone, being perfectly just, he provides them with the means, the freedom, to fulfill that obligation. Thus God gives parents the necessary authority over their children's education as the means to fulfill their obligation to provide for that education.

Pope Pius XI reiterated this fundamental truth in *Divini Illius Magistri*:

> The family therefore holds directly from the Creator the mission and hence the right to educate the offspring, a right inalienable because inseparably joined to the strict obligation, a right anterior to any right whatever of civil society and of the State, and therefore inviolable on the part of any power on earth.
>
> That this right is inviolable St. Thomas proves as follows: The child is naturally something of the father . . . so by natural right the child, before reaching the use of reason, is under the father's care. Hence it would be contrary to natural justice if the child,

> before the use of reason, were removed from the care of its parents, or if any disposition were made concerning him against the will of the parents. And as this duty on the part of the parents continues up to the time when the child is in a position to provide for itself, this same inviolable parental right of education also endures. "Nature intends not merely the generation of the offspring, but also its development and advance to the perfection of man considered as man, that is, to the state of virtue" says the same St. Thomas.[39]

Parents are entrusted with the authority and the obligation to see to the "development and advance to the perfection of man considered as man, that is, to the state of virtue."[40] This standard must guide all of their choices in educating their children or entrusting that education to others. As this development of virtue touches all aspects of mans' nature, we will consider the many facets of this process of educating.[41]

Education must be perfect, not in the sense that every day the process will be free from mistakes, but in the philosophical sense. Education must have a goal of the complete formation of the young person. Most schools of the modern era have as an end only the partial formation of the youth, primarily the formation of the intellect. Most do not even perform this well. Having been infected with the false philosophy of Rousseau, they allow the youth to "elect" their own courses rather than giving them what they need. The

39. Pius XI, *Divini Illius Magistri,* Nos. 32–33 (emphasis added).

40. Ibid., no. 33.

41. The explanation of education in this section is based on a sermon given by Headmaster Michael McMahon on September 10, 2011, for the opening of the academic year of Notre Dame de La Salette Boys Academy, a boarding school for eighth through twelfth grade operated by the Society of St. Pius X. Certainly the primary purpose of the Society as established by Abp. Lefebvre was the formation and sanctification of sacrificing priests. Immediately following that primary goal was another: restoring Catholic education. The foundation of truly Catholic schools could only come after the founding of truly Catholic seminaries, but the schools quickly followed the seminaries and now dot the globe with solid Catholic education. I am deeply indebted to Fr. McMahon and La Salette for the Catholic formation they have been providing to my oldest son since 2011. La Salette meets the definition of a perfect school outlined in this chapter as its program is directed to all the goals of education outlined in this section.

Church has been educating people for centuries and she knows what young men need to know.

Yet even those schools that might still offer a good academic formation are not perfect schools. To be perfect, something must be complete in its object and its means. A school must form the entire person. Human nature is comprised of a variety of elements. Man is physical; he has a body that must be trained. He is intellective, with a mind that must be cultivated. He possesses a will that must be trained through discipline and mortification. Most importantly, if he has been baptized, he possesses supernatural life that must be cultivated. To educate (with its etymology coming from the Latin "to lead out from") the whole person requires the formation of the entire human person on all of these levels. Every aspect of his natural and supernatural nature must be led out of the immaturity of youth into the maturity of Catholic manhood.

The body must be formed and trained through the prudent regimen of sports and physical work. Unlike modern schools, which seem always to tend to the extreme, sports programs must not be turned into a miniature version of the degenerate Pro Sports phenomenon that has even infected college athletics. Rather, sports is made noble by being properly oriented to an end rather than being an end in itself. Sports, or more accurately described physical *education*, is designed to form physical discipline and control of a young person's body. Yet sports address more than simply manual labor. They touch the social nature of Man. Training of the body is integrated into the social goal of a team which seeks to play as a unified whole. Thus, sports that require team coordination and leadership educate both physically and socially. This physical education must take into account the different aspects of feminine and masculine nature, therefore physical education for girls and the choice of types of sports must reflect that difference.

Above the physical level, we find the spiritual nature of man. His intellect needs to be formed in the wisdom of the ages. A rigorous and prescribed curriculum must be followed to ground the young in Theology, Latin, Philosophy, History, the Natural Sciences, Mathematics, Music, and the Arts. The human mind is made for order and structure, and so the sequence of studies must be designed to present an ordered system of human knowledge, in the original Latin sense of the word *scientia*. This order must come at the price of eliminating the ever increasing role of "electives" in mainstream schools. To elect a good course of study requires an informed election, which is only the result of education not a part of it. A teenage youth does not know enough about knowledge to make such elections. Some choice of subject matter may be permitted towards the end of a basic education, perhaps the election of a modern language. Yet the young must be led out of themselves not led by themselves.

The soul unites this intellect to the will. The power of the will is to choose the good and persevere in its attainment. This element of the complete formation must be attained through an ordered, almost monastic, schedule. The will of the young is weak and easily distracted by the wealth of apparent goods the world offers.[42] Along with the teenage crushes, all the modern distractions of video games, ipods, cell phones, social networking, the Internet, etc., must be restrained or eliminated to make room for the educating. We are told our modern teens cannot live without all of these. Yet I can attest based on my visits to La Salette Academy, which removes girls and gadgets from the lives of the boys, the young *can* live healthy and happy lives without all these distractions. To demonstrate that these rules are not just arbitrarily set as some prison rules, but aim to form a prudent Catholic man, at La Salette the boys are taught to use technology as a means to an end (rather than being made subservient to it). The boys are all taught to type on a computer in the junior year after having mastered the art of writing by hand (a lost art discussed later in this chapter). The seniors are permitted to use, under supervision, the Internet to apply to college. Thus, although the philosophy of La Salette is no doubt denounced by the world as "rigid" and "oppressive," it is in reality

42. This is one reason Fr. McMahon has established this academy in remote rural Illinois. Here the enticements of the false goods can be, for the critical period of this adolescent formation, removed. As Father noted, losing their heads over girls so typical of modern American boys is avoided because there are no girls around.

nothing other than Catholic prudence treating distractions as such. The young must be taught to use tools as instruments when necessary. This involves training the will to be detached, or unplugged, from technology. The battle for a prudent approach to technology is so important we will return to it later in this chapter.

The young also struggle with the virtue of perseverance. Even if they choose the real good, their wills need formation to persevere in the struggle to attain it. This is why their entire day must be structured for them and not left to their own whims. From an appropriately early rising through an ordered night, the young must learn perseverance through guided practice. For example, La Salette's school day starts with morning prayers and mediation at 7:10 and encompasses Mass, meals, classes, jobs, physical education, Rosary, and Compline. The routine is meant to train the will so that when the boys leave they will be able to follow their own regimen. What a contrast such a life presents to the modern American teenager, who is permitted to lie around in bed all day, eating when and where he chooses.

To anyone who persists in the belief that teenagers cannot live without being plugged into some electronic device, walk around La Salette during a period of recreation and you will see real boys interacting with other real people and real things. When I did, I passed through the recreation room where boys were playing ping pong and table soccer not on LED screens but with real objects in their hands. I heard a boy playing real music on a real piano. I walked through the gym to see balls flying, boys running, and laughter rising. Outside in the fields, a volleyball and a football game were underway. The boys did not need a Facebook account to share these moments. They did not need to text or tweet each other. They were actually living these events together. Unlike the zombie look of plugged-in teens, these boys looked alive, notwithstanding the "rigid" and "oppressive" rules of the academy. Clearly the formation of the will at La Salette involves the training of a balanced disposition.

Even if a school did all of the following things—educated the mind and body and trained the will—it would be imperfect. Man has not only a natural destiny but a supernatural one as well. Education must also form the supernatural life of man. It is for this reason that the first act of the academic year of traditional Catholic schools has always been the offering of the Holy Sacrifice of the Mass to Almighty God. The Mass must permeate a program of education. If that Mass is the true Mass, the Mass of All Ages, that education will be directed ultimately toward God. If the *Novus Ordo* permeates education, it has the potential of becoming a man-centered education. For this reason daily Mass in the Traditional Rite and at least weekly sung Mass is essential to the La Salette program. The boys are formed in serving Mass with the meticulousness of a seminary. Music, especially Gregorian chant and polyphony, is a hallmark of La Salette. The formation of the supernatural life continues through the public recitation of parts of the Divine Office, the daily public rosary, periodic pilgrimages, and retreats and spiritual conferences offered by visiting priests. All of these activities are not optional extras for a proper education but an essential element of its supernatural purpose.

Beyond all of the foregoing essential requirements, there is one further element necessary for the perfect formation of the young: the protection of their innocence. One would imagine that a father who had done all he could for the past fourteen years to protect his son from the wicked world of the degenerate modern pagans would be filled with trepidation driving away and leaving that son 700 miles from that safe environment of home. When leaving my oldest son at La Salette, I felt no trepidation. The Headmaster, Fr. Michael McMahon, and the other priests and religious as well as the laymen of the faculty have demonstrated through their fruits that I had not removed him from safety into danger. In conference for new parents, Fr. McMahon explained that he could not promise that none of the boys would break an arm or bruise a nose (to the sound of which most mothers must have squirmed), but he did assure the parents that La Salette is a spiritually safe place. Although he would not wish the boys to break a bone, breaking their innocence and their soul is of far more consequence than a mere bone which can be reset. Having given La Salette the rigorous investigation of a practiced lawyer, I am confident that while forming my son, La Salette will do this in an environment that will protect him from what he needs protection from during these critical years of transition. If only so many formerly Catholic schools had not abandoned the level of vigilance practiced at La Salette, the generations who lost their innocence in Catholic schools often at the hands of perverted authorities would look very different today.

Why am I so confident of the safety of this academy? First, I have studied the fruits, a test by which Our Lord told us we shall know those whom he would send. I have scoured the country talking to every graduate I could. To a man, I have found them to be mature, well-balanced Catholic gentlemen. For the past several years, half of the graduating class has gone to try a vocation at the seminary. By their fruits ye shall know them!

The critical evidence for me, however, is the personal responsibility of the leadership of the school. Education involves leadership and a leader must take responsibility. Father McMahon assured the parents that he would love our sons with the same love that we do. I believe he would lay down his life to defend the La Salette boys as would every natural father worthy of the name. Unlike those few religious orders or institutes still operating nominally Catholic schools, the personal responsibility of the priests is evident. While other religious hide behind lay boards and legal entities and lay headmasters distancing themselves from legal responsibility, the Society of St. Pius X proudly proclaims La Salette to be its school. One cannot spend a day at the academy and not see it as Fr. McMahon's school as well. He is not a mere chaplain or advisor. The boys are his life in the same spirit of Don Bosco. He is teacher, coach, headmaster, spiritual director, and in a certain sense father to the boys. Their admiration was evident in their eyes and demeanor as he walked between their two lines before Mass, inspecting, correcting, and instructing. It is a truism that responsibility focuses the mind. Since he is not shielded behind committees and lay boards, he stands first in the line of fire. If these boys were harmed in any way, he would stand first in line to bear the repercussions. His knowledge of this fact is clearly evident. This edge is what was lost when the traditional teaching orders adopted the obfuscated ways of the world to organize their schools to protect and isolate the religious from the line of fire. In so doing they lost the edge that parents face, responsibility for failure. Education must be done by those who take responsibility for their actions.

To educate requires one to take responsibility for maintaining a safe harbor in which to build the ship of maturity. Every aspect of man's nature must be led out of itself toward the natural and supernatural ends of that nature. Physically, intellectually, and spiritually, the young need to be formed. Only with such formation will they be able to sail out of the safe harbor to found families of their own.

The Need for Beauty in Education: Education and the Art of Penmanship

The principles on which education must be based will determine curricular choices. If education is seen as mere job training, the curriculum will be eviscerated of "impractical" subjects creating the gaping holes to be filled by silly electives. When my wife, my older daughter, and I travelled to Post Falls, Idaho to spend a weekend with the Dominican Teaching Sisters of Fanjeaux, my eyes were opened to an aspect of education that is apparently disappearing from the face of most schools: the art of handwriting. The purpose of our trip was to make a final decision and discuss arrangements for our daughter to begin high school as a border in St. Dominic School. Fortuitously, or perhaps providentially, we bought in the airport on the day of our departure from Idaho a copy of the *Spokesman Review*, the local paper of Spokane, Washington. On the front page appeared a story featuring the Dominican Sisters and St. Dominic School. The article explains:

> Cursive is a dying art.... The form of handwriting is briefly taught in mainstream classrooms, usually during third grade, and only practiced afterward as needed. Those lessons have been pushed out by technology and curriculum for standardized testing, local educators say.[43]

It goes on to explain that not only could the average high school graduate today not be able to reproduce the handwriting used to

43. Jody Lawrence-Turner, "Lack of emphasis on cursive has many debating," *Spokesman Review*, April 15, 2012.

pen important documents in our history (like the Constitution), but he would not even be able to read them. Handwritten script is as incomprehensible to most high school students today as Greek (which along with handwriting is a required subject in St. Dominic School)! The results of removing cursive writing from the curriculum are becoming evident. The story continues:

> Students can text, type and tweet, but ask them to sign their name in cursive, and it might bring a blank stare. . . .
>
> Instructors who have proctored the PSAT or SAT exams regularly tell the story that when students are asked to sign their name in cursive rather than print it, they aren't sure how to do so.[44]

This is the point to which the great era of free public education has brought us. Thanks to Jean-Jacques Rousseau and John Dewey, the fathers of modern public schools, our children have devoted twelve years of their lives to education and are not even literate enough to sign their own names! They are well versed in scoffing at their backward, ignorant, uneducated ancestors. They, unlike the exploited uneducated masses in the dark Middle Ages, are educated! Yet, whereas many of these ignorant medieval serfs could recite from memory many major passages of the Bible, government-educated youth cannot even sign their own name!

But these modern liberated students have so much more than their backward predecessors. They can text, blog, post, upload, chat, tweet, email, and multitask. Yet they lack some of the most basic skills commensurate with human nature: the ability to compose a coherent letter (without an automatic spell checker), conduct an ordered intellectual debate with a live person, or clothe the written word with elegant script. Our government-dominated education system is ordered by the first principle of America's state religion, Utilitarianism. Handwriting is seen as a waste of time. Why spend time learning how to write neatly and artistically when texting is so much *faster*? It is the content of the message that matters not the means of its delivery.

The Greco-Roman-Catholic Philosophical Tradition has always

44. Ibid.

stood against this false dogma of utilitarianism. The content of propositions is critically important. Is the message true? And in addition to truth, the other transcendental qualities of being are oneness, goodness, and *beauty*. What we do about the truth (good action) and how we explain and live the truth is also critically important (beauty).

This disregard of goodness and beauty has even infected the Church and is one explanation for the liturgical revolution. The defective *Novus Ordo* rite is still defended on the same false principle: "It is still valid." In other words, it can still *truly* cause the consecration of the sacred species so you may not criticize it. Completely dismissed are the questions "But is it a good rite; is it a beautiful rite?" All of the other elements of goodness and beauty in the Roman rite—incense, Latin, prayers in poetic and elevated language, chant, polyphony, vestments, etc.—are not *necessary* (utilitarianism) for the rite to be truly a Mass. They are, therefore, dispensable. Yet, as anyone who has found the truth, goodness, and beauty of the Roman rite knows, it is not just a valid consecration that matters, as Michael Davies would constantly quote the Catholics of the Western Uprising, "It is the Mass that matters." He, and they, did not say, "It is only a valid consecration that matters." By that phrase "the Mass," he meant the Mass in its entirety, in its truthful statement of Catholic doctrine, in the goodness of soul it inspired, and in the beauty with which it adorned the sacrifice. As goes the Church so goes civilization. Why did so many millions of Catholics accept a rite of Mass that, although useful in the sense of valid, lacks ordered beauty? The answer is an education that fails to cultivate an appreciation of beauty. The way one prays or writes matters as much as what one prays or writes.

Just as our churches have been stripped bare of goodness and beauty, so too have the schools, leaving utilitarian sweatshops of technically proficient computer operators. Our entire civilization is constantly being stripped of goodness and beauty to make way for the useful. The *Spokesman Review* article relates that "[c]ursive is absent from the 'Common Core,' the newest government learning standards for grades K–12, and K–12 public school districts in Washington are not required to teach it." Of course, handwriting has to be pushed aside for classes on how to use the brand new computers bought with the brand new money raised from the brand new taxes needed to feed the ever growing hunger of the government school system for money. We cannot find time to teach a useless skill like handwriting when we have to prepare everyone for the endless series of "standardized tests" to make sure the system is succeeding in producing "standardized" units of production who cannot even sign their own name. Church and state are not separated but joined in an unholy alliance to promote utilitarianism in worship, education, and culture.

Education has become a trade school for getting picked to join the ever decreasing wage slave labor pool. It is not about leading the mind out of darkness into truth, goodness, and beauty. It is about skills training and that does not include handwriting.

In contrast to the utilitarianism of the school systems (and parochial schools have become simply another arm of the government school system) stands St. Dominic School. Raised up on a mountainside just outside of Post Falls, Idaho, stands a majestic monument to Catholic civilization, a culture that required the beautiful to be part of education. The buildings of the school and chapel are reminiscent of a European alpine village. Blending beautifully with the natural surroundings, the pine trees, the sloping mountain terrain, the architecture, and adornments remind the young charges of the Sisters of their European, and hence their Catholic, heritage. One cannot help but feel surrounded by a sense of continuity (a *real* hermeneutic of continuity) and Tradition on the school grounds. This is not surprising, since unlike most Dominicans of the past two centuries, these religious have maintained an unbroken tradition of 800 years. They educate girls the way they always have. A phrase often heard during our visit in response to our questions and concerns for our daughter was: "That is no problem. We have seen that before. We have been doing this for 800 years." Such responses were not uttered with pride or braggadocio but with simple matter-of-fact humility. Whereas public and parochial schools across the country have gone in for every latest fad dreamt up by the cabal of education experts, the Sisters have quietly gone about doing what they have been doing for 800 years, teaching girls Catholic doctrine, grammar, composition, rhetoric, philosophy, mathematics, history, science, Latin, French, Greek, music, sewing, art, and *handwriting*, often with the same books used decades previously. Since they never fell for the newfangled methods and fads they do not need to restore anything. They have been using the traditional methods of education all along: recitation, memorization, dictation, oral lecture, class discussion, essay writing, and handwriting practice. Most importantly they have taught by their living example of continuity of tradition and civilization. As you wander the halls of St. Dominic School you will not see computers on every desk, wireless hotspots, or expensive audio/video equipment and all the other distracting gadgets of our times. On the contrary you will see the materials of education: blackboards, art supplies, pens, pencils, notebooks, and real *books*. You will also see ink wells and blotters or fountain pens, the ancient implements of the art of hand-writing. The teaching of handwriting also teaches important lessons about precision, hard work, and practice. The children start learning cursive in kindergarten by tracing with a pencil. They have to earn the right to use ink and dip pens. Writing with dip pens can also affect the way people write and compose thoughts. It requires precision, care, and concentration, or the ink becomes a blurred mess. As I considered this point I thought of my own graduate students who sit in class rapidly typing away simply recording every word uttered. Are they really thinking about what they are writing? Words are a unique gift to man that separates him from the brutes. Words should be treasured not tapped about thoughtlessly. If you have to stop every few words to dip your pen and if you have to write slowly to avoid smudging letters, you are forced to slow down and not just produce words like a machine.

Anne Marie Temple, a lay teacher at St. Dominic School and a curriculum advisor for another nearby school operated by the Society of St. Pius X, is quoted in the *Spokesman Review* as making another interesting observation regarding the effect on students who learn to write by hand:

> Cursive writing better corresponds to the nature of the language. It shows children immediately that words are unities, not simply

> groups of disconnected letters; it shows that sounds combine to form precise and definite words, which in turn represent ideas.[45]

Ideas seem to be the one thing the modern world has a hard time processing, and therefore the world leaves each man to his own ideas. Perhaps that is because the ideas are lost in a sea of words, not written but tweeted or texted.

My reading of the *Spokesman Review* article on the heels of my visit to St. Dominic School caused me to realize more of the implications of the Traditionalist cause. Clearly traditional religious and priestly orders and societies, like the Dominicans, are doing a great supernatural work in preserving the purity of the Faith and praxis. Yet as part of this primary mission, on the natural level these orders and societies are accomplishing nothing less than the preservation of civilization itself. Civilization is more than mere economic survival. A *civitas*, or city in the classical sense, is an ordered community of people committed to a common understanding of truth, goodness and beauty. Protestantism with its abstract teaching based on personal interpretation of scriptural texts has always spawned anti-cultural, anti-intellectual, and anti-civilization movements. Protestant rejection of religious truth gives way to Puritan rejection of goodness and beauty. Catholicism has never been a disembodied, abstract philosophy. It has always spread and grown through cultures and fostered civilization. Thus, by preserving the true Faith, traditionalists cannot help but preserve civilization itself. As Hilaire Belloc aptly wrote in his *Europe and the Faith*, "Europe is the faith and the faith is Europe."[46] By this, he meant that the Faith and European civilization were inextricably and indissolubly connected. One cannot exist without the other. This means that we cannot preserve the Faith without preserving the civilization that lives that Faith through goodness and beauty. Do children have to write with ink wells and blotters to save civilization? Obviously, they are not *per se* absolutely necessarily. Yet an education built on utilitarian foundations, even one that does transmit real truths, cannot preserve a civilization. A wholesale abdication on the cultural issues, of

45. Ibid.

46. Hilaire Belloc, *Europe and the Faith* (New York: Paulist Press, 1920), 191.

which civilized handwriting is a part, will eventually result in an abdication on the true Faith. Education must not only pass on an abstract set of dogmas, even if they are the true dogmas. The Truth must be written in a graceful, elegant hand.

The Attack on Civilized Education: Barbarians Inside the Gates (and on the Radio)

The vision of education we have been considering thus far is the antithesis of the utilitarian education promoted by liberal governments. As in many other areas, however, American conservatives have often become the unwitting allies of liberals, fighting to conserve liberal utilitarianism. Education is no exception. Often conservatives who rightly bemoan the poor state of American education merely advocate more of the same. They lack the vision of a perfect education and settle for a more effective utilitarian one. Their criticism ends up simply claiming that they can be more utilitarian in the result than the liberals rather than rejecting the errors at the root of the problem.

In the beginning of November 2011, purportedly "conservative" personality Rush Limbaugh went on a tirade against classical education, which provides an example of this phenomenon. Our society has for so long been utterly dominated by the false principles of the Enlightenment that even most of our "conservatives" have become the unwitting far-right fringe of the radical Left. Alas, today's conservatives are merely yesterday's liberals. And even Mr. Limbaugh, for all of his many good points, falls into this category, as is exemplified in his radio rant against classical education.

Conservatism was a term coined a few hundred years ago to describe politicians who wanted to conserve Western heritage and culture rather than overturning it in revolution. The central pillar of being conservative is supposed to be a commitment to remaining faithful to our cultural heritage, which means the Greco-Roman philosophical, literary, artistic tradition as transformed, corrected, enriched, and elevated by Catholicism. Yet today's shortsighted conservatives are only interested in conserving the current status quo in ruins scattered about after the most recent revolution. Rather than conserving the rich content of a worldview developed and pruned over millennia, "conservatives" like Mr. Limbaugh have no content to conserve. Despite their best efforts, in the end they conserve only an empty vessel that gets periodically refilled with the same poison after each successive revolution. Thus, today's conservatives conserve what their forerunners fought vehemently against just a few generations ago.

Let us take a closer look at Mr. Limbaugh's revealing rant and discuss how it is a prime example of liberal revolutionary thought couched in what passes for modern conservative attitudes. The radio bit was occasioned by a news photograph from the "Occupy Wall Street" crew, a sad set who do know at the very least that something is really wrong with our country, although they lack any sense of the actual problem or its solution. Apparently one protestor held a sign complaining about her useless "classical studies" degree and lack of employability.

Limbaugh constructed a dialogue between a fictional student choosing the classical studies major and the college laughing all the way to the bank with her tuition:

> At that point somebody at the university ought to say, "Babe, you are wasting your time in a nothing major. We are stealing your money. You're gonna be qualified for jack excrement when you get outta here." But they don't. Now, this is part of the trick, this is the ruse, and it's actually clever. . . . So here you have Miss Brain-dead freshly out of college with her Classical Studies degree who thinks that she wants to go classically study and that people also want to study classics studiously and classically, and she's going to be very hirable, very marketable and so forth. Gets out in the real world and finds her only chance is Occupy Wall Street and to write a note for a TV camera about how worthless her degree is. Well, that's what she does here. Her job prospects, zero. Yeah, they are, and they have been since you declared that major, and somebody shoulda told you that from the moment you declared the major in Classical Studies.[47]

47. Rush Limbaugh Show, "Deciphering the Sad Sack Story of a Classical Studies Scholar," Nov. 1, 2011. http://www.rushlimbaugh.com/daily/2011/11/01/deciphering_the_sad_sack_story_of_a_classical_studies_scholar.

Now this little gem is an example of classic utilitarianism—that categorical imperative for the incarnation of liberalism. The only good end or goal of life is material benefit, wealth, or pleasure (depending on which utilitarian you are reading, but they all boil down to the same thing). The value of anything—work, study, art, learning, education, or even people—is determined by what practical, material use we can get out of them. Truth—"What is truth?" as Pilate asked. As to goodness and beauty, we might suppose he would ask the same question about them. Can they buy you a new hybrid car or a vacation to Mauritius or a new PlayStation 27, or whatever it might be? No? Then they are "qualified for jack excrement." If studying the classic, perennial texts, ideas, and events of Western, that is, Catholic, culture cannot get you a high paying job then it's worth "jack excrement."

With all due respect, Mr. Limbaugh has no idea of the real purpose of education. So, for Rush and the other folks in Rio Linda, let's review: The word education comes from the Latin words *ex* ("out of") and *ducere* ("to lead"). The good of education is to lead the student out of ignorance and into truth. Unlike liberal Descartists or Modernists who create truth by merely thinking it up, classical education leads us out of ignorance by relying on tradition, coming from the Latin *tradere* ("to hand over"). Classical educators realize that we stand on the shoulders of giants. Through a combination of hard intellectual work (Aristotle, Cicero, Aquinas, etc.) and divine revelation (Scripture and sacred Tradition), Catholic culture has accumulated a vast collection of the true, the good, and the beautiful. Rather than starting from scratch on a *tabula rasa* ("clean slate"), as the Enlightenment destroyers of education proposed, classical study educates by handing on this tradition for each successive generation to make their contribution of conserving and organically increasing it through further study and integration of its contents within their times.

Contrary to this classical education of tradition, liberals from Jean-Jacques Rousseau to John Dewey to Rush Limbaugh dismiss all this as "jack excrement." It is dismissed as a collection of useless old books written by dead people. For the modern mind, education is supposed to be practical, hence our pathetic excuse for public and, in almost every case, private school systems' focus on the practical, the "useful." Most graduates of high school leave without having read Virgil, Dante, Socrates, Aristotle, Aquinas, Shakespeare, or without knowing the difference between a substance and an accident or what caused the Punic Wars or the Crusades or what makes Mozart different from Bach or Gregorian chant. They are too busy learning "how to think for themselves" rather than learning what to think. This "learning how to think for yourself" nonsense is code for practical education. We do not need to teach you anything; we just need to teach you how to think so you can go discover "your own truth" without being burdened by the "prejudices" of a several thousand-year-old civilization.

Connected to the "learning to think for yourself" mantra, we witness the obsession with "math and science" among the government, the teachers' unions, and the experts. Now these are useful subjects! They can get you a job discovering the next techno-gadget to be made by slave labor in China, or the next equation that can be used to create a derivative product that will squeeze another 1 percent profit margin for Wal-Mart stock.

Do not misunderstand me—I am not attacking math and science. From the time of Aristotle's schoolroom with Alexander the Great, they have held an important place in a classical education. Yet they have been exalted to supernatural status because they are seen as "useful" in accomplishing what liberalism has been about for centuries, making beaucoup bucks with as little effort as possible by exploiting everything and everyone. After all, if I do not exploit, somebody else will. That is just survival of the fittest, one of the few absolute truths that modern schooling makes sure is never questioned when learning to "think for yourself."

Let us return to Limbaugh's manifesto to see more of the confusion that remains when one is not led away from ignorance by classical education:

> Tell me, any of you at random listening all across the fruited plain, what the hell is Classical Studies? What classics are studied? Or, is it learning how to study in a classical way? Or is it learning how to study in a classy as opposed to unclassy way? And what about

> unClassical Studies? Why does nobody care about the unclassics? What are the classics? And how are the classics studied? Oh, cause you're gonna become an expert in Dickens? You're assuming it's literature. See, you're assuming we're talking classical literature here. What if it's classical women's studies? What if it's classical feminism? Who the hell knows what it is? One thing I do know is that she, the brain-dead student, doesn't know what it is, after she's got a major in it. Because all she knows to do with it is go down to Occupy Wall Street and complain and write a note for the cameras.
>
> As I say, this is deviously clever. Socialists, liberals work undercover for decades taking over higher education, and then they dilute it and they make higher education anything but higher. There's really nothing special about it unless you go specific into the law or medicine where you really have to know it. But most of these majors are useless, such as black women studies, women's studies, whatever studies. Postmodernist theory in the new modernist world, whatever they get a degree in.[48]

If Mr. Limbaugh had actually received a classical education he would know what the classics are. They are Greek philosophy, Roman law, art based on principles of order and symmetry and reflecting the reality of creation, Euclid, Latin and Greek grammar, philology and etymology, mystery plays, Shakespeare, Chaucer, Dante, and the mistress of all, theology. Limbaugh parrots the false arguments of the liberals of a few generations ago. Like Pilate they mock: "What are classics?" Why is Dante's *Divine Comedy* a classic and not an obscure black woman's scribbling of a ditty in sub-Saharan Africa? Why is Aristotelianism classic and not existentialism? Why is Latin a "classic" language and not Ebonics of South Los Angeles? With such questions as these they long ago ripped Latin out of our primary (yes, primary) and secondary schools. They substituted *The Color Purple* for *The Merchant of Venice* and the Beatles (as was actually taught in my freshman "Catholic" high school art class) for Mozart, and replaced philosophy with "critical thinking." The answer to these questions, by the way, is that they are classics because they have been and will always express truth, goodness, and

48. Ibid.

beauty—the transcendental properties of being. This insight is part of classical knowledge going back at least to Aristotle's text on metaphysics, or the science of being.

Rush Limbaugh rightly recognizes that there is a big problem with education. It has replaced the study of the classics with the study of the novel, the ludicrous, and the latest thing someone dreamed up while "thinking for themselves." Feminism, black women studies, women's studies, whatever studies— postmodernist theory in the new modernist world are all fabrications inserted in the place of classical studies from Kindergarten to graduate school. The liberals know if "educators" can fill as many heads as possible with these nonsense "subjects," they will take up space that could have been occupied by the tradition that is no longer handed down through education. They thereby neutralize the resistance.

Like the Rush Limbaughs of the world, even if they sense the absurdity of modern education they will not know what they are missing and will not know the difference between the true and the novel. Having lost sight of the glory of the true, Limbaugh grasps onto anything he can still comprehend, which is all utilitarian liberalism wants him to comprehend. Law and medicine, they are practical! You can get a job with those degrees.

Even if that may still be the case for the moment, what kind of doctors and lawyers are we producing without a classical education? The kind of doctors who cannot understand that killing a baby in the womb is murder or that trying to clone a human person is false, evil, and will result in ugliness. As a lawyer, I can tell you from first-hand experience that it produces lawyers who think that what is ethical is whatever the latest rules of professional conduct stipulate. If they allow you to lie in a certain case or do everything you can to free a guilty person, then even that is ethical.

Like Rush, I will concede that maybe people with these "practical" degrees can get jobs, but getting jobs with a total lack of classical formation is really dangerous. These people will be in charge of the life or death of individuals and nations, and yet they will learn nothing about what makes a system of living cells a person or what makes a collection of people a civilization. By the way, legal and medical degrees were never part of a classical education. To enter these professions one had to receive training (not education) in these arts only after completing a classical education.

And in that regard I must clarify one point. I am not hereby advocating everyone attend a four-year college and incur hundreds of thousands of dollars of debt to do it. Without understanding the reasons, Rush is actually right in his conclusion that most university degree programs are a scam. The reason for this is that they are not truly educating; they are not handing over the knowledge needed to lead minds out of ignorance. With very few exceptions, mostly located in the fly-over states, universities and colleges are not teaching the classics. They are forging a chain in the debt slavery of our modern economy in exchange for a degree in what Limbaugh calls the "un-Classical Studies" or whatever name it goes by in course catalogues.

To be educated by the classics does not require enrollment in a six-figure college. I know a husband and wife who were both home-schooled through high school and never attended college. Yet they are more educated in the classics than most college graduates I see in law school. The classics were formerly taught in grammar school (so called because they actually taught grammar) and high school. Surviving slates from schools of the so-called "medieval" period evidence the fact that seven-year-olds were conversant in Latin grammar and literature.

Even in our own country, which built up an educational system after the gutting of the classics had been well underway, a large amount of classical education survived into the nineteenth century. At least students were required to know something, rather than knowing they could "think for yourself."

I came across a copy of an eighth-grade final exam from Salina, Kansas from 1895. It was evidently transcribed from the original document on file at the Smokey Valley Genealogical Society and Library in Salina, and reprinted by the Salina Journal. Remember when your grandparents talked about only finishing the eighth grade and we all wondered how they survived? I doubt if even half of the material tested here below is taught by the twelfth grade in Salina public schools today. Much of this knowledge would likely be considered "useless" by Mr. Limbaugh and a lot of other "conservatives" today. This test does not require a true classical education. It lacks many subjects, including theology—this coming from late nineteenth-century America, which had been living with Jefferson's wall of separation for over a century. Theology was expelled from schools long before prayer. It also ignores much of classical, non-American history. This is the land of *tabula rasa* par excellence, after all (that is, after the non-Catholic settlers erased the earlier writings of the natives on the slate).

Yet the following test does prove something. When classical education is replaced with practical education, within a century even the little bit of remaining practical learning eventually drains away. Take the test yourself, if you dare. Then ask yourself, would a population able to complete this exam to finish eighth grade have fallen for the nonsense of the politicians sitting in Congress and the White House today? Could those politicians pass this exam? Could Rush Limbaugh?

8th Grade Final Exam: Salina, KS—1895

Grammar (Time, 1 hour)

1. Give nine rules for the use of capital letters.
2. Name the parts of speech and define those that have no modifications
3. Define verse, stanza, and paragraph.
4. What are the principal parts of a verb? Give principal parts of "lie," "play," and "run."
5. Define case; illustrate each case.
6. What is punctuation? Give rules for principal marks of punctuation.

7–10. Write a composition of about 150 words and show therein that you understand the practical use of the rules of grammar.

Arithmetic (Time, 1 hour 15 minutes)

1. Name and define the Fundamental Rules of Arithmetic.

2. A wagon box is 2 feet deep, 10 feet long, and 3 feet wide. How many bushels of wheat will it hold?

3. If a load of wheat weighs 3,942 lbs., what is it worth at 50 cts/bushel, deducting 1,050 lbs for tare?

4. District No. 33 has a valuation of $35,000. What is the necessary levy to carry on a school seven months at $50 per month, and have $104 for incidentals?

5. Find the cost of 6,720 lbs. coal at $6.00 per ton.

6. Find the interest of $512.60 for 8 months and 18 days at 7 percent per annum.

7. What is the cost of 40 boards 12 inches wide and 16 feet long at $20 per meter?

8. Find bank discount on $300 for 90 days (no grace) at 10 percent.

9. What is the cost of a square farm at $15 per acre, the distance of which is 640 rods?

10. Write a Bank Check, a Promissory Note, and a Receipt.

US History (Time, 45 minutes)

1. Give the epochs into which US history is divided.
2. Give an account of the discovery of America by Columbus.
3. Relate the causes and results of the Revolutionary War.
4. Show the territorial growth of the United States.
5. Tell what you can of the history of Kansas.
6. Describe three of the most prominent battles of the Rebellion.
7. Who were the following: Morse, Whitney, Fulton, Bell, Lincoln, Penn, and Howe?
8. Name events connected with the following dates: 1607, 1620, 1800, 1849, 1865.

Orthography (Time, 1 hour)

1. What is meant by the following: alphabet, phonetic, orthography, etymology, syllabication?
2. What are elementary sounds? How classified?

3. What are the following, and give examples of each: trigraph, subvocals, diphthong, cognate letters, linguals?

4. Give four substitutes for caret "u."

5. Give two rules for spelling words with final "e." Name two exceptions under each rule.

6. Give two uses of silent letters in spelling. Illustrate each.

7. Define the following prefixes and use in connection with a word: bi, dis, pre, semi, post, non, inter, mono, sup.

8. Mark diacritically and divide into syllables the following, and name the sign that indicates the sound: card, ball, mercy, sir, odd, cell, rise, blood, fare, last.

9. Use the following correctly in sentences: cite, site, sight, fane, fain, feign, vane, vain, vein, raze, raise, rays.

10. Write ten words frequently mispronounced and indicate pronunciation by use of diacritical marks and by syllabication.

Geography (Time, 1 hour)

1. What is climate? Upon what does climate depend?

2. How do you account for the extremes of climate in Kansas?

3. Of what use are rivers? Of what use is the ocean?

4. Describe the mountains of North America.

5. Name and describe the following: Monrovia, Odessa, Denver, Manitoba, Hecla, Yukon, St. Helena, Juan Fernandez, Aspinwall, and Orinoco.

6. Name and locate the principal trade centers of the United States.

7. Name all the republics of Europe and give the capital of each.

8. Why is the Atlantic Coast colder than the Pacific in the same latitude?

9. Describe the process by which the water of the ocean returns to the sources of rivers.

10. Describe the movements of the earth. Give the inclination of the earth.

Conclusion

The family is the society at the foundation of the commonwealth. Throughout this chapter we have surveyed the attacks on the definition of the nature and ends of the family. The American commonwealth no longer contains a consensus on the nature of the family. With a majority of Catholics supporting the legal recognition of non-families in same-sex "marriages," we see that the natural law foundation of the family as the lifelong indissoluble union of one man and one woman for the purpose of the procreation and complete education of children has been rejected. Christ longer reigns in broken homes that lack the authority of the head and the love of the heart. Beginning with Vatican II's rejection of the hierarchically ordered ends of marriage, we have seen the decomposition of marriage, familial authority, and the education of the young. When Christ does not reign, someone else will reign. When reality is swept away, a false apparent reality will arise. The fundamental problem with the family is the denial of the reality of the family and its purpose established by the eternal law and known through the natural law. We will close this chapter to consider a real lawsuit representative of the fruits of denying reality. A society that cannot distinguish between a marriage and a perversion of nature has lost all grip on reality.

Amber Duick filed a lawsuit against the massive Toyota Motors company and its high-flying advertisement firm, Saatchi & Saatchi, as a result of a virtual prank they played on her. Putting aside the issue of whether Miss Duick should be able to sue over this matter and if so what she should recover, the August California appellate court opinion allowing her case to go to trial on the merits reveals some frightening facts about what Toyota and Saatchi were doing in a plan to supposedly sell cars.

Saatchi & Saatchi devised an advertising campaign to promote Toyota's Matrix. It was targeted at twenty-year-olds whom Saatchi thought would find it fun to "punk" their friends (i.e., play an online practical joke on them). As we shall see, it was a pretty dark joke. The program was called "YourOtherYou." Print and billboard advertisements encouraged young people to sign up a person on whom they wanted to play the prank on the program website providing personal information about their "friend." They would then choose one of five virtual characters to use in their prank. Duick's friend apparently chose Sebastian Bowler, about whom we will learn later. Other choices included a heavy metal fanatic. The aim of the prank was to frighten the chosen "friend" by making him think the "virtual" stranger was real and that he possessed personal information about them—phone number, home address—and was on his way to visit them in the real world. Saatchi & Saatchi even went to the trouble of creating online identities for the virtual characters, including websites, MySpace pages, etc. The ad agency went so far as to record an album for the virtual heavy metal fanatic's virtual band. Saatchi & Saatchi were proud of their virtual universe—before the lawsuit, that is. In 2008 Saatchi creative director Alex Flint is reported to have said about the campaign, "Even when you get several stages in, it's still looking pretty real. I think even the most cynical, anti-advertising guy will appreciate the depth and length to which we've gone."[49]

According to the court's opinion, the registration of Duick by someone who knew her triggered Toyota to send an email to her inviting her to participate in a "personality evaluation." A link in the email brought her to a website where she was asked to accept the "Personality Evaluation Terms and Conditions" in order to participate. Buried in the legalese of the agreement were statements that described the program merely as "an interactive experience." The second paragraph of the form stated, "If you review and agree to the Terms and Conditions detailed below . . . you may participate in a five-day digital experience through Your Other You. . . . You may receive email messages, phone calls, and/or text messages during the five-day experience." A subsequent paragraph also states, "You understand that by agreeing to these Terms, you are agreeing to receive emails, phone calls, and text messages from Toyota during the five-day experience of Your Other You." But Duick did not

49. See Kim Zetter, "Court Approves Lawsuit Against Toyota over Cyberstalking Ad Stunt," *Wired*, Sept. 12, 2011. http://www.wired.com/threatlevel/2011/09/toyota-punkd/.

receive emails identified as coming from Toyota or as part of her "experience." That would have spoiled the prank. Rather, she received emails from the apparently real but really virtual Sebastian Bowler. I quote from the California opinion to show what happened next.

> The text of the first email [from Bowler] reads, "Amber mate! Coming 2 Los Angeles Gonna lay low at your place for a bit. Till it all blows over. Bringing Trigger." Duick received another email from Bowler the following day, accurately stating her previous home address, describing it as a "Nice place to hide out," and advising her that "Trigger don't throw up much anymore, but put some newspaper down in case." The email also provided a link to Bowler's MySpace page, which portrayed him as a 25-year-old Englishman and "a fanatical English soccer fan who enjoyed drinking alcohol to excess"; the page also displayed photographs of a pit bull dog.
>
> Additional emails from Bowler to Duick over the next few days purported to describe his cross-country journey by car to visit her, including photos and videos of his travels and references to his efforts to evade law enforcement ("I seem to have lost the coppers for now, so I'm all good, mate"; "Had a brush with the law last night. Anyway, hopefully I'll have lost them by the time I get to your place"). One message explained that Bowler "ran into a little problem at the hotel," and Duick subsequently received an email from an individual identifying himself as "Jimmy Citro," purporting to be the manager of a motel and billing Duick for the damage Bowler had done to the motel's property. The final email included a link to a video revealing that Bowler was a fictional character and that the entire sequence of emails was an elaborate prank, all part of an advertising campaign for the Toyota Matrix.[50]

So the whole point of this attempt to advertise cars was to frighten Duick into thinking she was being harassed by a sleazy pit bull-owning criminal on the run from the law and to make her fear she was being pursued by a motel for damage caused by this stalker. He indicated he was coming to visit her in the real world and he had her address to prove that he knew where she lived. If anyone out

50. *Duick v. Toyota Motor Sales, U.S.A., Inc.*, 131 Cal.Rptr.3d 514 (2011).

there has any idea how this is supposed to get Miss Duick to want to buy a car, let me know!

Apparently, a bunch of (likely) six-figure-income executives at Toyota and Saatchi & Saatchi think it is perfectly moral to go to elaborate lengths to lie to people, to scare them into thinking they are being stalked. Oh, it is all ok because it is not "real." It is all only in the virtual world of emails and Facebook pages, so who cares? Remember, this is not a bunch of truant teenagers doing this in their garage. This was designed with great care (and presumably great expense) by professional businessmen. This is where the undiscriminating embrace of the virtual universe has led our sorry excuse for a culture. Car companies peddle their wares by scaring innocent women. It's all legal, they tried to argue in court, because after all she "clicked through" our contract and agreed to be bound by our terms and conditions, which authorized us to do this to her. So clicking on a virtual button on a virtual screen binds Miss Duick to a virtual contract to allow a virtual stalker to harass her with emails and threats. There is no moral problem here according to Toyota's logic because it is all not real; it's virtual.

This lawsuit, again regardless of whether her damage claims seem excessive or not, proves that the cyberspace world that our economy has been busily constructing with massive government funding is a major occasion of sin. By blurring the distinction between fiction and reality, it tempts people to believe that what they do online has no moral significance because it is only fictional, virtual. I would guess, or at least hope, that the high-flying executives at Toyota would feel some moral compunction not to stalk Miss Duick and threaten her themselves. Yet they apparently saw nothing wrong with doing it through a virtual Bowler.

This is the mess we have created by an undiscriminating approach to technology. Whatever we can do we should (with government subsidies to boot). This has been the reigning societal attitude. The Church has joined the bandwagon with the Pope himself going online with his own YouTube station. The whole *zeitgeist* accords with the Church's embrace of progress and modernity at Vatican II. The Church wanted to become hip and so she threw out her traditions to embrace the "modern man." Technology is hip, so we all have to embrace it wherever it leads. Like the modern ecumenism, we don't know where technology is taking us but we are on for the ride; fasten your virtual seatbelts. Thus, instead of acting like the moral guardians the clergy are supposed to be, their voices warning of the grave prudential dangers of many of these technologies have been deafeningly silent. Schools, Catholic among them, install computers and internet access in as many classrooms as they can, often applying for government money to do so. "Get the kids online" has been the policy rather than educating them properly to be wary of the moral hazards. Today's children will be tomorrow's Toyota executives and advertising gurus. If this type of stunt is what the reigning generation sees fit to implement, I shudder to think what the next generation raised with a Facebook account before they are out of diapers will do. *Ab Cyberspace libera nos Domine*!

3

The Foundations of Economic Society

As we observed in the Introduction, the household is not self-sufficient. The art of household management or economics is not merely an internal art. Households must interact with one another to meet their needs. Exchange transactions among households are the basis of economic activity. As argued in Chapter 1, all of human life must be under the empire of Christ the King. There can be no separation between Church and state nor between Church and economy. This chapter will examine the foundation of principles of Catholic economics, all of which flow from the primary principle that all of economics must be regulated by the eternal law, the constitution of Christ the King.

There are some who argue that the phrase "Catholic economics" is nonsensical: There can be no "Catholic" economics; there is only economics. We will return in the final pages of this chapter to refute the claims of these economic liberals. For now, we can state that all of economic activity involves human action, investing, buying, selling, laboring, etc. Any human action has moral implications. We are whole beings. We cannot compartmentalize our existence. We cannot be Catholics on Sunday or Catholics with respect to our religion but something else Monday through Friday at the office. To claim economics is somehow devoid of moral significance is to deny that it is a human activity.

In the same vein economic liberals will often seek to disqualify the Church from speaking on economics, claiming "it is just a science." Even if economics were a science, which it is not, it cannot on its own answer the important questions about what we should do. Leo XIII shortcut this line of argument when he said in *Rerum Novarum*, "We approach the subject with confidence, *and in the exercise of the rights which manifestly appertain to Us*."[1] Pius XI echoed this statement more strongly in *Quadragesimo Anno* when he proclaimed, "there resides in Us the right and duty to pronounce with supreme authority upon social and economic matters," and later stating that these issues are "subject to Our supreme jurisdiction."[2] This was not a new idea. These pontiffs were not stating a new truth, but they were merely reminding people that this has been the case since the beginning of Christianity. Church history is filled with cases of economic issues being settled by the Church in councils, papal decretals, ecclesiastical courts, and various synods. The very first Ecumenical Council of the Church, in Nicaea, issued canons dealing with an economic issue, usury. The papal archives are littered with these questions, from *Naviganti*, dealing with sea loans, to *In Civitate*, dealing with credit sales, to *Vix Pervenit*, summarizing the teaching on usury. Due to particularities of modern times, some people have the impression that the Church's morality is only concerned with sexual and marital morality. Economic issues were just tacked onto this history in recent times as an addendum. Nothing could be further from the truth of history.

Catholic economic doctrine is not something new. The Church did not create a social and economic doctrine in recent times to supplement its sexual morality. The doctrine Leo XIII and Pius XI speak about is merely the continuation of a long tradition going back to the ancient pre-Christian world. Aristotle had placed economics as a sub-discipline of politics (itself a part of ethics) and which Christians later understood to be itself subordinate to theology. The principles expounded in *Rerum Novarum* and its progeny are not part of the perennial teaching of the Catholic intellectual tradition. To dispel this false accusation throughout this chapter and the next, I have purposefully chosen to rely heavily (and perhaps disproportionately) on sources that predate *Rerum Novarum*. I did this not because *Rerum Novarum* and its progeny say something different from the sources on which they rely. To the contrary, they merely

1. Leo XIII, *Rerum Novarum*, no. 16 (emphasis added).
2. Pius XI, *Quadragesimo Anno*, no. 41.

restate and apply the earlier teachings. I emphasize the earlier sources to emphasize the point: Economic doctrine has a long genealogy in Catholic doctrine and philosophy.

The False Dichotomy

A final preliminary point to the discussion of Catholic economics is that the discussion of Catholic economic teaching has been unduly limited by imposing on it a debate over whether the Church's teaching supports communism or capitalism. The Liberation Theologians stand on one side claiming it supports Marxist ideas, whereas the Libertarians (or the economic liberals) claim it requires *laissez-faire* capitalism. Essentially, these two ideologies of communism and capitalism are seeking the same end but with different means. They both propose wealth maximization as the ultimate end of human society. They each promise more prosperity through central planning or the free market. Their argument is over how much the government should exercise its monopoly over interference with economic activity, with economic liberals saying not at all and communist economic tyrants saying all the time. This is essentially an argument over means, not ends. The end is the same: more wealth; the difference lies only in the means and the principle of distribution. Constraining the debate in this way (to discuss only the means of attaining and distributing the ends) prevents us from considering the deeper questions: What is the proper end of economic activity? "Economics" cannot answer that deeper question of ends because, as Aristotle recognized, economics is a subordinate discipline. It is subordinate to politics, which focuses on the ends of civil society. Economics merely studies the means.

Now before we leave this image of communism and capitalism, I think we should observe that, despite their stated principles, the two systems really produce great wealth for a select few. Capitalism purports an equal opportunity for all to gain wealth. Yet in its Darwinian aspect of survival of the fittest, it really ends up providing great wealth for the "fittest"—the most efficient, the most proficient at playing in the capitalist system. According to capitalism's definition of justice, this result is just, for those who win are meant to win because they are the most able. Thus a result of concentration of wealth in a small group of hands is just; the invisible hand of the free market produced this result, therefore it must be just. Communism purports to say that there will be more wealth for everybody. But that end goal is in practice quickly qualified to apply to the long off utopian day that will succeed the dictatorship of the proletariat. In the interim period the reality is that it produces more wealth for the Party, the communist officials running this dictatorship of the proletariat. In their application in the twentieth century, communism and capitalism thus produced the same result: wealth concentrated in the hands of a small group of people.

This limitation of the debate to the most efficient ends to produce wealth enables those advocating liberal capitalism to dismiss the Church form the debate. They frame the debate in terms of which system, communism or capitalism, works better. The evidence from that system clearly indicates capitalism. Yet the Church enters the debate not to argue over which system works better but to interject the larger question: What do we want to achieve by the system? Thus, the economic liberal's position boils down to "It works! And communism failed." In light of the emerging economic system collapse, that argument might have to be modified to: "It took longer than communism to collapse" or "it let the party go on a lot longer than communism." Accepting for the sake of argument that current crises will pass and that capitalism does work in that it produces more wealth in the aggregate, that does not answer the question:. Is that a good thing? How is that wealth used? Proving that a means is effective in no way proves that it should be used. It may well be very efficient to use a machine gun to execute people, but that does not answer the question whether you should be executing them in the first place. Capitalism does not answer those kinds of questions. It just accepts the proposition that more wealth is an absolute good, and whoever has wealth was the most able and thus the result is just. We will see that Catholic economic doctrine has a better answer than "it seems to work at getting more wealth."

When looking at how Catholic economic thought answers these big questions, I will not be presenting my opinion or my answers, but the answers of the great thinkers in the Catholic intellectual tradition in their own words. In selecting the words of great Catholics, I placed an emphasis on the thinkers of the twelfth, thirteenth, and fourteenth centuries because it was in the twelfth century that Europe saw one of the greatest economic revivals of history. The great economic disasters of the tenth century eventually gave way to a great revival of commerce and economic activity beginning in the twelfth century. We will thus be looking at the writings of those who have experienced the functioning of effective economic revival using Catholic moral principles. In this section, we will also look at a variety of sources, philosophy, theology, canon law, and literature. Doing so will help us uncover the *sensus Catholicus* on these matters.

Faced with an apparently never-ending series of economic crises, from the housing crisis of 2007 onward through the auto industry bankruptcy to the European debt crisis of 2011–2013, many may be willing to consider ideas and principles that under more prosperous times were ignored. The Catholic philosophical and intellectual tradition offers a comprehensive system of economic thought that provides much material for critiquing the reigning economic philosophy and identifying within it the causes of the current crises. It also offers the philosophical blueprint for an alternative model for the future. The Catholic philosophical tradition offers insights for understanding the nature of wealth and its acquisition, economic justice in exchange, the nature of property, and the lending of money. In essence, it offers a comprehensive alternative economic philosophy to those developed and disseminated in the nineteenth and twentieth centuries. This chapter sets forth the foundational principles relating to the tools of the economy, wealth, property, and business. The next chapter digs more deeply into the details concerning the use of these tools in particular contexts and examines the Catholic doctrines of just price and usury. These chapters argue for the reintegration of this system into the ongoing debate about the economic future of our world. Just as the restoration of the Catholic natural law definition of marriage is at the heart of restoring the family, the restoration of core Catholic natural law principles is indispensable to the restoration of the economy.

Putting First Things First— The Proper Attitude Toward Profit and Wealth: Is It the Economy that Matters?

What does Catholicism think about wealth generation and economic activity in relation to ultimate ends? We will start with a quotation from St. Thomas: "Temporal goods are subjected to man that he may use them according to his needs, not that he may place his end in them and be over solicitous about them."[3] So our first principle of Catholic economic thought is that we have to keep economic matters in their proper place: secondary. Contrary to a famous campaign slogan, it is not the economy that matters; it is the Holy Sacrifice of the Mass that matters. As important as economic concerns are, we cannot let them become an end in and of themselves or become overly focused on them. Now we are composed of a spirit *and a body* and thus temporal goods are important to us. We need temporal goods to enable us to think about spiritual things. They are not, however, an end in and of themselves. This teaching of St. Thomas is thoroughly rooted in the Gospels. There are several biblical passages that thinkers like St. Thomas turned to for guidance. The first one lays out several distinctions very important for this discussion. It is the familiar story of the Rich Young Man:

> And behold one came and said to him: Good master, what good shall I do that I may have life everlasting? Who said to him: Why asketh thou me concerning good? One is good, God. But if thou wilt enter into life, keep the commandments. He said to him: Which? And Jesus said: Thou shalt do no murder, Thou shalt not commit adultery, Thou shalt not steal, Thou shalt not bear false witness. Honour thy father and thy mother: and, Thou shalt love thy neighbor as thyself. The young man saith to him: All these I have kept from my youth, what is yet wanting to me? Jesus saith to him: If thou wilt be perfect, go sell what thou hast, and give to the poor, and thou shalt have treasure in heaven: and come follow me. And when the young man had heard this word, he went away sad: for he had great possessions. Then Jesus said to his disciples: Amen, I say to you, that a rich man shall hardly enter into the

3. Aquinas, *Summa*, II–II, Q. 55, art. 6, Reply to Objection 1.

> kingdom of heaven. And again I say to you: It is easier for a camel to pass through the eye of a needle, than for a rich man to enter into the kingdom of heaven.[4]

First the young man asks a real lawyer's question: What must I do to stay out of jail? What is the minimum I have to do to avoid hell and attain salvation? Asking a lawyer's question, he receives a lawyer's answer: What is the law? Summing up the answer is the word "justice." We must avoid being unjust to God and to our neighbor, as exemplified in the Ten Commandments. Then the young man says, I have done all this. Our Lord replies, "if thou wilt be perfect" there is more you can do; sell what you have and give to the poor and follow me. This answer saddened the man (for he was rich) and he thus departed from Our Lord. This exchange presents a critical distinction in this area, which will appear throughout the economic philosophy of Catholic doctrine. This is a distinction between acts of justice and acts of perfection. Justice is the law, the minimum required. This category contains principles of economic justice. To violate them is to break the divine and natural law. The second category contains counsels of perfection, things we are encouraged to do but which are not individually required to be done. What is interesting about this passage is that after the rich man, having kept the laws of justice, refuses to follow the counsels of perfection, Our Lord warns that "a rich man shall hardly enter into the kingdom of heaven." So Our Lord does not say that is ok that you parted company with me over only an optional counsel of perfection; you did the minimum. He says the opposite. For one merely avoiding economic injustice, it will be difficult to be saved. Failure to perform any individual counsel of perfection does not condemn one to hell; yet one's general attitude towards these higher standards can prevent the attainment of this greatest end. Although we are not required to do all that is encouraged by the higher counsels, our refusal to embrace them demonstrates that one is overly solicitous of earthly things, or reveals an excessive attachment to our temporal riches. This point is overlooked by many who argue against Catholic

4. Matthew 19:16–24.

economic principles on the grounds that many teachings are only "optional" and therefore unnecessary. A Libertarian might argue that he is personally in favor of charity as a good thing, but it has nothing to do with economic principles because it is only optional. Although counsels of perfection may be "optional" in that any one of them may not be necessary for salvation, an attitude of deliberately turning away from them is a turning away from salvation.

Wealth: A Necessary Occasion of Sin

One way to think about wealth in light of this passage is that wealth is a necessary occasion of sin. Some amount of wealth is necessary for life, yet having it can be a temptation to sin by becoming overly attached to it and as a result parting ways with Our Lord, as did the Rich Young Man. This is a nuanced understanding of wealth that dissenters from Catholic economic doctrine often overlook. The Church does not embrace wealth as an ultimate good, yet it does not condemn it as an intrinsic evil. It embraces wealth and yet holds it at a distance as a necessary occasion of sin. If we recognize wealth as such a necessary occasion of sin, we can deal with it in the proper fashion, with our eyes open and having taken the proper precautions.

Saint James in his epistle draws our attention to this same point. In this passage he speaks to the rich, warning them of the dangers to salvation wealth can produce: "Go to now, ye rich men, weep and howl in your miseries, which shall come upon you. Your riches are corrupted: and your garments are moth-eaten. Your gold and silver is cankered: and the rust of them shall be for a testimony against you, and shall eat your flesh like fire. You have stored up to yourselves wrath against the last days. Behold the hire of the labourers, who have reaped down your fields, which by fraud has been kept back by you, crieth: and the cry of them hath entered into the ears of the Lord of Sabaoth. You have feasted upon earth: and in riotousness you have nourished your hearts, in the day of slaughter."[5] Wealth is not corrupt itself; but that of the rich men addressed has become corrupted by the over-attachment to it (it has been horded

5. James 5:1–5.

as seen by its being moth-eaten). This over-attachment caused these rich people to violate principles of economic justice (defrauding laborers of their just wage, for example). Thus our attitude towards wealth affects even our ability to comply with the minimum of justice. If we make wealth an end in itself, we face a real danger of being tempted to bend the rules of economic justice to amass this end.

Now that we have placed wealth in the category of something to be treated with care, we need to focus more on the main principle of Libertarian economics, that which drives the system: the desire for profit. The maximization of individual wealth preferences is what is seen by economic liberals as what makes the system work. This desire for profit drives the force of the invisible hand of the market. Here is what Henry of Hesse says about the desire for profits: "Whoever has enough for these things [to sustain oneself, to perform pious works, to make reasonable provision for future emergencies, or to support offspring] but still works incessantly to gain riches or a higher social status, or so that later he may live without working, or so that his sons may be rich and great—all such are driven by damnable avarice, physical pleasure, and pride."[6] Having spent ten years in a corporate law practice, the words "works incessantly to gain riches" describes many people in the sphere in which I trod daily. Henry's point is that the desire for wealth, much like the desire for other things, is not bad in and of itself, but it needs to be constrained. It needs to be proportionate to the ends to which it will be put. The constraints on the desire for wealth are not excessive but rather very prudent. One may seek enough wealth to satisfy temporal needs, to save for future uncertainties, to perform pious works (e.g., to go on pilgrimages). Yet there is an outer limit. To possess enough for all this and still desire more exceeds the bounds of prudence. The profit motive in the economic liberal's philosophy cannot accept this limit. Profit is always good and more profit is always better.

6. Henry of Hesse, *De contractibus*, in John Gerson, *Opera omnia*, 4 vols. (Cologne, 1483–4), 4, cap. 12, fol. 191ra.

Sufficiency—The Mean Between Two Vices

Importantly the virtue of restraint in the desire for temporal goods can be seen as the mean between two vices. This concept of the mean in an Aristotelian sense is often misinterpreted in the post-Hegelian modern age to mean the synthesis of the two vices—a little of this vice and a little of that one. This is not the sense in which the mean is used by Aristotle and Aquinas. The mean for Aristotle is like a virtue sitting at the top of an inverted parabola. If it leans too far to one side it will fall off into one vice. If it leans to the other side it falls into the contrary vice. Thus virtue involves a sort of prudent tension keeping both vices at bay lest we fall into either vice. In this sense the virtue of a restrained desire for wealth lies between the two vices of being overly solicitous for wealth and being irresponsible. Jean de Meun in his great literary work *The Romance of the Rose* summarizes this concept when he says, "Wealth and beggary are two extremes. The mean is sufficiency."[7] Sufficiency, the desire for enough wealth (for the enumerated purposes listed above) is virtuous, but being solicitous for more and not caring for sufficiency are the opposite vices. Saint Bernard agrees with this conclusion: "In themselves, as regards man's Spiritual welfare, they [riches] are neither good nor bad, yet the use of them is good, the abuse is bad; anxiety about them is worse; the greed of gain still more disgraceful."[8] The proper use of wealth is virtuous; its abuse—the greed of gain—is vice. We need to have this balance, not falling into either extreme of not caring about our temporal needs and excessive greed. This balance is contrary to the American mythology of wealth. For example, the "American Way" encourages you to work harder to get more in your retirement account so you can buy a luxury villa in Florida and so that you can "live without working."

Finally, St. Thomas uses an image from nature to demonstrate how being properly solicitous for temporal goods requires holding such desire in its proper constraint—a befitting time. "The ant is

7. Guillaume de Lorris and Jean de Meun, *The Romance of the Rose*, trans. Frances Horgan (Oxford: Oxford University Press, 2009), 173.

8. St. Bernard of Clairvaux, *De consideratione*, trans. George Lewis (Oxford: Oxford University Press, 1908), 47.

solicitous at a befitting time, and it is this that is proposed for our example. Due foresight of the future belongs to prudence. But it would be an inordinate foresight or solicitude about the future, if a man were to seek temporal things, to which the terms 'past' and 'future' apply, as ends, or if he were to seek them in excess of the needs of the present life, or if he were to forestall the time for solicitude."[9] We may seek profit, but doing so in excess is like being irresponsible about them (forestalling the time for solicitude), a vice. As we have seen, economic liberals often attempt to falsely argue from nature about the inevitability of profit maximization. Interestingly, St. Thomas, who is falsely claimed to be the father of their praxology, uses an image from nature to prove that sufficiency is evident in nature's not being overly solicitous for profit.

So we have seen that the profit motive cannot be an end in and of itself. Wealth is neither good nor evil in and of itself; the use to which wealth is put needs to be considered. Wealth must not become the focus of all of our ends.

The Basis of Wealth—Private Property

Now we have considered wealth to some extent, but the possibility of wealth presupposes the institution of private property. The liberal Catholics who hold economic liberalism to be an article of the Faith love this topic, believing that it proves the Church supports their liberal ethic. They point to Leo XIII's acknowledgement of private property in *Rerum Novarum* and conclude therefore the Church supports private property. This conclusion is true in general but not in the way it is often meant by liberals. The Church does not defend private property in the same sense as a Libertarian does. We have to read Leo XIII in *Rerum Novarum* in light of what the Catholic Church has always understood by the "right" to private property. I am going to refrain from using the term the "right" to private property as I do not believe the word "right" accurately conveys the concept of property taught by Catholic principles. I will use the term the "institution" of private property, for the concept

9. Aquinas, *Summa*, II–II, Q. 55, art. 7, Reply to Objections 1 and 2.1–2.

involves much more than mere "rights." Private property involves duties, which duties give rise to certain rights.

For our purposes I am going to pass over the philosophical debate over whether the institution of private property existed in the natural law from the beginning or whether it was established after and as a result of the Fall (although I do not mean by doing so to imply this debate is of no importance). We will deal with private property as part of the natural law at least after the Fall.

Saint Augustine in addressing the place of private property in the natural law says, "We must ascribe to the true God alone the power to grant kingdoms and empires. He . . . grants earthly kingdoms both to the good and to the evil, in accordance with his pleasure. . . . It is beyond anything incredible that he should have willed the kingdoms of men, their dominations and their servitudes, to be outside the range of the laws of his providence."[10] We can observe two things from this statement. God wills the institution of private property by including it in the natural law, again ignoring for the moment when that occurred. Secondly, since God willed such an institution, it is senseless to assert that it is outside of his province. It is like saying, "Thank you very much for the private property, God, but now you may go back to heaven and let us do with it as we please." This is the classic enlightenment view of God as clock maker who winds up the world and then detaches from it. That is not the true God, the God whom the Church proclaims.

So what is private property and why does it exist? Why did God place it in the natural law? The debate about the nature of property goes all the way back to Plato and Aristotle. Plato advocated a common ownership and use of property in his *Republic*. Aristotle, in his *Politics*, argued for the superiority of private ownership. Christian thinkers made their own Aristotle's arguments in favor of private property, which were essentially that private property (1) better keeps peace among men; (2) provides an efficient allocation of work and avoids labor shirking and complaining; (3) is needed to practice the virtue of liberality; and (4) provides pleasure of ownership. The

10. Augustine, *City of God*, Bk. V, ch. 21, ch. 11. http://www.newadvent.org/fathers/1201.htm.

Christian thinkers tended to downplay the final reason given by Aristotle by merging it into the penultimate one.[11] Saint Thomas provides a great summary of several centuries of thought on this question. I am going to quote the passage at length, as it is so important to understanding the nature of the institution and why it exists:

> Two things are competent to man in respect of exterior things. One is the power to procure and dispense them, and in this regard it is lawful for man to possess property. Moreover this is necessary to human life for three reasons. First because every man is more careful to procure what is for himself alone than that which is common to many or to all: since each one would shirk the labor and leave to another that which concerns the community, as happens where there is a great number of servants. Secondly, because human affairs are conducted in more orderly fashion if each man is charged with taking care of some particular thing himself, whereas there would be confusion if everyone had to look after any one thing indeterminately. Thirdly, because a more peaceful state is ensured to man if each one is contented with his own. Hence it is to be observed that quarrels arise more frequently where there is no division of the things possessed. The second thing that is competent to man with regard to external things is their use. On this respect man ought to possess external things, not as his own, but as common, so that, to wit, he is ready to communicate them to others in their need. Hence the Apostle says (1 Timothy 6:17–18): "Charge the rich of this world . . . to give easily, to communicate to others," etc.[12]

Saint Thomas's definition of private property contains two parts. First it involves the ability to acquire and to dispose of things. We usually refer to these two concepts by the term "ownership." He explains why this ownership is helpful to human society. It solves what modern economic theory would call a prisoner's dilemma. It thus has efficiency benefits. Secondly, he explains that private property brings order to human affairs. Order in human society is a good. Third, St. Thomas points out that, connected to order, private

11. See Odd Langholm, *Economics in the Medieval Schools* (Leiden, The Netherlands: E. J. Brill, 1992), 152–53.

12. Aquinas, *Summa*, II–II, Q. 66, art. 2.

property promotes peace and harmony, states of existence conducive to growth in the spiritual life. All of these reasons demonstrate that private ownership of property is not an end in and of itself but only an instrumental end necessary or useful to attain other goods. Now nothing that is a means can be treated as an absolute. It must always be evaluated in terms of the end it serves. Notice, although there are efficiencies caused by the institution of private property, efficiency (getting more stuff) is not the only justification proposed. It creates goods for the community other than the ability to produce more wealth.

The second aspect of the definition of private property is an ability to use the material good involved in the exercise of private property. So it is possible to acquire things "as your own" but not to use them completely "as your own" but "in common." The right to use may not be exercised solely with an eye to the individual benefit of the owner. Individual use must be considered in light of the common good. This does not mean we are obligated to use property against our interest or in a personally harmful way, but we need to use property in a way that harmonizes with the common good. This second aspect of the definition conflicts with the modern, Libertarian sense of private property—the right to do with *my* stuff *as I see fit*. My home is my castle! As the Thomist Henri Grenier explains, "The adherents of economic liberalism, in virtue of the principles of their doctrine, which leads to individualism, do not recognize in a positive manner the existence of the social character of private ownership. Moreover they deny it at least implicitly from the fact that they claim for the individual a liberty in economic matters which is too absolute."[13] In contrast to modern economic liberals, the Catholic tradition holds that "[p]rivate property remains in some way common as regards its use."[14] Due to this modern exaggeration of private property as an absolute, St. Thomas's understanding of the limitations on our use of private property is difficult for us to comprehend. To aid in doing so it is necessary to contemplate how we go about acquiring objects of private property. Here, Giles of Rome can

13. Grenier, *Thomistic Philosophy*, 383.
14. Ibid.

provide a useful insight. "There may be no lordship with justice over temporal things or lay persons or anything else which is not under the Church and through the Church: for example, this man or that cannot with justice possess a farm or a vineyard or anything else which he has unless he holds it under the Church and through the Church."[15] Giles is describing the origins of property in terms of the feudal system. This system of dividing property is based on the correspondence of rights and obligations. The head of the feudal system, the king, invests someone with a fief—land that becomes the vassal's property. This vassal in turn invests other vassals with parts of this land, which in turn pass to them. Each vassal is, however, invested with his fief only after he takes an oath to fulfill the obligations associated with the property. The feudal lord's use of his fief is limited by the rules of the feudal system. He may not just decide one day to tell all the serfs to get off of his land as he has decided to hire workers to farm it, claiming "a man's home is *his* castle!" He has the right to benefit from the produce of his fief but does not have the right to do with it whatever he chooses.

In addition to the duties running down from the lord of the manor, he has duties running up to the person from whom he received the fief. He must render service to his lord and must obey the laws and customs set down by his overlord with respect to the fief. The essence of this specific system of rights and obligations as applied to the lands of Europe was seen as providing principles which could be abstracted to understand the nature of property philosophically. God as creator owns everything; He is the ultimate overlord. Everything Men use, they receive from Him. God has granted it to us for private use by dispersing it as he sees fit to be used under the Church, meaning in accordance with the natural law as taught by the Church. The idea is that the Church as Christ's representative on earth is the seniorial overlord of all property owners. Thus, we owe duties to the Church with respect to what we do with our property. Further, as overlord, the Church has the right to teach rules regarding our use of the property allocated to us. If the duke

15. Giles of Rome, *De ecclesiastica potestate*, trans. R.W. Dyson (Suffolk, UK: Boydell and Brewer, Ltd., 1986), 68.

of a manor breaks the feudal laws regarding the use of his fief established by his overlord, he has violated the rights of the overlord who granted the fief. The terms of grant, the promise to honor the obligations connected with the property, have been broken. Under this view we cannot understand "property rights" without understanding the "obligations" embedded in the system of distribution of that property. "Our" property is not "ours" absolutely in that our use of property is limited by rules established by God and his Church. This ultimate connection between private property and the greater goods common to all men is summarized in the centuries-old expression of a primary principle of natural law: "the common ownership of all things,"[16] by which is not meant abolition of private property but that private property is to be used consistently with the common interests of all men. In the next section we will see how the obligation to give alms (or use some of our property to aid those in need) is one of the restrictions on our use of property due to this principle.

Before turning to this topic, however, we need to say a word on how individuals acquire property. We have established that it is held from God through the Church, but in what manner is it acquired? John Fortescue, commenting on Genesis, explains the origin of this process:

> [I]n which words there was granted to man property in the things which he *by his own sweat* [my italics] could obtain.... For since the bread which man would acquire in sweat would be his own, and since no one could eat bread without the sweat of his own countenance, every man who did not sweat was forbidden to eat the bread which another had acquired by his sweat.... And thus the inheritable ownership of things first broke forth. For by the words *bread* our elders teach us, we are to understand not only what is eaten and drunk but everything by which man is sustained; and by the word *sweat*, all the industry of man.[17]

16. Gratian, *Decretum*, D.1 C.7, in *The Treatise on Laws*, trans. Augustine Thompson and James Gordley (Washington, DC: Catholic University Press, 1994).

17. John Fortescue, *De natura legis naturae*, trans. Ewart Lewis, *Medieval Political Ideas* (Oxford: Routledge, 2012), 135.

Passages such as this are often seized on to justify the notion that "you can eat what you kill." The products of your sweat are yours to do with as you wish. Yet such a view takes the process of acquiring property out of the context of the overall system. Yes, we acquire property through work, but our use of the property once acquired is still governed by the obligations God has decreed as ultimate overlord. Thus, although the feudal knight would receive his fief through work (performing a military service to the lord), this work produced the fief but did not exempt him from the feudal obligations attendant to the fief. We earn the right to particular property through our work, but once obtained we hold that property subject to the rules of the true owner, God. Such an idea is at odds with both the communists' and the libertarians' notion of property. To the communist, the state takes the place of God and owns all property. Work does not give rise to property rights. The state distributes property in its caprice. To the Libertarian, property exists without obligation. It is acquired by work and once acquired its use is within the sole discretion of the owner.

Charity, Justice, and Almsgiving

Almsgiving or acts of charity are often characterized by Libertarian Catholics as a subject of free choice. You may have encountered the argument: "Charity is great. Libertarianism encourages it by encouraging the production of excessive wealth that can be used in almsgiving. Everyone is free to perform charity if they so choose." This argument can be summarized as "almsgiving is optional. If you want to do it that is great for you." Catholic teaching on the other hand sees almsgiving as more than a mere pious option.

Peter Lombard placed together two apparently contradictory texts from St. Augustine: "Justice is in the relief of misery" and "Almsgiving is a work of mercy."[18] The first passage appeared to consider almsgiving, the relief of misery, an obligation of justice. The second passage in contrast asserts that almsgiving is an act of mercy. By definition, mercy is not something required by justice but

18. Peter Lombard, *Sententiae in IV Libros Distinctae*, 4 vols. (Grottaferrata, Italy: Collegium S. Bonaventurae ad Claras Aquas, 1971–1981), 330, 188.

something above and beyond the requirements of justice. It is not merciful to do what justice demands. There is a reconciliation of this apparent contradiction. Saint Thomas's explanation of this reconciliation is well reasoned, as always: "Hence whatever certain people have in superabundance is due, by natural law, to the purpose of succoring the poor. For this reason Ambrose says, and his words are embodied in the Decretals (Dist. xlvii, can. Sicut ii): 'It is the hungry man's bread that you withhold, the naked man's cloak that you store away, the money that you bury in the earth is the price of the poor man's ransom and freedom.'"[19]

Thus, each man is obligated in general to give alms from the amount of wealth he possesses that is above and beyond abundance. We met the concept of abundance in the prior chapter; it was the list of licit reasons for acquiring wealth. Superabundance is above and beyond these. If we have gained wealth to this magnitude we are obligated to give alms to those in need out of this superabundance. The obligation is so great that if we fail to fulfill it, our retention of this property is a theft; we eat another man's bread. Our use of this superabundance is restricted by this obligation. In the age of Christendom, consistent failure to comply with this obligation could result in being compelled by an ecclesiastical court to do so. Judges could compel charity in cases of necessity out of superabundance.[20]

Yet this obligation is not owed to a particular person. We are not obligated to give alms to a specific person. As to the gift of alms to a particular person, it is an act of mercy towards him individually. The general obligation to give alms exists pursuant to general justice, yet it is not a particular obligation in particular justice to any specific person.

There is a second obligation of almsgiving beyond superabundance. Saint Thomas continues:

> Nevertheless, if the need be so manifest and urgent, that it is evident that the present need must be remedied by whatever means be at hand (for instance, when a person is in some imminent dan-

19. Aquinas, *Summa*, II–II, Q. 66, art. 7.

20. Brian Tierney, *The Idea of Natural Rights* (Grand Rapids: Wm. B. Eerdmans Publishing Company, 1997), 74.

> ger, and there is no other possible remedy), then it is lawful for a man to succor his own need by means of another's property, by taking it either openly or secretly: nor is this properly speaking theft or robbery.[21]

Thus, when a person is in extreme need we are obligated to give to him the property we have, not qualified by superabundance, which will enable his survival. This obligation is clearly one of particular justice, for if we fail to perform it the one in need may take what he needs. Since all property is God's in the first place and since God wills that owners are obligated to use their property to aid one in extreme need, the one in need has property rights in that which he needs to survive, exemplified by the fact that St. Thomas says taking it is not theft or robbery. The man is taking what belongs to him. Translating this concept into modern legal parlance: extreme necessity establishes a property right in the one in need with respect to the goods of another. Now I must emphasize that this obligation to give succor is limited to cases of *extreme* need. So you cannot take your neighbor's wallet to pay for a new plasma TV because you really "need" it. Extreme necessity involves real danger of actual survival.

Catholic teaching has identified two instances when almsgiving is not optional but required. Saint Thomas uses these instances to reconcile the statements of Augustine: "Accordingly we are *bound* to give alms of our surplus, as also to give alms to one whose need is extreme: *otherwise* almsgiving, like any other greater good, is a matter of *counsel*."[22] Augustine was therefore not contradicting himself. In certain cases (superabundance and in cases of extreme need) almsgiving is a requirement of justice. Our acceptance of our property from God is bounded by these requirements. When these conditions are not present, then almsgiving is optional, a counsel.

In the first instance, where almsgiving is required by justice out of superabundance, we may wonder to whom is the almsgiving owed. Absent extreme necessity, it is not owed to individuals as individuals but to God as overlord. Since the Catholic institution of private property is rooted in relationships (the lord to his vassal),

21. Aquinas, *Summa*, II–II, Q. 66, art. 7.
22. Ibid., II–II, Q. 32, art. 5 (emphasis added).

Catholic thinkers have worked out orders of preference in giving alms based on relationships. Thus, one should look first to needs in one's family in preference to strangers. If there is none in one's family in need, among strangers, some gave priority to groups, such as all Christians, the old, the sick, and those who fell blamelessly from wealth to poverty.[23] An example from English literature explains the order thus: "Nevertheless we must keep order in giving and take need to the cause and to the manner of need in them that we give alms to, for why some be poor by their will and some against their will. And they that are poor by their will, some are poor for the love of God and some for the love of the world. They that be poor for the love of God must be helped passing other, for their poverty is profitable, perfect, and virtuous."[24]

Catholic teaching, ever vigilant to prevent extreme interpretations of moral norms, places two qualifications on the obligations to give alms. First, superabundance is not a mechanical formula; it depends on the facts and circumstances of a particular station in life. Thus, what is superabundance for the prince of a kingdom is not the same for an artisan. The determination of superabundance depends on the station in life of the person considered. Saint Thomas explains, "Yet it would be inordinate to deprive oneself of one's own, in order to give to others to such an extent that the residue would be insufficient for one to live *in keeping with one's station* and the ordinary occurrences of life: for no man ought to live unbecomingly."[25]

23. See, e.g., Gratian, *Decretum*, D. 86, cc. 14, 16, 17, cols. 300–1. http://www.columbia.edu/cu/lweb/digital/collections/cul/texts/ldpd; Brian Tierney, *Medieval Poor Law: A Sketch of Canonical Theory and Its Application in England* (Oakland, CA: University of California Press, 1959), 56–57, 150, note 34.

24. *Dives and Pauper*, pt. 2, Commandment ix, xiii, p. 286, lines 50–6, quoted in Diana Wood, *Medieval Economic Thought* (Cambridge: Cambridge University Press, 2004), 61.

25. Aquinas, *Summa*, II–II, Q. 32, art. 6 (emphasis added). Even St. Thomas recognizes that for certain noble causes it may be permissible to give more than would ordinarily be prudent: "Yet I say this without prejudice to such a case as might happen, supposing that by depriving himself of necessaries a man might help a great personage, and a support of the Church or State, since it would be a praiseworthy act to endanger one's life and the lives of those who are under our charge for the delivery of such a person, since the common good is to be preferred to one's own."

Consistent with the needs of one's station in life, one is obligated to give to the poor out of superabundance. There is no one-size-fits-all definition of superabundance. In addition, if one can assist another who is in extreme necessity, there is an obligation to give beyond superabundance. Besides these two instances of required almsgiving, doing further is a matter of permissible mercy regulated by prudence. Thus, charitable almsgiving is both a requirement and an option.

Thus, in contrast to Plato's argument, property should be owned privately, but its use is another matter. There are obligations with respect to our common use of property. Leo XIII does not defend private ownership as an absolute. He says, "consequently, a working man's little estate thus purchased should be *as completely at his full disposal* as are the wages he receives for his labor. But *it is precisely in such power of disposal that ownership obtains*, whether the property consist of land or chattels."[26] Leo XIII defends not the Libertarian distortion of private ownership but the Catholic sense that includes "limits of private possession," which mean limits to the use of private property. For Leo XIII as for all Catholics before him, private property "rests on the principle that it is one thing to have a right to the possession of money and another to have a right to use money as one wills. [I]f the question be asked: How must one's possessions be used? The Church replies without hesitation in the words of the same holy Doctor: 'Man should not consider his material possessions as his own, but as common to all, so as to share them without hesitation when others are in need.'"[27]

Being in Business

Now that we have considered the root of economic activity—wealth and property—we can begin to consider what one does with these instruments. What does Catholic teaching say about the choice of being engaged in commerce, as distinguished from working in agriculture or being an artisan? Commerce is the work of buying and selling. Is such a choice licit?

26. Leo XIII, *Rerum Novarum*, no. 5 (emphasis added).

27. Ibid., no. 22.

This question is addressed by Catholic thinking on two levels, the general and the individual. First, the question of whether trading and commerce is permissible at all as a profession must be addressed. Secondly, individual business transactions must be examined to see if they comport with justice. Before addressing these topics, I wish to make one caveat. I am not here addressing which institution is charged with enforcing the norms of the natural law regulating business. As we conclude that certain businesses or forms of transactions are illicit, it does not follow that the civil law must necessarily prohibit it. I ask you not to conclude that just because Catholic teaching prohibits a form of economic activity, that the government ought always and everywhere to prohibit it. Natural law is enforced in different fora. The internal forum, the confessional, is the proper locus for certain of the issues addressed. In other cases an external forum is more appropriate. Even if an external forum is appropriately designated to address a particular issue, there remains the question of whether a civil or church court is more suited to ruling on the matter. Do not make an unwarranted assumption about what the government should and should not prohibit. This is a second-level inquiry governed by principles of political prudence. In this chapter I am attempting to lay out the principles of economic justice and not the political judgments regarding the scope of legal action.

The process of buying goods to resell to others (trade) met with great biblical skepticism. Now I would guess that 90 percent of Americans have probably never even considered this possibility that trading in goods could be morally problematic. The American economy seems based on buying goods (from China) and reselling them to American consumers. As with the biblical skepticism regarding wealth, the Bible does not state that being in commerce is *ipso facto* impermissible. It expresses skepticism; such a profession is dangerous. "A merchant shall hardly keep himself from doing wrong. . . . As a nail sticketh fast between the joinings of the stones; so doth sin stick close between buying and selling."[28] Saint Ambrose echoes this biblical theme: "Why do you change the industry of nature into

28. Ecclesiasticus 26:29, 27:2.

fraud? Why do you diminish the abundance for the people? Why do you produce scarcities? . . . This you call industry; this you term diligence, which is the deceitfulness of craft, which is the cunningness of fraud. . . . This I call robbery and usury. . . . Your gain is the public's loss!"[29] He is not saying that all merchants are evil but that there appears to be a real near occasion of sin in that merchants easily succumb to these frauds and deceits. Aristotle shared this skepticism in his discussion of the proper political order. He argues that a merchant who regulates his profits by his needs was involved in natural and legitimate acquisition,[30] but "business" engaged in to amass wealth and not just satisfy needs was unnatural because it had no limits and was an "*appetitus divitiarum infinitus* [an infinite appetite of riches]."[31] Since a desire for riches has no limit, one must be imposed by human reason. This is why Gratian recommends that those in a weakened spiritual state, such as penitents, refrain from engaging in business.[32] It is dangerous and as penitents are still recovering from the effects of prior sin, they should not put themselves in such a position of danger. Commerce may be a necessary occasion of sin (it is necessary to some extent to enable necessary exchange transactions), but it is still an occasion of sin.

What precisely does a tradesman do? Given dangers identified by the authors, under what circumstances can one choose such a path? The following passage from St. Thomas addresses both questions.

> A tradesman is one whose business consists in the exchange of things. According to the Philosopher (Polit. i, 3), exchange of things is twofold: one, natural as it were, and necessary, whereby one commodity is exchanged for another, or money taken in exchange for a commodity, in order to satisfy the needs of life. Such like trading, properly speaking, does not belong to tradesmen, but rather to housekeepers or civil servants who have to pro-

29. Ambrose, *De officiis ministrorum*, Lib. III, cap. 6. http://www.newadvent.org/fathers/34013.htm.

30. Aristotle, *Politics*, I, 1256a, b.

31. Ibid., I, 1257a, b.

32. Gratian, *Decretum*, Causa XXX, question III of second part *De poenitentia* (*quia difficile est inter ementis vendentisque commercium non intervenire peccatum*; "Penitents should avoid commerce because it is difficult to avoid sin.")

> vide the household or the state with the necessaries of life. The other kind of exchange is either that of money for money, or of any commodity for money, not on account of the necessities of life, but for profit, and this kind of exchange, properly speaking, regards tradesmen, according to the Philosopher (Polit. i, 3). The former kind of exchange is commendable because it supplies a natural need: but the latter is justly deserving of blame, because, considered in itself, it satisfies the greed for gain, which knows no limit and tends to infinity. Hence trading, considered in itself, has a certain debasement attaching thereto, in so far as, by its very nature, it does not imply a virtuous or necessary end.... Nevertheless gain which is the end of trading, though not implying, by its nature, anything virtuous or necessary, does not, in itself, connote anything sinful or contrary to virtue: wherefore nothing prevents gain from being directed to some necessary or even virtuous end, and thus trading becomes lawful. Thus, for instance, a man may intend the *moderate* gain which he seeks to acquire by trading for the upkeep of his household, or for the assistance of the needy: or again, a man may take to trade for some public advantage, for instance, lest his country lack the necessaries of life, and seek gain, not as an end, but as payment for his labor.[33]

We see that engaging in buying and selling to acquire the things necessary for oneself or one's family (or household) does not make one a "tradesman." One is not trying to profit from the activity but merely obtain needed goods. This former type of exchange is distinguishable from people who engage in trading solely for the purpose of profit. After expressing concern over such activity, he concludes it is morally neutral. It is not inherently virtuous but not intrinsically evil. Thus, the act of being in the business of trading for profit must be evaluated in light of the reason for seeking the profit. As Gratian explains, seeking profit merely for its own sake is disgraceful:

> Everyone who in the time of harvest or grape gathering, not out of necessity but on account of greed, gathers together the year's food harvest or wine, by a proverb of credit, he gathers together one peck for two denari (silver coins), and he continuously stores it up

33. Aquinas, *Summa*, II–II, Q. 77, art. 4 (emphasis added).

> until it may be sold for four denari or six, or more, we call this disgraceful profit.[34]

According to St. Thomas, to be licit the intention of profiting from trade must be limited in two ways. First it must be oriented towards a proper good such as the support of one's family or the poor or for the common good of the community. Secondly, the amount of profit sought must be moderated (subjected to a limit). One limit is that the profit must be proportional to the value added by the merchant to the goods transferred. John W. Baldwin provides an excellent overview of the way in which Catholic writers used these concepts to work out a hierarchical system of evaluating different uses of commerce and concluding which were licit and which were not. He addresses the specific question when, if ever, it is licit to buy something for one price and sell it for a higher price:

> First of all there is the case of one who buys goods for his own or household use with no intention of reselling these goods at a profit. At a later date, he discovers that he is forced through circumstances of necessity (*necessaritas*) or expediency (*utilitas*) to sell these goods. . . .
>
> The second category deals with the artisans and craftsmen and occurs when one buys goods cheap and then by changing or improving them, he is able to sell them at a higher price. The higher price for which he sells the goods is justified by both the expenses (*impendium*) and the labor (*labor*) he as an artisan has expended upon the goods in order to improve them. This type of business (*negotiatio*) is essentially honorable (*honestus*) and permitted always to the laity. . . .
>
> The final category of buying cheap to sell dear is exclusive of the first two. If one buys goods cheap *with the sole motive of selling them later at a higher price* for profit *without having changed the form of the goods* through added expenses or labor and without being compelled to do so by necessity or expediency, then that one

34. Gratian, *Decretum*, Causa 14, q. 4, C, IX. *Item Iulius Papa. Quicumque tempore messis uel uindemiae non necessitate,sed propter cupiditatem conparat annonam uel uinum, uerbi gratia de duobus denariis conparat modium unum, et seruat, usque dum uendatur denariis quatuor aut sex, aut amplius, hoc turpe lucrum dicimus* (my translations).

> is conducting a commercial enterprise (*negotiatio*) in the truest sense of the word. This pure merchandising, although permitted (*licitus*) to the laity was unconditionally forbidden to the clergy. To the laity it could be an honorable (*honestus*) or a shameful (*turpis*) affair. If no labor or expense were involved, for example if one made profits by observing the market and buying in times of plenty and selling in times of famine, the enterprise was immoral. . . . If, however, heavy expenditure had been made or if the merchant was fatigued by hard labor, then the enterprise was assessed as honorable, unless some other unworthy means intervened.[35]

In considering these ideas, one contemporary issue comes to my mind: the pricing of fuel. One study concluded in 2008 that almost two thirds of the price of gas was due to oil speculation.[36] Another more recent study attributed 40 percent of the price of gas to Wall Street speculation.[37] Among other information, this report claims:

> Even those inside the oil industry have admitted that speculation is driving up the price of gasoline. The CEO of Exxon-Mobil, Rex Tillerson, told a Senate hearing last year that speculation was driving up the price of a barrel of oil by as much as 40%. The general counsel of Delta Airlines, Ben Hirst, and the experts at Goldman Sachs also said excessive speculation is causing oil prices to spike by up to 40%. Even Saudi Arabia, the largest exporter of oil in the world, told the Bush administration back in 2008, during the last major spike in oil prices, that speculation was responsible for about $40 for a barrel of oil.

Fuel speculators are people who do nothing other than try to buy today and sell tomorrow at a higher price. As what they buy is purely synthetic, they add no value to the product. They do not

35. John W. Baldwin, "The Medieval Theories of the Just Price: Romanists, Canonists, and Theologians in the Twelfth and Thirteenth Centuries," *Transactions of the American Philosophical Society* 49, no. 4 (1959): 1–92 (emphasis added).

36. F. William Engdahl, "Perhaps 60% of today's oil price is pure speculation," *Global Research*, May 2, 2008. http://www.globalresearch.ca/perhaps-60-of-todays-oil-price-is-pure-speculation/8878.

37. Bernie Sanders, "Wall Street greed fueling high gas prices," *CNN*, February 28, 2012. http://www.cnn.com/2012/02/28/opinion/sanders-gas-speculation/index.html.

transport it; they do not store it; they do not refine it. They merely speculate to take advantage of price movements for a profit. As money has poured out of the mortgage markets (due to another crisis) and into the fuel futures markets, are we witnessing the rotten fruits of this pure speculative trading?

Now if one of the limits on legitimate trading activity is a moderation of profit, how does one define and quantify what is moderate as opposed to excessive profit? William of Rennes explains:

> Although business can scarcely be conducted without sin, merchants may receive a *moderate profit* from their wares for the maintenance of themselves and their families. Since they work for all and perform a kind of common business by transporting merchandise back and forth between fairs, they should not be held to pay their own wages. From the merchandise itself they can accept a *moderate profit*, which is regulated by *the judgment of a good man*, because the amount of profit permitted cannot be exactly determined in shillings, pounds, or pennies.[38]

Note first that William places the same qualification on the definition of a legitimate merchant: he must actually add some value to the goods sold. As to determining the moderate profit, he explains there is no generally applicable mathematical formula. He uses the concept of the "judgment of a good man." This was a reference to a concept in Roman law of referring a difficult factual determination to an experienced man who demonstrated expertise in applying right reason. In a Catholic context, the "judgment of a good man" is the advice of a well-informed confessor, one who possesses the grace of office to assist in discerning the proper moderation of profit in a particular case.

Yet our economic system exalts the pure profit principle. More profit is always better, or in the words of the character Gordon Gekko of the film *Wall Street*, "Greed is good." Pure speculation is the goal of thousands of analysts and traders on Wall Street. The public celebrates people like George Soros who have made enough specula-

38. William of Rennes, *Glossa* to *peccant* II, 7 para. 9, p. 235 in *Summa Sancti Raymundi de Peniafort, Barcinonensis, Ordinis praedicator, De poenitentiaet matrimonio, cum glossis Ioannis de Friburgo* (Farnborough: Gregg Press 1967).

tive profit to fund a country not care for the needs of his family. The subprime mortgage crisis was driven in part by speculative trading in credit default swaps that amplified astronomically the losses created by a small percentage of homeowners defaulting on loans.[39] Not many questioned these vehicles of speculation when profits were coming in. Questions only arose when losses were manifest.

Beyond fulfilling these general requirements for conducting legitimate commerce, moderating profit based on the assessment of a confessor and having a worthy purpose for which profit is sought, each individual transaction of a merchant is also subject to further moral principles regulating particular economic transactions. Even if being a merchant in general is being conducted in a Catholic manner, the Catholic merchant must make sure that individual transactions are in and of themselves made on just terms. It is to the justice of individual exchanges that the next chapter turns. Before descending to the level of such details, we will close this chapter by returning to the objections of the economic liberals touched on in the opening pages of this chapter. We will conclude by exposing the dangerous premises of economic liberals.

Unlimited Greed or Rational Constraint?

The central assumption underlying all of liberal economic thought in contrast to Catholic economic doctrine is greed. Now economic liberals do not always use that word; they may call it "profit motive" or "self-interest" or "wealth maximization," but all of these terms boil down to the same thing.

More clever economic liberals will mask this principle by saying that it is only valid within the economic "framework." Once wealth is generated, morality may have something to say about what one does with it; but within the analysis of the process of production, profit maximization is the supreme criterion for evaluating economic choices: which alternative generates more wealth is the key to

39. For more detail on the legalized gambling conducted through credit default swaps, see Brian M. McCall, "Gambling on Our Future: The Federal Government Fiddles while the Common Law Could Protect Our Future," *Arizona State Law Journal* (forthcoming).

choosing human action (even if some concede that morality can put demands on the further use of this wealth). All other considerations eventually distill to this sole criterion. Social responsibility, charitable giving, concern for the safety of workers, and other values may be considered by economic liberals, but only after maximum profit or wealth maximization is attained. A decision to donate computers to a school is justified for a board of directors only to the extent the enterprise hopes to derive at some point a greater amount of wealth than expended in the donation through advertising or customer good will. This is why participants in a system controlled and ruled by liberal economic thought may be decent people, men who want to make moral choices, but their philosophy precludes the "intrusion" of such morals into the decisions of a business enterprise, wherein the generation of profit is the complete good to be sought. This move exempts economic liberals from the moral (divine and natural) law's requirements of justice and fairness. Again, some economic liberals make exceptions for a few egregious offenses against the natural law, such as fraud and violence. Yet man is subject to the entire divine and natural law. We are not free to pick and choose which norms to observe and which to leave outside of our artificial "framework."

Now one with a *sensus Catholicus* likely knows this philosophy is flawed. We will explore Catholic economic doctrine to see exactly why it is flawed.

As St. Thomas teaches, relying on Aristotle, men act in accordance with ends. We choose actions that, in light of all the relevant facts, appear to attain a particular end. Now some ends are incomplete; they do not perfect all of the aspects of man's nature. Some ends are more complete; they encompass more aspects of man's nature. The ultimate or most complete end of man is eternal salvation, the beatific vision. In attaining this end, man's nature is perfected. Below this perfect end are other necessary ends that must be pursued in order to make the perfect end attainable. The highest natural end is the living of a virtuous life in peaceable society. Below this complete natural end, the creation of sufficient temporal wealth is one of the incomplete ends comprising it. In order to come to know, love, and serve God and live well with our neighbor in this world so as to attain his ultimate end, happiness in heaven, man must satisfy the physical needs of his bodily nature. The satisfaction of human temporal needs provided by wealth is therefore one of the ends towards which man's nature, and hence natural law, directs him. We cannot lose sight of the fact that this end is only intermediate, incomplete. Wealth or profit is not a final end in and of itself; it is a means to other ends and as such must be morally evaluated as a means. It must therefore be limited to the extent it conforms to the ultimate natural and supernatural ends of man. We see here that the economic liberal's fatal error is that he makes of an incomplete end the complete criterion of decision within a "framework" he arbitrarily uses to insulate economic activity from the same degree of moral scrutiny that governs other human activity.

The effect of doing so is that the attainment of wealth becomes infinite. When an incomplete end is treated as a complete end it is distorted, and the proper orientation of man towards his true end is obscured. This is why man is required to place limits on the increase of wealth as a criterion of economic decision making just as he must place due limits on his concupiscent appetite. The desire for wealth, much like the desire for other things, is not bad in and of itself but it needs to be constrained and properly oriented to a higher end. The generation of wealth according to Catholic economic doctrine must be placed under constraint just as the desires of concupiscence must be subjected to reason. Henry of Hesse explains it thus: "Whoever has enough for these things [to sustain oneself, to perform pious works, to make reasonable provision for future emergencies, or to support offspring] but still works incessantly to gain riches or a higher social status, or so that later he may live without working, or so that his sons may be rich and great—all such are driven by damnable avarice, physical pleasure and pride."[40] To possess enough for all this and still desire more exceeds the bounds of prudence. Constraints on the desire for wealth are not excessive but rather very prudent. There is an outer limit to acquisitiveness.

Saint Bernard agrees with this conclusion: "In themselves, as regards man's Spiritual welfare, they [riches] are neither good nor

40. Henry of Hesse, *De contractibus*, in Gerson, *Opera omnia*, 4, cap. 12, fol. 191ra.

bad, yet the use of them is good, the abuse is bad; anxiety about them is worse; the greed of gain still more disgraceful."[41] The proper use of wealth is virtuous; its abuse—the greed of gain—is vice.

Liberal economic philosophy says any choice that increases net wealth is a good choice; the principle acknowledges no limit. The profit motive in the economic liberal's philosophy cannot accept the limit defended in Catholic economic philosophy. Profit is always good and more profit is always better—again, within the "framework" that economic liberals use to exempt "economics" from full moral scrutiny, while protesting that outside the "framework" capitalists can be moral and generous people when it comes to deciding how they will use their wealth.

Saint Thomas uses an image from nature to demonstrate how being properly solicitous for temporal goods means holding such desire in its proper constraint—a befitting time. "The ant is solicitous at a befitting time, and it is this that is proposed for our example. Due foresight of the future belongs to prudence. But it would be an inordinate foresight or solicitude about the future if a man were to seek temporal things, to which the terms 'past' and 'future' apply, as ends, or if he were to seek them in excess of the needs of the present life, or if he were to forestall the time for solicitude."[42] We may seek profit, but doing so in excess is—as is being irresponsible about them (forestalling the time for solicitude)—a vice.

Before proceeding in this argument I must pause to clarify that recognizing a necessary moral restraint on the profit motive is not analogous to asserting that the government must impose this restraint in all circumstances. The question of what is the appropriate balance among the Church's public law, local government, national government, and personal restraint as directed by a confessor is a question about the appropriate means. This is a large topic in itself; for centuries and in light of differing circumstances, the balance between the internal forum (confession) and the various external fora (civil and ecclesiastical courts) has gone on and will continue. Yet proponents of economic liberalism often attempt to

41. St. Bernard of Clairvaux, *De consideratione*, 47.

42. Aquinas, *Summa*, II–II, Q. 55, art. 7, Reply to Objections 1 and 2.

confuse the issue by raising this topic as a red herring. They conflate the argument that morality requires this restraint with the advocacy of a totalitarian police state. Economic liberals in doing so avoid having to argue the real issue: the profit principle cannot be the sole criterion of evaluating the justice and morality of economic choices.

Returning to the necessary restraint, recall it is the other ends of man's existence. What are these other ends? They are none other than the supernatural and natural ends of man. For example, living justly or rendering to others their due is an end of the social nature of man. Justice is one of the cardinal virtues man must strive to perfect on his path to the complete end. Thus, it is illicit to obtain profit by use of means that violate commutative justice (which includes more than fraud). Liberal economic thought rejects this constraint. This is to say nothing of the divine law in light of which man's actions must be judged.

The Old Economic Liberal Canard: Economics Is Just a Science!

The Catholic economic liberal Dr. Thomas E. Woods, Jr. has argued that "economics is a science whose purpose is to employ human reason to discover how man's ends can be reached. What those ends should be is a matter for theology and moral philosophy to decide."[43] Whatever most efficiently gets us to the chosen end is the right economic choice. Yet Catholic morality does not permit ambivalence about means. Even if one's ends are good (as determined by theology and moral philosophy, as Dr. Woods would say), the means chosen must also be morally just. Thus, to claim that economics is merely the science of "means" is defective. The choice of means is not morally neutral. Means have moral implications.

A typical argument is that a low wage (one below the intrinsic value of the work performed for that wage) is acceptable if the free market will bear such wage (due to a large number of unemployed workers, for example).[44] It is argued that even the worker paid an

43. Thomas Woods, *The Church and the Market* (New York: Lexington Books, 2005), 31.

44. Ibid., 50ff.

unjust wage is better off in the end because the profit made by the employer increases overall wealth for society, or put in a favorite expression of economic liberals, a rising tide raises all boats. Conceding for the moment that this assertion is factually true (despite its being counterintuitive), Catholic economic doctrine prohibits paying an unjust wage as a means to this end. Even if more wealth is created for the economy or more people have jobs, if this end is achieved by a violation of justice, this end cannot justify an unjust means. A worker has been paid less than the value of the work performed. Society may have more wealth, but the end of man called justice has been violated by the use of an unjust means. So economics is "value free"[45] simply because it refuses to consider the moral values that restrain making use of unjust means.

Now the reason economic liberals cannot see the error of the ends justifying the means is that they assert that economic actions are amoral—they have no moral implications. Tom Woods, for example, says "absolutely nothing in the body of economic law derived through praexology involves normative claims" and "it is absolutely senseless to argue that . . . economic law should be subordinate to moral law."[46] Dr. Woods asserts this based on an understanding of economics as merely the study of human action to discover independent natural laws or operations.[47] Since these laws are part of "nature," they are not moral or immoral; they just exist. He even compares economic laws to the law of gravity.[48] The fatal flaw in this thinking is that all human actions involve *choice*. Human actions are not like gravity, predetermined and independently operating. Choices always have moral implications; they are either morally licit or illicit choices. Dr. Woods is correct; economics involves the study of human actions. Yet unlike the study of naturally existing gravity, all chosen human acts have moral implications and natural and divine restraints.

Take for example one of Dr. Woods's favorite examples of an

45. Ibid., 31.
46. Ibid.
47. Ibid., 16.
48. Ibid., 43.

"economic law" akin, in his mind, to gravity: supply/demand price relationships.[49] When supply goes down or demand goes up, prices go up. He asserts that empirically this can be observed and therefore the movement of prices up as supply declines, or demand increases, is morally neutral; it just happens by force of an economic "law of nature." This assertion is false. Prices are not autonomous forces independent of human choice. Prices go up because *people choose to increase them.* Now, it may be true that since the dawning of the Liberal Age people raise prices in these contexts because they believe, erroneously, that they have no choice: "Since prices always rise with supply decreases, I have to raise my prices." In a Catholic age, however, when people were not drunk with the propaganda of economic liberalism, this was not the normal reaction. The causes, nature, and duration of the supply shortage, or demand increase, had to be considered before a guild, or a public authority, or a father confessor would permit a merchant to increase prices. Thus, prices could be altered, *but only if there existed a morally licit reason to do so*, such as a sustained increase in the cost of transportation of the goods.

Further, unlike *liberal* economics as defended by Dr. Woods, *Catholic* economics holds it morally impermissible to increase prices due to a particular need of a buyer of goods or services. As explored further in the chapter on the just price doctrine, St. Thomas teaches that it is unjust for a seller to charge more because a buyer is in particular need of a good.[50] To use another example offered by Dr. Woods,[51] if a crisis such as the terrorist attacks in New York were to occur and people were deprived of their homes, it is unjust to increase the cost of a hotel room by 185 percent simply because more people want rooms. Dr. Woods claims, however, that allowing this price-gouging is a good thing because it allows the resource—the room—to go to the person who values that resource the most. Actually it allows the room to go to those with the most wealth, who may not be the people who value the room the most. A person of modest means who has no other place to find shelter for

49. See ibid., ch. 2.

50. *Summa*, II–II, Q. 77, art. 1.

51. Woods, *The Church and the Market*, 46–47.

his family may place a greater value on the room than a millionaire who just does not want to spend a night with his in-laws. The difference is the man of moderate means has less wealth with which to *express* his greater value of the room.

Dr. Woods raises a red herring at this point, arguing that keeping room rates in a time of crisis at normal levels will cause a waste of limited resources with a family taking up two rooms when they would only use one if the prices were higher.[52] First of all, it is *precisely the wealthier room-renter*, not the lower-income family, that is more likely to hog rooms by renting more than one for his comfort, so the argument fails on that account. In any case, since this outcome again involves human choice, it is not inevitable. This hotel owner can simply require that in emergencies a family of four may only rent one room so that others in need can occupy the second room. There is no need to increase the price by 185 percent to achieve a just rationing of scarce resources. Since Dr. Woods has started from the false moral premise that prices and other economic decisions are independent of human moral choice, he argues falsely that economic choices should be allowed to fall where they may, as a ball dropped can only fall to the ground due to the law of gravity.

In the end, this obscuring of the human moral choice involved in all economic actions becomes a façade behind which wealth can be pursued without moral limits. No, economics is not a discipline about invariable independent forces such as physics. It is the study of human actions relating to the means of creating temporal goods. Every human action and all means to ends must be oriented to and limited by the ultimate ends of man. This simple truth has been under attack for centuries by economic liberals. It is time that Christ's truth, the natural law, be given its proper place within the discipline of economics. The only desire of man that can morally be unlimited is the desire for God. The desire for wealth must be subject to just limits, with God and his law in view at all times. The operation of his law in particular transactional settings will be the focus of the next chapter.

52. Ibid., 47.

4

The Details of Economics: Money, Debt, Just Price, and Usury

EXCHANGE IS AT the heart of economic activity. Since each household cannot produce everything it requires for its sustenance, they enter into exchange transactions. To adapt an example used by Aristotle, one family might be shoemakers and another might be house builders. The shoemakers will need a house and the house builders will need shoes. They acquire what they need through exchange. This chapter examines principles that govern exchange transactions. Money is at the heart of modern exchange transactions. Money is a medium or method of exchange that facilitates more exchanges than simple bartering. Since a house builder is not likely to be interested in exchanging a house for a number of shoes equal to the value of a house, money can be used to bridge the gap. Due to the prevalence of money in a large economy's exchange transactions, this chapter will begin with a consideration of money and its perversion by the debt masters of the modern economy. After considering modern money, this chapter will consider two of its uses: the exchange of money for goods for a just price and the lending of money for others to use, or usury.

The Problems of Modern Paper Money

Aristotle realized that money serves two purposes: a measure facilitating exchanges and a store of value for future use. Bartering enables only limited exchanges. One requiring shoes must find someone requiring something he has. The buyer may have equivalent value but not in a form the seller needs. Money breaks the impasse. Money equal to the value of the shoes can acquire what the seller needs. Money thus measures the value of things without reference to specific goods. Money can thus serve as a yard stick to equate value. Second, money facilitates more transactions by bridging time. A buyer may need shoes when the shoemaker may need nothing. The transaction would have to wait until the shoemaker was in need. If the buyer pays in money, the shoemaker can keep that money for later necessity, perhaps to buy a house.

The fourteenth-century scientist and philosopher Nicholas Oresme identified the first of these functions of money by explaining that it is an "instrument artificially invented for the easier exchange of natural riches" and a balancing "instrument for the exchange of natural riches." Money is important to society because it is essential to facilitate necessary exchange transactions, both those that are contemporaneous and over the course of time. Money can be used as a standard measure of comparison among unlike goods. As Aristotle points out, goods cannot be compared in a linear manner. One shoe is not equal to one house but only a fraction of the value of a house. A standard monetary system provides a system for equating value among disparate things. For example, a shoe might be worth $10 but a house $100,000. In this case, it is the monetary unit of the dollar with all of its denominations that allows the comparison of value between shoes and houses. In this case a shoe is worth 1/10,000 of a house. By using money the house builder does not have to transfer 1/10,000 of a house for shoes (which would be utterly impractical) but rather a monetary unit representing 1/10,000 of a house. In a similar manner, the metric system allows the comparison as to length among objects of dramatically different size. The length of a house can be equated in size (perhaps 40 meters) to the length of a shoe (perhaps 33 centimeters) by use of the metric system. Likewise they can be equated in value through the monetary system of the dollar or the pound. Because not all exchanges are simultaneous, the secondary purpose of money is to store value for future use over time. To use the prior example, the home builder may keep some of the money he received from building a house until he needs a pair of shoes. Thus, a medium of exchange can facilitate both contemporaneous exchange, and a store of value can facilitate exchanges over extended periods of time.

In light of this definition of money as a medium of exchange, several conclusions about the nature of money can be drawn. First, as St. Thomas Aquinas observes, money is not natural but artificial wealth. He distinguishes between these two categories of wealth thus: Natural wealth is that which serves man as a remedy for his natural wants, such as food, drink, clothing, cars, dwellings, and such like, while artificial wealth is that which is not a direct help to nature, as money, but is invented by the art of man, for the convenience of exchange, and as a measure of things salable.

Natural wealth consists of things that can be used directly to satisfy human needs (food, clothing, etc.). These things are defined by the need they satisfy. Food is anything that satisfies hunger. Yet money does not directly satisfy needs. It instrumentally satisfies those needs by facilitating exchanges ordered to the acquisition of natural wealth that satisfies them. Although there are certain essential qualities that money will necessarily contain to function as such, as something designed by the art of man, money does not have an essential composition. It can assume a variety of forms as long as they satisfy the instrumental purpose of facilitating the comparison of values, the exchange of goods, and the storing of value.

Further, as St. Thomas observes, money is not an end in and of itself. It does not directly satisfy any need. As a mere instrumentality, money is not used as an end itself but as a means to achieve other ends (current or future exchange transactions). Once money is seen as a mere instrumentality either to effect present exchange transactions or to store value for future ones, it can only be normatively evaluated in the context of its particular use. As Aquinas says:

> All other things from themselves have some utility; not so, however, money. But it is the measure of utility of other things.... And therefore the use of money does not have the measure of its utility from this money itself, but from the things which are measured by money according to the different persons who exchange money for goods.[1]

1. St. Thomas Aquinas, In *Quator Libros Sententiarum* III, 37, i, 6, quoted in Diana Wood, *Medieval Economic Thought*, 74.

In other words, because money can only be used to trade for other things (now or in the future), its use cannot be evaluated normatively in isolation but only in the context of a particular exchange transaction. Analogically, a yardstick functions only in its use to measure. If used to measure the amount of poison to kill someone, it is an immoral use. If used to measure the size of a beam to build a house, it is a moral use. We must examine in more detail the ways in which money can be used.

Even though the use of money can only be evaluated in context, anything selected to be used as money can be evaluated in light of its ability to fulfill the measuring and comparison functions of money. Many things have been used over the millennia for money (cattle, tobacco, gold, silver, paper, etc.). Their suitability to serve as a medium of exchange can be evaluated in light of how well they fulfill the purpose of money. The more stable its purchasing power, the better it serves its function. Saint Thomas observes: "it ought to be so established that it [money] retains the same value more permanently than other things."[2] Thus, a relatively stable element such as gold is more appropriate than fresh fruit, which will rapidly decay. The opposite is also true. The more instability in the purchasing power of money, the less it serves its function and the more difficult and unjust become exchanges. As A.N. Fielding commented: "Money must be made a just measure of value. If it is not, every money transaction perpetrates injustice.... And injustice means sooner or later the disintegration of the existing social order."[3]

To achieve both its measure and store functions, money's value must be clear. If a shoemaker is to resolve on parting with shoes for a set economic value, money can facilitate this transaction if it is a reliable measure. It can serve as store of value only if certainty exists about its future value. Likewise, one would abandon measuring a room in feet if the size of a foot unpredictably changed throughout the time of taking measurements.

The history of money over the past few centuries has been a

2. Aquinas, *Commentary on the Nichomachean Ethics*, trans. C.J. Litzinger, OP (South Bend, IN: Dumb Ox Books, 1964), Book V, Lecture IX.

3. Quoted in Fahey, *Money Manipulation*, 71.

movement from the use of some valuable commodity, such as precious metals, to paper receipts representing deposits of such goods, to paper representing nothing. Thomas Jefferson noted the dangers of detaching the monetary system from some external anchor and relying solely on a printing press when he noted, "That paper money has some advantages, is admitted. But that its abuses also are inevitable, and, by breaking up the measure of value, makes a lottery of all private property, cannot be denied."[4] Since the supply of paper on which to print money is practically limitless, the stability of money is destroyed absent some other constraint.

What Is Our Current Money?

During the nineteenth century, most of the paper being used as a medium of exchange consisted of banknotes, which were simply written promises of private banks to hand over the named amount of gold or silver in the paper. Since the banks issuing these notes were not actually required to hold the gold or silver they promised to pay on issued notes, the value of these notes varied wildly. As a result of this system, "there were wild fluctuations in the amount of notes issued by banks, and the quality of the notes ranged from valuable and reliable, on the one hand, to worthless."[5] In response to a financial panic involving bank runs in 1907, the federal government enacted the Federal Reserve Act, which created the Federal Reserve System (FRS). The FRS consists of twelve regional Federal Reserve Banks and a Board of Governors that oversees the system. The topic of the FRS is large indeed. We will only focus on its role in controlling the money supply.

Originally the Federal Reserve Banks functioned as central banks that held the legally required reserve deposits that banks were required to have in relation to all their promises to pay out real money. The Federal Reserve stood ready to lend money (or gold) to member banks if they were short of funds to meet obligations. The

4. Thomas Jefferson to Josephus B. Stuart, Letter, May 10, 1817. http://yamaguchy.com/library/jefferson/jeff_18.html.

5. Ali Kahn, "The Evolution of Money: A Story of Constitutional Nullification," *University of Cincinnati Law Review* 67 (1999): 393, 429.

whole system still maintained a nexus to gold as Federal Reserve Notes (banknotes issued by the FRS) were redeemable in gold.[6] A bank faced with redemption requests could borrow Federal Reserve Notes from a Federal Reserve Bank. The Federal Reserve Note was a promise of the Federal Reserve Bank to redeem in legal money of the United States, i.e., gold coin. Then came the Great Depression. One of the measures enacted was an abandonment of internal gold redemption. The promise to redeem Federal Reserve Notes in gold was abolished and deleted from the notes. It was illegal to contract for the payment of gold, and coins were confiscated.[7] The United States government still agreed to exchange US dollars for gold in international transactions until 1971, when the final curtain came down on the gold standard and US dollars ceased to have any legal connection to gold.[8] Thus, Federal Reserve Notes ceased to be redeemable for gold. After the abandonment of gold redemption, what then do the familiar green bills in our wallets legally signify? Federal law mandates that Federal Reserve Notes "shall be redeemed in lawful money on demand."[9] Federal law then defines these same Federal Reserve Notes as "lawful money."[10] Thus, the dollar bill at home in a piggy bank represents the right to demand that the Federal Reserve Bank redeem it for another Federal Reserve Note. If that sounds circular, that is because it is!

Now putting these elements together, here is how America's (and likewise most of the rest of the world's) monetary system works. Banks create money by lending to customers. When a customer needs a loan, the lending bank just creates the money to lend out of thin air by noting in its records that the borrower's account has been increased by the loan amount. The bank in essence promises to lend to the borrower money it does not have in exchange for the borrower's promise to pay the amount the bank promises to pay back to the bank. The bank is limited by how much money it can

6. See ibid., 436–37.

7. See Lewis D. Solomon, "Local Currency: A Legal and Policy Analysis," *Kansas Journal of Law & Public Policy* 5 (1996): 59, 64.

8. Ibid., 65.

9. 12 U.S.C. §411 (1934).

10. 31 U.S.C. §5103 (1982).

create to lend by fractional reserve requirements. The amount of money it can create is limited by the amount of reserves it owns. Reserves essentially are the amounts credited to its account at a Federal Reserve Bank plus physical Federal Reserve Notes it possesses in its vaults. All credits at Federal Reserve Banks can be withdrawn in Federal Reserve Notes, which as we have seen represent the right to exchange them for other Federal Reserve Notes. Thus, the FRS can print as many notes as it needs, since the only thing the notes promise is to print more like them. Now banks can increase the amount credited to their Federal Reserve Bank account in several ways. The most common method would be to sell government securities they own back to the Federal Reserve Bank. The Federal Reserve Banks do not themselves have reserve requirements since they are the reserve banks and they therefore can purchase as many government securities as they want and pay for them with a credit on their records to the seller, such credit being redeemable only in Federal Reserve Notes.[11] Although there is more complexity to the monetary system, this explanation demonstrates the essential elastic nature of the currency.[12] The FRS can make more money by buying US government securities (thereby creating bigger reserve account balances for member banks). It buys these securities with promises to pay Federal Reserve Notes, which it is capable of printing without limit (in the unlikely event a bank actually demands payment in physical notes). Member banks can then create more money to loan to their customers as a result of the larger account balances with a Federal Reserve Bank. If the FRS wants to reduce the amount of money in the country, they can sell US government securities to member banks, which pay for them by reducing the balances in their reserve accounts. This reduction reduces the amount of money banks can lend.

To give a sense of the importance of bank-created money, which is essentially a bank's promise to pay Federal Reserve Notes on withdrawal from accounts at the bank, we can briefly examine some sta-

11. See ibid.

12. In fact, the stated purpose of the Federal Reserve System is to "furnish an elastic currency." Federal Reserve Act, Pub. L. No. 63–43, 38 Stat. 251 (1913).

tistics published by the Federal Reserve. As of December 2010, there was $916 billion of physical currency in circulation, whereas the total of all other components of what the FRS considers money equivalents (M1 and M2) was $9,732 billion.[13] Thus, physical currency only accounted for approximately 8.6 percent of the total money and money substitutes (limited only to M1 and M2) in the US economy. In 2000, the amount of currency was only $597 billion, whereas the other components of M1 and M2 were only $5,436 billion.[14] As noted earlier, even though the amount of bank credit functioning as money is connected in a sense to the amount of physical currency, the FRS system has the ability to increase the currency by printing more Federal Reserve Notes to satisfy its obligations to its depositors.

13. Figures derived from Federal Reserve Statistical Release: Money Stock Measures, June 2, 2011. http://www.federalreserve.gov/releases/h6/Current/. M1 is comprised of (1) currency outside the US Treasury, Federal Reserve Banks, and the vaults of depository institutions; (2) traveler's checks of nonbank issuers; (3) demand deposits at commercial banks (excluding those amounts held by depository institutions, the US government, and foreign banks and official institutions) less cash items in the process of collection and Federal Reserve float; and (4) other checkable deposits (OCDs), consisting of negotiable order of withdrawal (NOW) and automatic transfer service (ATS) accounts at depository institutions, credit union share draft accounts, and demand deposits at thrift institutions. M2 is comprised of M1 plus (1) savings deposits (including money market deposit accounts); (2) small-denomination time deposits (time deposits in amounts of less than $100,000), less individual retirement account (IRA) and Keogh balances at depository institutions; and (3) balances in retail money market mutual funds, less IRA and Keogh balances at money market mutual funds. All figures are taken from those that have been seasonally adjusted by the Federal Reserve. These calculations do not reflect all money substitutes since they exclude things such as bank deposits above $100,000.

14. Figures are taken from *Monetary Trends* published by the Federal Reserve Bank of St. Louis, August 2001. For this year, M1 was defined to include the sum of currency held outside the vaults of depository institutions, Federal Reserve Banks, and the US Treasury; travelers checks; and demand and other checkable deposits issued by financial institutions, except demand deposits due to the Treasury and depository institutions, minus cash items in process of collection and Federal Reserve float. M2 was defined to include M1 plus savings deposits (including money market deposit accounts) and small denomination (less than $100,000) time deposits issued by financial institutions; and shares in retail money market mutual funds (funds with initial investments of less than $50,000), net of retirement accounts.

As should be obvious, physical currency is virtually insignificant in importance in comparison to the money substitute of credit at banks created out of thin air by the banks themselves as loans to their depositors. Further, there is no external limit to the amount of money this system can create. Whereas the volume of gold coins is limited to the amount of gold a country acquires through production or export trade (with some room for tinkering by shrinking the size of each coin), our current system is limited only to the extent the policy makers in the FRS think they should limit the money supply. There is no external limit, no direct connection to the productiveness of the economy. Money and money substitutes have lost all connection to reality.

One explanation for the seemingly never-ending series of financial crises may be the great uncertainty surrounding money and its sustainability as a reliable store of value for later use. The twentieth century had already seen a severe loss of certainty in the stability of currency as the number of inches in a foot (to use the analogy) was gradually severed from any fixed referent (such as gold) as well as the loss of an ability to even know the number of all dollars comprising the overall yardstick. The number of available US dollars is not only the printed dollar bills in circulation but also the amount of money banks may lend in excess of amounts of deposits held. Under current law of fractional reserve banking, banks can lend more money than they have in deposits. Thus, unlike in past centuries when one of the fundamental obligations of governments was to control the reliability of the yard stick by authenticating the money supply, private banks now create money virtually at will in order to lend it out for their own profit. Put simply, we all know a dollar today will not be worth the same in the future; how much so is an open question.

Added to this existing uncertainty are billions of dollars on loan/invested into banks and auto companies as bailouts and stimuli. They act as an overhang of inches that could at any moment dilute the size of the yardstick. Beyond the technical economic debates over whether this can be controlled and compensated for, I suggest it is time for a more fundamental debate about the obligations of government to provide a stable measure of exchange and a real store of reliable future value.

The Ballooning of Debt Money

Our problems involve not only paper money but a special kind of paper money, one based purely on debt. The political news of 2011–2012 was abuzz with the issue of raising the federal debt limit, the amount Congress authorizes the government to borrow. Although controlling profligate government spending is a serious issue, the debt ceiling debate is really a red herring. Although the recent congressional debate may generate political capital, rising debt is a necessary component of a money system built on debt.

Our monetary system requires an ever increasing debt, public and private. Our paper money is used to represent the right to receive the specified amount of gold. A US $100 bill was a claim ticket entitling its holder to receive physical gold. The twentieth century saw a Democrat (Franklin Roosevelt) and Republican (Nixon) president work in tandem to eliminate all connection between paper money and gold. (Truly this was a bi-partisan issue!) United States dollars today literally are debt. Money is created as debt. New money enters the economy in the form of debt. Banks, not Uncle Sam, create money out of thin air and then lend it to their customers. As we have seen, a stroke of a keyboard is all that is needed to credit the account of a borrower with the loan proceeds that did not exist prior to the loan. The only limit on the bank's ability to create such money is the reserve requirement set by the Federal Reserve, which is controlled by the banks themselves. Banks can only create and lend nine times their reserves. Yet the Fed can create more reserves by buying government securities (government debt) in the market with its own invented money, which appears as a credit in the reserve accounts of member banks.

Since all money is created as a loan, these loans have to be repaid at some point, and as loans accrue interest, the amount repaid is always larger than the amount borrowed. Since all our money is created as debt, that means more debt has to be created to invent the money to pay the interest on the original loans. This is the origin of the debt treadmill. Unless the Fed bought government debt, the banks would not be able to create more money to loan, and there would not be enough money in the economy to service all the historic debt. The result is that unless the system creates more debt money, everyone (public and private) will not have enough money to service existing debt. The system is a balloon that constantly must be inflated with new debt money to keep up with debt service on the old debt money. This is why all the political ranting over the debt level is a faint whisper in a hurricane. Yes, increasing federal debt is bad; yet it is necessary to keep the monetary system churning. Without new debt/money, the system would grind to a halt. Recall 2008 when the entire economy ground to a halt because banks stopped lending. Debt is necessary to the creation of money to keep up with debt payments. Ultimately the only end of the federal debt crisis lies in reforming the monetary system.

Historically money was created as a result of increased economic productivity. Ancient Egypt used receipts for deposited grain as money. The more grain produced and deposited in silos, the more money produced. For over two thousand years, the West used precious metals as the base of its money. The more precious metals discovered, mined, and processed, the more coins were available as money. Although none of these monetary systems were perfect, as they were open to some manipulation and fraud, the base of the system was real wealth production. The base of our monetary system is debt, an obligation when combined with interest that by definition must always grow. To default on government obligations or not raise the debt level would cause our monetary system to implode. The only real solution then is to change the system to one based on production not debt.

The government cobbled together a deal at the eleventh hour to raise federal debt of $14.3 trillion by $2.4 trillion. At the signing, President Obama commented, "It's an important first step to ensuring that as a nation we live within our means." Although I agree there needs to be a next step, I doubt he has the same step in mind. For most politicians, it is merely a painful step on the same road. We really need to get off the current road and get on one going in a different direction.

In 1976, total household debt was $818.8 billion, which increased to $13.386 trillion by 2010. In 1976 total debt (business, government, and private debt) was $2.1 trillion, which figure had risen to $36.113

trillion by 2010. The reason is simple: the monetary system needs more money to keep servicing debt, so total debt must rise to cover total interest.

Thus cutting federal spending no matter how admirable it may sound in and of itself will not solve our problems. In fact, it creates new ones. Without increased government borrowing, the money creation machine cannot function. The federal debt along with private debt must rise to make money. We are enslaved to debt. The answer: we must get off the money as debt road and re-establish a monetary system on a foundation other than debt. For an example of a possible next step on an alternate road, consider H. R. 6550 introduced in Congress in December 2010. Nothing has happened with this proposal while the politicians ran around scaring everyone with the May 2, 2011 (then extended to August 2, 2011) deadline to raise the federal debt ceiling limit. Now is well past the time to explore this new road rather than simply raise the debt ceiling year after year.

The Debt Masters: The Federal Reserve

On Thursday, November 19, 2009, the House Financial Services Committee approved 46–23 the Paul-Grayson "Audit the Fed" amendment with broad bi-partisan support. It would repeal a law that prohibits a full audit of the activities of the Federal Reserve System. More than 300 congressmen sponsored it in the House despite rather fierce opposition from Rep. Barney Frank, then chairman of the Financial Services Committee.[15]

One of the fundamental obligations of government is to provide a sound and stable monetary system. In order for business exchange transactions to occur, people need a reliable system to measure and compare economic values. In 1913 our government ceded that responsibility to a joint venture between government and private bankers. The Fed is comprised of banks jointly owned by the federal government and private banks. Profits made by the Fed are allocated

15. After the Audit the Fed bill was defeated, some provisions of the original bill did make their way into The Wall Street Reform and Consumer Protection Act of 2009—Financial Stability Improvement Act of 2009 (Public Law No: 111-203).

among the member banks and the government. The federal government has devolved to this public/private entity its right to print legal tender, the only money accepted for the payment of all debts.

The Fed wears many hats: it makes monetary policy, it implements that policy through lending and acquiring financial assets; it prints money at will; it participates in financial transactions for profit. Yet, unlike both private banks and all aspects of the government, the Fed is immune from independent periodic auditing with respect to many of its most important activities. These include not only its policy-making decisions but also financial transactions entered into by the Fed (including transactions with foreign banks and governments). Thus, not only has government relinquished its obligation to protect and stabilize our measure of exchange, it has relinquished it to a market participant that has been shielded behind a wall of secrecy since 1913.

Chairman of the Fed Ben Bernanke has vehemently resisted the Audit the Fed legislation, claiming it would interfere with the Fed's independence in making monetary policy. First of all the Fed is *not* independent. It is not a private actor. It is a creation of government, which exists by will of the government. All other branches and agencies of government function in the light of day with their decisions and activities subject to public review and comment. Even if the Fed were a private entity (which it is not), businesses of its nature are subject to audit and review by the independent auditing firms and public agencies such as the SEC and IRS. The Fed has the benefit of keeping one hand in private for profit economic activity and another hand in making public policy regulating that activity. Is it too much to ask that the citizens of Oklahoma, whose representatives created and sustain this entity and who will be left paying the bill if it collapses, have a right to at least know what the Fed is doing and with whom it is transacting? Fortunately an overwhelming majority of congressmen think so. Although pursuant to the Dodd-Frank Act, the Fed does now have to release some information about its activities, hopefully someday the Fed will be subject to the same rigorous auditing standards as public corporations.

This triple power of paper currency, debt-based money, and the secretive government private bank, the Fed, are at the root of the monetary woes of our country. Given this triple powerhouse is not going to be abolished anytime soon, since it is supported with all the wealth and force of those who profit from it, what can local communities do to ease the harmful effects?

Why States Need Local Money

Although most living today know nothing other than a joint federal/commercial bank monopoly of money, this was not always the case. For most of our nation's history, a variety of local and regional currencies competed in the monetary marketplace. The few experiences of national currencies ended in disaster; the Revolutionary War Continentals and Civil War Greenbacks are examples.

A local currency alternative offers two main benefits. First, it encourages and promotes local reinvestment. Businesses and employees who receive a portion of their income in local currency are encouraged to reinvest (spend) it locally. Secondly, it provides for a disaster recovery plan in the event of a collapse of the national currency. Although such a thought was inconceivable to our parents, warning signs of hyperinflation or other collapse of the dollar have surfaced lately. Although nobody can predict the future, the ingredients of a dollar collapse are clearly present: massive dollar creation by the federal government through its bailout printing press at the Fed and the quiet movement of many countries away from the US dollar as an international reserve currency (a movement made inevitable by Nixon's closing of the gold window in the 1970s). Much of the US dollar's international strength is anchored in the Middle East petroleum countries. With the growing political instability of late (especially with its anti-American variety), a flight from dollar assets could result. National currency collapses are interspersed throughout history, and not just among developing nations. From Diocletian's Roman Empire to the Weimar Republic, powerful nations have seen their money lose all value quickly. I am not saying this will happen, but if it were to occur, having a local currency in circulation could provide a back-up method for keeping local exchange transactions in motion.

Local currencies can take on a variety of forms and features. Ithaca, New York has had a local program called "Ithaca Hours" in circulation since 1991. It uses a currency unit linked to the average hourly wage. Parts of Massachusetts have also adopted a local program. According to the BerkShares website, "over one million BerkShares" have been "circulated in the first nine months and over 2.7 million to date. Currently, more than four hundred businesses have signed up to accept the currency."[16] Adopting a local currency certainly involves navigating some legal issues, not least of which is the risk that the federal government will tyrannically suppress the program (as happened to state bank notes, which were taxed out of existence in the late nineteenth century, paving the way for a national monopoly). Yet our state government working together with local businesses can develop a program and incentive structure to launch a local currency alternative. The time to do so is now—before another financial collapse is rolling across the country.

Even with efforts to build a local currency alternative underway, much of the economy is still dependent on the unreliable debt-based paper money controlled by the Fed and its shareholder banks. The instability and unreliability of our debt-based money system makes the analysis of the use of that money more complicated. As we shall see in the rest of this chapter, the use of money in exchange transactions is subject to moral evaluation under the principles of just price and usury doctrines. The inscrutability of a debt money system where the value of money is always in flux makes the application of these doctrines more complicated. It becomes equivalent to measuring the perimeter of a room with a ruler that is constantly changing its size.

Rediscovering Catholic Just Price Doctrine

In a general sense, St. Thomas Aquinas predicted the paralysis of our financial and economic system that occurred in the financial collapse of 2008 when he predicted that in a society where unjust exchange transactions dominate, eventually all exchanges will cease to occur.[17] Saint Thomas also points out that although human law

16. See http://www.berkshares.org.

17. St. Thomas Aquinas, *Commentaries on the Ethics*, Bk. V, Lecture IX, no. 980 ("Without just exchange, no exchange will happen and it is needed for society").

does not and cannot prohibit all injustice,[18] society cannot escape the consequences of transgressing the divine law that leaves "nothing unpunished."[19] Thus, at least part of the explanation for the current economic and financial crisis lies in continuous and systemic violations of natural justice by our economic system. Now, there is likely not one product or market or factor completely responsible for these injustices. Yet there is one area of economic justice, understood in light of Catholic doctrine, that has certainly been largely ignored in twentieth- and twenty-first- century America—the just price doctrine. The search for causes and solutions to our perpetually recurring economic crises must therefore involve in part a re-acquaintance by our society with this element of Catholic truth.

As early as Aristotle, philosophers recognized the necessity of the exchange of goods. A house builder needs shoes and a shoemaker needs a house.[20] As the exchange is to be mutually beneficial to each party (each needs what the other is to exchange), the costs should not be born disproportionately by one party.[21] If unequal exchanges were to occur, they would serve as random instances of wealth redistribution; if wealth were to be redistributed at all it should be done according to a normative scheme not on the basis of random individual transactions.[22]

An apparent contradiction existed in the philosophy of Aristotle (as well as Plato). Although recognizing the need for exchange of goods (exchange was necessary to society), Aristotle was skeptical of tradesmen (those engaged in retail exchange) and only reluctantly allowed them into his ideal community.[23] The theory of the just

18. Aquinas, *Summa*, II–II, Q.77, art. 1, Reply to Objection 1.

19. Ibid.

20. Aristotle, *Ethics*, V, 5; Aquinas, *Commentary on the Ethics*, Bk. V, Lecture VIII, no. 976.

21. *Summa*, II–II, Q. 77, art. 1 ("Now whatever is established for the common advantage, should not be more of a burden to one party than to another").

22. See James Gordley, "Equality in Exchange," *California Law Review* 69 (1981): 1591.

23. Diana Wood, *Medieval Economic Thought*, 71, 111; see also Aristotle, *Politics*, I, 1256a, b; 1257a, b.

price can be seen as a reconciliation of the apparently contradictory acceptance of exchange transactions but wariness of those who facilitate them. Aristotle was interpreted as arguing that exchange is necessary for society, but exchange was not possible unless equality was maintained in an exchange.[24] It was those tradesmen who engaged in unequal exchanges who were to be restrained, and it was these who gave rise to the skepticism.

Based on Aristotelian theories of justice as the mean, advocates of the just price theory assert that voluntary exchanges need to be proportional in value. No person should profit from another's loss.[25] In an exchange, justice is found in an equal exchange, but injustice is found in an unequal one as the mean is not maintained.[26] Yet equality does not mean identical items be exchanged (this would defeat the idea of exchange). A proportionality of value needs to be maintained. So if a shoemaker were to exchange with a homemaker, one would not exchange one shoe for one house but rather that number of shoes which equate to the value of the house.[27] Since a homebuilder will not necessarily need so many shoes, money was invented to serve as a method for achieving this proportion.[28] With the invention of money, value can be expressed in prices quantified in a standardized manner by that money. A just price is thus a price that equals the value of the thing being purchased.[29]

It is important to note that equality in exchange is not to be con-

24. See Aristotle, *Ethics*, Bk. V, 1133a, 21–25 ("If this [reciprocal equality] is not observed, there will be neither exchange nor sharing"); see also Aquinas, *Commentary on the Ethics*, Bk. V, Lecture IX, no. 980; Wood, *Medieval Economic Thought*, 71.

25. Justinian, *Digest*, 50.17.206 (*Iure naturae aequum est neminem cum alterius detrimento et injuira fieri locupletiorem*). http://www.archive.org/stream/digestofjustiniao1monruoft/digestofjustiniao1monruoft_djvu.txt.

26. Aristotle, *Ethics*, Bk. V, 1131b32–1132a7.

27. See ibid., 1133a19–1133a25.

28. See ibid., 1133a19–1133b29.

29. See Fortescue, *De natura legis naturae*, in Ewart Lewis, *Medieval Political Ideas* (New York: Alfred A. Knopf, 1954), 135 (in discussing the origin of private property by commenting on Genesis 3:17–19, Fortescue explains that the investment in labor (sweat) is a licit and just way to acquire property or wealth: "in which words there was granted to man property in the things which he *by his own sweat* could obtain.... For since the bread which man would *acquire in sweat would be*

fused with the communist notion of equality of wealth. Equality in exchange does not require that wealth be equalized but that exchanges between individuals not occur on unequal terms. To use the example of the shoemaker, he may increase his wealth by investing more labor in the production of more shoes, which he then exchanges for their just value for other items of production or wealth. His overall wealth may increase (due to his labor), but it is not at the expense of those to whom he sells shoes; they transfer wealth equal to the value of the shoes they receive.

Now Christianity built on these Aristotelian principles when it asserted that Christians could not benefit from the loss of another in an exchange. In contrast, pagan Roman law had acknowledged that parties to exchange transactions had some freedom to take advantage of each other: "it is naturally permitted to parties to circumvent each other in the price of buying and selling."[30] Yet St. Paul, in a passage that strikingly parallels the Roman law text, claims that the divine law is contrary to such permissiveness. He says:

> For you know what precepts I have given to you by the Lord Jesus. For this is the will of God, your sanctification . . . that no man overreach, nor circumvent his brother in business: because the Lord is the avenger of all these things, as we have told you before, and have testified.[31]

Thus, Christians are obligated by divine "precept" and the "will of God" not to overreach or circumvent one another when exchanging goods. This obligation has been referred to over the course of Catholic centuries as the just price doctrine. One of the most concise statements of the normative requirement of paying a just price is that of St. Thomas Aquinas:

his own, and since no one could eat bread without the sweat of his own countenance, every man who did not sweat was forbidden to eat the bread which another had acquired by his sweat. . . . And thus the inheritable ownership of things first broke forth" (emphasis added)).

30. Justinian, *Digest*, 4, 4, 16, para. 4; 19, 2, 22, para. 3. "In buying and selling natural law permits the one party to buy for less and the other to sell for more than the thing is worth: thus each party is allowed to outwit the other."

31. 1 Thess. 4:2–3, 6 (the omitted intervening verses refer to precepts against sins of the flesh).

> Now whatever is established for the common advantage, should not be more of a burden to one party than to another, and consequently all contracts between them should observe equality of thing and thing. Again, the quality of a thing that comes into human use is measured by the price given for it, for which purpose money was invented, as stated in Ethic. v, 5. Therefore if either the price exceed the quantity of the thing's worth, or, conversely, the thing exceed the price, there is no longer the equality of justice: and consequently, to sell a thing for more than its worth, or to buy it for less than its worth, is in itself unjust and unlawful.[32]

Saint Thomas explains that the purpose of exchange transactions is to mutually benefit both parties. They are exchanging things because each will benefit from the thing exchanged by the other. Since the intended purpose is mutual benefit, the burdens should be mutual and not disproportionate. It is unjust for one party to bear the cost of a mutually beneficial transaction. To sell something at a variation from the just price disproportionately burdens one party and is therefore unjust in itself. However, St. Thomas continues by explaining that to achieve such equality it is sometimes just to compensate a party for losses incurred in accomplishing the exchange. He says, "On such a case the just price will depend not only on the thing sold, but on the loss which the sale brings on the seller. [H]e may charge for the loss he suffers."[33] The converse of the legitimate right to be compensated for costs incurred is not true. It is not licit to exact a profit above the just price because the other party has a particular need for the item exchanged. "Yet if the one man derive a great advantage by becoming possessed of the other man's property, and the seller be not at a loss through being without that thing, the latter ought not to raise the price, because the advantage accruing to the buyer, is not due to the seller, but to a circumstance affecting the buyer. Now no man should sell what is not his. . . ."[34] Here is an example. I buy your deceased grandmother's wedding ring in a

32. Aquinas, *Summa*, II–II, Q. 77, art. 1.
33. Ibid.
34. Ibid.

pawn shop for $200 and I have it appraised and find it to be worth $200. If we agree that I will sell it to you for $2,500 because you really want it, since you have no memorabilia of your grandmother, I have violated the moral law by selling for more than the just price. Notice a non-Catholic market definition of economic morality would have to conclude there is nothing wrong with our transaction since *you agreed to pay* $2,500. The ring was worth more to you, thus I am free to extract this higher price from you. Now St. Thomas does remark that people who derive special advantages from a sale are free to give a gift out of gratitude. But a freely given gift is different from a required term of transaction on the part of the seller.

This statement of the just price doctrine (no one should pay more or less than a thing is worth) begs at least two questions necessary to apply the norm to real exchanges: (1) What is something worth? And (2) should all unjust exchanges be corrected? Each question will be addressed in turn.

Value is determined by the relation that a thing bears to the satisfaction of a human need.[35] Therefore the just price is the common estimation of the satisfaction of human needs achieved by a particular thing.[36] The common estimation may or may not be the prevailing market price, where "market price" is defined as whatever a buyer is willing to pay. If the agreed market price corresponds to the common estimation of the value of human need satisfaction, then the two will be identical. What is significant about common estimation is that it is *common.* A particular or unique need or desire of a buyer or a community is not a legitimate factor in determining the just price.[37] Just because a buyer is starving and without food,

35. Aquinas, *Commentary on the Ethics*, Lecture IX, 981.

36. See John T. Noonan, Jr., *The Scholastic Analysis of Usury* (Boston: Harvard University Press, 1957), 85.

37. See *Summa*, II–II, Q. 77, art. 1 ("Yet if the one man derive a great advantage by becoming possessed of the other man's property . . . the latter ought not to raise the price, because the advantage accruing to the buyer, is not due to the seller, but to a circumstance affecting the buyer"). See also Justinian, *Digest*, 35.2.63 (*Pretia rerum non ex affectu nec utilitate singulorum, sed communiter funguntur*; "The prices of things do not come out of the desire or utility of each individual but they are derived commonly" (my translation)); ibid. at 9.2.33 (stating the same concept).

this does not entitle the seller to ask a price more than the common price for such food. Those who simply declare that there can be no moral limitation on freely agreed prices or that the price agreed by buyers and sellers in a free market is by definition a just price have no reason to condemn the sale of bread for $25 commonly bought and sold for $2.00 to a family about to starve because their food supply was destroyed by a natural disaster. Catholic economic theory clearly condemns such a price and requires restitution.

How does one know the common estimation of value or price? In Roman law (and later European law rooted in Roman Law), there were two possible methods: the price could be fixed *ex ante* by the legitimate governmental authority (as is done with utility company prices in modern times) or it could be determined in an *ex post facto* proceeding by the judgment of a good man (*ad abitrium boni viri*), or what we would call in modern times an expert.[38] Depending on the particular facts, sometimes this expert was in a public forum, an ecclesiastical or civil court, and sometimes he was a priest in the internal forum of the confessional.

Given the difficulty of determining an exact just price in the absence of a fixed legal price, when should the human law require rectification of an *ex ante* incorrect assessment of the just price by contracting parties as determined *ex post facto* by an expert? Saint Thomas Aquinas argues that a sale at any variation from the just price violates the normative principle of equality in exchange, but the law only requires restitution for knowingly contracting at an unjust price[39] or when the error was without knowledge (*absque fraude*) but the variation from the just price is great

38. See Baldwin, "The Medieval Theories of the Just Price," 33, 49. See also Diana Wood, *Medieval Economic Thought*, 143.

39. *Summa*, II–II, Q. 77, art. 1 (Here he uses the word deceit (*fraus*), a term that requires acting with knowledge). See also Huguccio, *Summa Decretorum*, quoted in Baldwin, "The Medieval Theories of the Just Price," note 118 ("*Credo tamen nec ecclesiam nec aliquem hominem ex scientia certa debere plus accipere quam res valeat, presertim si plus offertur per licitationem;* "I believe, nevertheless, neither a church nor any man, with certain knowledge, ought to accept more than a thing is worth, especially if more is offered in the bidding" (author's translation; emphasis added)).

(*nimius excessus*).[40] The limitation of a legal remedy only to cases of intentionally contracting at variance to the just price or an unintentional great difference does not mean abandonment of the more rigorous normative principle.[41] Yet the recognition that the just price can change over time[42] and cannot always be determined with exact precision but can only be estimated necessitates that only intentional or notable variations should be corrected by the force of law.[43] For example, Roman law only required restitution to one who sold land for less than one half of the just price.[44] The post-Roman period of Western Catholic law saw the gradual

40. Aquinas, *Summa*, II–II, Q. 77, art. 1, Reply to Objection 1 ("Accordingly, if without employing deceit the seller disposes of his goods for more than their worth, or the buyer obtain them for less than their worth, the law looks upon this as licit, and provides no punishment for so doing, unless the excess be too great").

41. Ibid. ("On the other hand the Divine law leaves nothing unpunished that is contrary to virtue. Hence, according to the Divine law, it is reckoned unlawful if the equality of justice be not observed in buying and selling.") Yet even under the divine law (which represents the normative principle embodied in the legal requirement to make restitution), the necessary imprecision in knowing the exact just price necessitates restitution only if the variation is notable. See ibid. ("he who has received more than he ought must make compensation to him that has suffered loss, if the loss be considerable (*notabile damnum*). I add this condition, because the just price of things is not fixed with mathematical precision (*punctaliter determinatum*), but depends on a kind of estimate (*aestimatione*), so that a slight addition or subtraction would not seem to destroy the equality of justice").

42. Justinian, *Digest*, 35.2.63.2 ("Sometimes place or time brings a variation (*varietatem*) in value; oil will not be equally valued at Rome and in Spain nor given the same assessment (*aestimabitur*) in periods of lasting scarcity as when there are crops. . . ."). See also Aquinas, *Summa*, II–II, Q. 77, art. 3, Reply to Objection 4 (discussing whether a merchant with knowledge that merchants with a greater supply of the goods sold are about to arrive in a location needs to disclose the likely downward price effect).

43. For a discussion of why human law must be in accord with divine law but need not always strictly enforce the principles of justice in all cases, see Aquinas, *Summa*, I–II, Q. 96, art. 2 ("Now human law is framed for a number of human beings, the majority of whom are not perfect in. Wherefore human laws do not forbid all vices, from which the virtuous abstain, but only the more grievous vices, from which it is possible for the majority to abstain; and chiefly those that are to the hurt of others, without the prohibition of which human society could not be maintained: thus human law prohibits murder, theft and such like").

44. Justinian, *Code*, 4.44.2, 4.44.8.

expansion of this remedy to a wider range of transactions than the original Roman remedy, yet it never corrected all deviations from the just price.[45]

One inference drawn from this two-part analysis of when the civil law should correct unjust prices is that the law should correct even some unintentional violations. Putting aside difficulties of determining with perfect precision the common estimation of a type of goods, the thing sold may have a hidden defect that makes the particular thing worth less than the common estimation. Saint Thomas explains that if the defect is later discovered, the seller must repay a portion of the price attributable to the impairment of value. Although one may not be culpable for unwittingly selling something at an unjust price (due to the defect), once the defect is discovered, the seller is obligated to compensate for the defect:

> But if any of the foregoing defects be in the thing sold, and he knows nothing about this, the seller does not sin, because he does that which is unjust materially, nor is his deed unjust, as shown above (59, 2). *Nevertheless he is bound to compensate the buyer, when the defect comes to his knowledge.* Moreover what has been said of the seller applies equally to the buyer. For sometimes it happens that the seller thinks his goods to be specifically of lower value, as when a man sells gold instead of copper, and then if the buyer be aware of this, he buys it unjustly and is bound to restitution. . . .[46]

Thus, the just price doctrine is a requirement of transactions independent of the obligation not to lie or commit fraud (for example, by denying a known defect).

The recognition that the just price for particular goods could change over time led to the development of a corollary theory to address situations when a buyer pays for a purchase at a different time from that stated in the contract (in modern terms, a credit sale). The theory of *venditio sub dubio* allowed a seller of goods to charge more than the current just price if payment was to be separated from delivery by time and there was legitimate doubt as to the

45. See Baldwin, "Medieval Theories of the Just Price," 22–27.

46. Aquinas, *Summa*, II–II, Q. 77, art. 2.

just price of the goods at the applicable future time.[47] Two conditions must be met to licitly charge more than the current just price: There must be a real doubt that the current just price would remain the same at the time of payment, and the agreed price must not clearly be in excess of a reasonable estimate of the future just price.[48] A price clearly in excess of the expected just price constituted disguised usury for a loan. Many who considered the issue recognized that although certain credit sales at higher prices could be licit, the risk of evasion of usury and just price normative principles was great and therefore counseled caution.[49]

Just price theory held that normatively nobody should sell something for more than its common estimation of value plus costs of sale. A particular need or desire of the buyer for the good was an illegitimate factor in determining price. The exact just price could vary over time and unless fixed by law could only be arrived at by estimation. This doubt and variability of price restricted those cases where the human law would correct errors to notable variations or unreasonable estimates of future prices in credit sales. Yet the divine law leaves nothing unpunished. Despite the civil law's allowance of unjust exchanges, the society will still bear the consequences.

It seems apparent that the Catholic doctrine of the just price is generally absent from our current economic discourse. It is almost a daily occurrence to hear people say, "I got a great deal" (implying either that the person paid less than the just price or the predeal price was in excess of the just price and the deal was merely a return

47. Gregory IX, *Naviganti* ("[S]omeone who pays ten shillings in order that the equivalent measures of grain, wine, or oil will be handed over to him at some other time shall not be considered a usurer, even if they then turn out to be worth more, so long as there is a reasonable doubt whether they were going to be worth more or less at the time of settlement. By reason of the same doubt even someone is excused who sells cloth, wine, oil, or other goods so that after a certain amount of time he gets back more for them than they are worth at the time of the sale. . . ."); Innocent IV, *Commentaria apparatus quinque libros decretalium*, XIX, ch. V, *In Civitate* (Minerva GmbH, 1570).

48. See *In Civitate.*

49. Raymond de Roover, *San Bernardino of Siena and Sant'Antonino of Florence: The Two Great Economic Thinkers of the Middle Ages* (Boston: Baker Library, 1967), 29–30.

to a just price level). I would like to end this consideration of just price doctrine by considering one particular application: the housing market. Most people would agree that this segment of our economy played an important role in the economic problems. Was there some aspect of it that suggests routine violation of just price doctrine?

Although our culture has become accustomed to calling the mortgagor of a property the owner, to what extent does one really "own" a house subject to a mortgage? Ownership is "[t]he bundle of rights allowing one to use, manage, and enjoy property, including the right to convey it to others."[50] Yet one who has acquired a home subject to a mortgage does not possess the right to do these things absolutely but only contingently on repayment of the loan supported by the mortgage plus required fees. If one doubts the restriction on ownership, consider the result of attempting to convey the property without discharging the mortgage. The rights of the home owner can better be described as contingent ownership or "[o]wnership in which title is imperfect but is capable of becoming perfect on the fulfillment of some condition."[51]

Economically, a mortgaged financed home purchase is a credit sale of property by the mortgagee. The bank in essence purchases the property and then agrees to resell it to the borrower over time at an increased price (the amount of the mortgage plus the interest factor). The fact that the lender requires some of the purchase price to be paid quickly (by only financing 80 percent or 90 percent of the price) does not alter this re-characterization. Although the bank does not take record legal ownership in our current legal system, economically it is no different.[52] The lender is entitled to enforce the sale of the property to the borrower at a predetermined price (varying depending on the exact time of completion of the purchase, or in the current legal terms, at maturity or prepayment)

50. Bryan Garner, ed., *Black's Law Dictionary*, 8th ed. (Eagan, MN: West, 2004).

51. See "ownership" in ibid.

52. Such a re-characterization of the legal form of a mortgage into its economic reality is similar to the re-characterization of certain transactions which in form appear to be leases into a secured sale. See Uniform Commercial Code §1–203 and §9–109(a)(1).

regardless of the real value of the house at the time of repayment. If the borrower does not pay by at least the times required, the lender has a right to use the force of law to remove all indices of ownership from the borrower (i.e., cancel the sale).

Re-characterized in this way, just price law, and the corollary of *venditio sub dubio*, can be used to evaluate the normative justice of the standard terms of such transactions. First, there must be genuine doubt that the current price of the residential property will be higher at the time of repayment. Second, the total price (meaning the total amount paid by the borrower to the lender, including fees, interest, charges, points, etc.) must not be so great as to clearly exceed a reasonable estimate of the value of the property at the time of payment plus the costs of entering into the transaction (legal and documentary fees). A simple example will illustrate the analysis. A agrees to buy a house from B for $100,000 and obtains from C a 100 percent mortgage at the following rates and amortized over the following periods. In each case a 1 percent origination fee is charged and reimbursement of transaction costs is excluded, assuming that C only passes through the actual cash cost so C receives no net benefit from these payments.[53]

Annual Fixed Interest Rate	Years of Amortization	Total Payments to Lender	Equivalent Percentage Increase of Total Payments Over Original Price of the House
6%	30	$216,850	116.9%
6%	15	$152,890	52.9%
10%	30	$316,930	216.9%
10%	15	$194,425	94.4%

53. See Brian M. McCall, *The Church and the Usurers* (Washington, DC: Sapientia Press, 2013), Chapter 6 for a more detailed consideration of the housing market and these hypothetical examples.

The final column of the above table shows the implicit assumed rate of increase in the just price of the property over the life of the payments on the credit sale (this assumes the original $100,000 was the just price at the starting point). The just price theory then asks whether such percentage increases in property values appear reasonable. These percentages are significantly above the historical increase of housing prices. United States house prices increased a total of only 10 percent from 1975 to 1995.[54] From 1975 to 2004, housing prices appreciated annually at a more rapid annual rate of 2.23 percent (still significantly below annual interest rates) or cumulatively around 42 percent for the entire nineteen-year period.[55] Following further rapid appreciation, the current decline in housing prices seems to have begun in 2007 with an initial decrease in prices of 1.3 percent.[56] Such simple calculations suggest in general that at least some mortgages are priced at a level in excess of what just price theory would consider just in a case of a credit sale. (All of this assuming that the historic increases in housing prices were in themselves just increases of the common estimation of housing.)

Although the above analysis is simplified, it demonstrates the strong inference that unjust exchange transactions have pervaded throughout our historic housing markets. At least some of the causes of our current dilemma lie in a system that has been built without the foundation of just price requirements. As with so many social and economic problems, the Church's doctrine holds the answers to why this current crisis occurred and how we fix it. As Leo XIII commented about earlier economic turmoils, "the question under consideration is certainly one for which no satisfactory solution will be found unless religion and the Church have been called upon to aid."[57]

54. Charles Himmelberg, Christopher Mayer, and Todd Sinai, "Assessing High House Prices: Bubbles, Fundamentals, and Misperceptions," *Journal of Economic Perspectives* 19 (2005): S67, note 4.

55. See ibid.

56. US Dept. of Housing and Urban Development Office of Policy Development Research, "U.S. Housing Market Conditions," *Hud User* (May 2008). http://www.huduser.org/periodicals/ushmc/spring08/USHMC_Q108.pdf.

57. Leo XIII, *Rerum Novarum*, no. 24.

Usury: What Is It? How Do We Avoid It? Why Do Our Shepherds Ignore It?

Usury, which we can define for now as profit charged for a loan, is one of the most critical economic issues for our time for two distinct reasons. First, this sin is pervasive in our finance capitalist economy. A particularly pernicious usurer of our time, payday lenders were non-existent thirty years ago, but by 2005 there were over 20,000 payday loan retail outlets nationwide, more than McDonalds, Burger King, Sears, JC Penny, and Target Stores combined.[58] It is a sin that surrounds us, yet we hear almost nothing of it from the shepherds and theologians of our day. Those whom I refer to as the "economic modernists" (this includes both the Liberation Theology brand and the Libertarian Michael Novak brand) of our century have struck a deal with the Father of Lies. Deny some of the truths God has revealed in exchange for the promise (illusory) of economic prosperity. The Liberation Theology folk made this deal with a Mephistopheles dressed in the gray garb of communism. The Libertarian school made it with him dressed in the slick hand-made Italian suits of Wall Street. The clothes and terminology changed, but the deal was the same. Deny Catholic economic teaching in exchange for economic "progress" and prosperity. The deal with communism has been exposed for what it is, and the deal with libertarianism is the latest great façade to be showing its cracks (record mortgage foreclosures, "liquidity" problems, the collapse of the assumed Wall Street bedrock of Bear Stearns). Usury permeates the Libertarian version of finance capitalism. This fact was evident over eighty years ago to the great theologian and economist Fr. Bernard W. Dempsey, who argued that capitalism had created a new form of the sin of usury which he called "institutional usury."[59] This new sin was not committed by individual usurers but by a monetary and credit system built on and sustained by a systemically usurious monetary system. Notwithstanding the obvious failure of the prom-

58. See Brian M. McCall, *The Church and the Usurers: Unprofitable Lending for the Modern Economy* (Washington, DC: Sapientia Press, 2013).

59. Fr. Bernard W. Dempsey, *Interest and Usury* (Washington, DC: American Council on Public Affairs, 1943), 216–228.

ised reward, our shepherds and theologians hold up their end of the bargain and fail to warn and teach the faithful about the dangers of usury. The faithful therefore have a duty to inform themselves about this topic.

The second major reason for a closer review of usury is that it is one of the favorite tools of the moral modernists. They use the history of usury as a purported example that proves *Pascendi* and Vatican I wrong. The Church can change moral teaching such as that on contraception and abortion; it happened in the past with usury. The Church prohibited usury, they claim, and now the Church allows it. This infiltration of modernist argumentation is exemplified by examining *The Dublin Review*, a Catholic journal founded by Cdl. Wiseman and others in the early nineteenth century. In 1873 and 1874, the journal published a two-part article that explained the divine law on usury and the history of its application by the Church.[60] Although experts may dispute some historical details and arguments in these two articles, they solidly defend the Church's teaching on usury as just, consistent, and correct. "It is false to say that . . . she [the Church] has ever changed her principles of morality; or that she now concedes in practice what she condemns in theory."[61] Less than a hundred years later, the same *Dublin Review* (or at least the periodical bearing the same name!) published an article entitled "Authority, Usury and Contraception" by John T. (now US judge) Noonan. The autumn 1966 article (a copy of which I own containing what appears to be excellent notes of the late Michael Davies, and which was very useful in composing this chapter) holds out the hope that the Church will revise the teaching on contraception just as the teaching on usury was changed. The article attempts to argue that despite the usury doctrine being supported by more weighty authority than the contraception rule, theologians worked out "modifications, alternatives and changes which effectively sapped the force of the old rule." Noonan suggested the Church in 1966 "was on a threshold, perhaps, of a development [in the teaching

60. "Usury," *Dublin Review* (Autumn 1873): 323–48; "Usury and the Canon Law," *Dublin Review* (Winter 1874): 69–99.

61. Ibid., 93–94.

on contraception] analogous to that on usury."[62] What a radical change in less than a century! So that we are equipped to defeat this false argument claiming the "development" of doctrine, we need to understand the teaching on usury accurately.

Our task is not an easy one for several reasons. First, as Dempsey understood, we live in an economic system that has institutionalized usury. We are so inundated with it that our intellect has been darkened in its ability to perceive it. Second, the explanation of the divine prohibition of usury is inextricably linked to Aristotelian and Thomistic philosophy, which has been almost completely ignored in our modern educational system. The Church spoke about usury in the language of Aristotle and St. Thomas. To understand the Church's statements we need to rediscover the language in which the teaching is expressed; we need a philosophical Rosetta Stone. Third, new forms of economic transactions have arisen over the centuries, and Catholics have been faced with the often difficult task of understanding these new transactions so as to properly apply the teaching on usury. In making these applications of the unchanging law to new facts, theologians and members of the hierarchy can make factual errors that later can be corrected. Also, theologians can issue provisional or qualified conclusions about the application of the theory to new situations while they continue to consider the question. This process of applying the law of usury to new facts is further complicated by the fourth difficulty: the language of economics and of our legal system has shifted the meaning of critical terms used by the Church to define and explain the moral law on usury. "Interest," "loan," "money," and "usury" have very different definitions in our common language today, and we run the risk of not realizing that the Church was using these terms as originally defined in Roman law and Aristotelian philosophy and not as misused today. Finally, we need to distinguish two functions of the teaching authority of the Church that are often conflated. One is the proclamation of the unchanging divine moral law. Second is the application of that law to specific factual situations. An

62. John T. Noonan, Jr., "Authority, Usury, and Contraception," *Dublin Review* 509 (Autumn 1966): 201.

example using contraception is useful. The Church has always taught that "any use whatever of marriage, in the exercise of which the act of human effort is deprived of its natural power of procreating life violates the law of God and nature and those who do such a thing are stained by a grave and mortal flaw."[63] Next the Church needs to guide the faithful in discerning whether particular actions (such as newly discovered techniques for identifying a wife's fertile period and then restraining from marital acts at such time) are "an act of human effort" which deprives marriage "of its natural power of procreating life." In explaining that under certain grave conditions such periodic continence does not constitute such an act of human effort, the Church is not "changing" or "modifying" the moral law but merely making a judgment as to whether that law (as always understood) applies to these facts. Another example can be found in the teaching on the just war. John Paul II declared that the US war in Iraq did not constitute a just war. If a subsequent pontiff were to declare that John Paul II did not correctly apply just war moral principles to this specific war and in fact it was a just war, the Church would not have "changed" its teaching in any way. One pope would have corrected the erroneous judgment of a prior pope about this particular war. (Note: I am not suggesting I believe John Paul II was incorrect, but merely positing this as an example to illustrate the point.) Putting these difficulties together, we can see how some can reach an erroneous conclusion that the Church modified the moral law of usury when the Church or a particular theologian explains that a type of economic activity does not constitute usury. It would be as if the definition of the word "abortion" were transformed into that which we now call "adoption," and then someone found a statement by the Church that "abortion" (as redefined to mean adoption) is permissible by married couples and reached the conclusion that the Church changed the moral law when in reality the world merely changed the meaning of a term.

We will therefore examine what the Church has always taught on usury. We will next examine how economic changes made it neces-

63. Pius XI, *Casti Connubii*, No. 56 (Vatican City: Libreria Editrice Vaticana, 1930).

sary for the Church to apply the moral law to new factual scenarios. In a several-centuries process of this application we can discern two strands of arguments: one faithful to the unchanging moral law and the other going beyond the mere application to new facts and arguing for a change in the moral law. Our modern confusion on usury stems from secular society's effectively embracing this second flawed approach. Finally we will examine some practical applications of the usury teaching to our lives in the twenty-first century.

To discern what Scripture and Tradition have taught, we need to define some terms. This is somewhat tedious but necessary in this complicated area. To begin, we will start with some statements from the last major papal document that focused exclusively on usury, *Vix Pervenit* of Benedict XIV. The pope writes, "The nature of the sin called usury has its proper place and origin in a *loan* contract."[64] He continues, "any *gain* which exceeds the amount he [the lender] gave is illicit and usurious."[65] The two highlighted terms are critical to this summary of the doctrine. If a particular transaction is not a loan, then any gain cannot be usury (although it may be licit or illicit as a result of a moral principal other than usury, as when, for example, a merchant sells a product for more than its just price). Secondly, only "gain" is usury. We need to examine carefully what these two terms signify.

In modern law and speech, the word "loan" has a broad meaning. It can be used to describe when a person gives money to another to buy food or medical care and expects repayment of that money at another date. It can refer to an investor who provides capital to a business for a time and expects the return of his capital and a profit. Further, it can describe when a person gives another a piece of property (like a car) to be used for a while and requires the return of that same property. The Roman law had distinct terms to identify all of these transactions, which are now signified by our word "loan." Since most of the examples of the infallible teaching of the Church

64. Benedict XIV, *Vix Pervenit* (Vatican City: Libreria Editrice Vaticana, 1745), no. 3, I (emphasis added).

65. Ibid.

on usury use these Roman law terms, we need to understand that the law of usury only applied to those situations designated by the Roman word for "loan" (*mutuum*) and not the modern term.

The *mutuum* involved the transfer of ownership of a fungible good that was consumed in first use and required that the borrower return at a later time property of the same kind and quantity provided to him. This definition only covers the first example we cited above. The other examples were identified by other terms, such as *societas*, *census commodatum*, and *conductio locatio re*. One could not commit usury when engaging in these other transactions (again, other sins were possible but not usury).

Before progressing, we need to understand the concept of "consumed in first use." The *mutuum* only applied to the transfer and retransfer of this type of property. It is something that cannot be used without its destruction or loss. Tangible property can be divided into three groups of things: (1) those that can be used without their total loss, (2) those that can only be used by their total loss, and (3) those things which have different possible uses, some of which consume the thing and some of which do not. A house can be lived in and not destroyed. Wine cannot be used (for drinking or cooking) without consuming it. A potato can be used without consuming it (for example, by planting it as a seed potato) or by consuming it (eating it). From about 325 through the fourteenth century, money was thought to be exclusively or almost always in the second category of things that are consumed in first use. Due to the expansion of commerce, more opportunities to use money in a productive way (like the seed potato) became common. Many theologians began to consider whether money was actually in the third category of things that can be used in first use or used productively. Money could be used without consuming it completely (like planting a seed potato to grow more potatoes).

The next important concept in the pope's statement is "gain." The sin of usury occurs when a lender of a fungible thing consumed in first use requires that he be put in a better position than he was in before the loan. It is licit to require equality in position. Now we must distinguish gain from compensation for a loss. If a man steals my car and crashes it, he then is obligated to give me a new car of similar quality in restitution. I do not gain; I merely return to my original position. The Roman law called the payment to compensate for loss *quod interest* or the "difference." The original meaning of our word "interest" was not payment of gain for a loan but payment in compensation for a loss. For example, Marcus borrows 100 ducats from Linus and promises to pay it back in two months. Linus needs the money back in two months to pay his son's tuition at the university. Linus pays the money back two months late, and as a result Linus has to pay a ten ducat fine for paying tuition late. Marcus should pay Linus ten ducats in "interest" to compensate him for that loss. This payment is not usury, as it is not a payment for the use (consummation of money) but merely compensation for the harm done by not returning the money when agreed.

Thus far, we have established that the sin of usury is important for two reasons: (1) it pervades our economy, and (2) it has been erroneously used as a purported example of the Church changing her teaching. We established the essential terminology for discussing usury, which was defined as the seeking of gain on a loan of a consumable thing. In the first millennium of the Church's teaching in this matter, money was considered something that could only be consumed in use. The sin could only arise in a loan of such a consumable. Usury could not be committed in the rental of a field or plough. Second, the prohibition of usury did not affect the right of a lender to charge a borrower for loss or harm caused by the borrower. With this background we can further explore the nuances of the Church's teaching on usury. In particular, we will consider some more specific applications of this core teaching to the investment in businesses and to the discovery that money may be a thing that has a dual use: consumption and production.

Many historians falsely accuse the Church of being opposed to a productive economy. Citing usury, intellectuals such as Weber and Tawney claim the Church's teaching discouraged investment.[66] As we have seen, usury only applies to the loan of a consumable. The

66. See e.g., Max Weber, *Economy and Sociology: An Outline of Interpretive Sociology* (University of California Press, 1978); R.H. Tawney, *Religion and the Rise of Capitalism* (1926); republished Mentor (1953).

Church taught that money could be invested in productive assets or ventures and the investor had a right to ask for a share of the production his money helped to create. Two common forms of investment specifically approved by the Church have been the *census* and *societas*. The former involved the purchase of a share of the future fruits of a productive asset over a specified time. For example, an investor could buy a right to a percentage of the crops *produced* by a farm over the period of his life. As this was not the loan of money with a requirement that the money be repaid but the purchase of an interest in land, usury could not occur. The *societas* was a partnership ("society" comes from the Latin word). Christians were permitted to pool their resources and their labor in a common enterprise and then agree among themselves (within limits) how to share the rewards of their enterprise. These investments in productive assets and enterprises were not forbidden by the Church. In a true *census* or *societas*, one could not commit usury as no money was loaned (although one could be capable of other sins in these transactions, e.g., fraud or embezzlement). Throughout the late Middle Ages and the Renaissance, various theologians attempted to discuss whether certain changes to these forms of investments transformed them from business investments into loans of money. To generalize, many of the new features were a result of methods of allocating the high risk of ventures based on exploration of the newly discovered lands and the dangers of the seas associated with it. For example, some partners in a *societas* would agree that some partners would exchange their right for a higher share of the profits for a smaller but more certain share. Although theologians, prelates, jurists, and even popes sometimes disagreed about how to analyze these changes, their disagreements do not concern the definition of usury but its application to novel and more complex situations. The situation was complicated since some people tried to evade the prohibition of usury by cloaking loans in the name (but not the substance) of these other forms of activity. Some in the Church conservatively advised against otherwise permissible activity in order to deter such immoral evasions. Yet such a prudential judgment likewise belongs to the realm of the application of usury teaching not the teaching itself.

Some who analyzed these new business structures, both Protestants and Catholics, reacted to the complexity involved by abandoning the ancient objective definition of usury for a subjective criterion. They argued that usury only existed in charging for a loan out of a motive of wanting to do harm to the borrower. Since they couldn't read the hearts of the lender they would assume if he charged a large amount (biting usury) his intention must be harmful. Their approach offered no principled way of determining how much of a charge was excessive. Is 10 percent, 30 percent, or 200 percent excessive? Those who adhered to the true Catholic understanding knew it was not intention that made the sin (although one's intention could affect the level of culpability of the usurer). Usury was the charging of a gain on a loan. Some situations may be difficult to discern what in substance was transpiring (and in fact due to the difficulty some people may not be culpable of committing the sin—or at least a mortal sin) if they were unaware that it involved usury. The general principle was clear: investment in business assets or ventures was not usury. Usury was the charging of gain on a loan of money. If the transaction was not a loan there could be no usury. The test was objective, albeit often difficult to apply.

The second aspect of usury that spurred controversies at the same time was the understanding of "gain." As we have seen, the Church's teaching did not require a lender to lose money (receive back less than he lent). Christ's statement "Lend hoping to receive nothing in return" was understood as a counsel to perfection not a commandment on pain of sin. Thus, to give money to those in need was charity; to lend and ask for equal recompense was just. Prior to the late fifteenth century, the money system was stable, and gold and silver coins retained a relatively stable value. Also, there were very limited opportunities to invest excess money in productive ventures. Both of these factors of the economy began to change as Europe entered the sixteenth century. The influx of newly discovered gold and silver deposits from the New World,[67] combined

67. As the supply of coined money increased, this naturally caused the value (purchasing power) of individual coins to decline.

with the increased debasement[68] of coins by some European princes, caused the monetary system to experience dramatic fluctuations in value. People began asking when they could charge "interest" (understood as discussed in the prior chapter as a compensation for loss) on loans as a result of these factors. A simple example will illustrate the new concerns. In 950, Beowulf has 100 gold coins in a treasure chest. He lives in an area of England constantly under assault by the Danes. The only economy is subsistence farming. He lends ten gold coins to Canute, who pays him back ten gold coins in a year. Beowulf puts the ten coins he receives back in his chest where they remain. The coins contain an identical amount of gold and can purchase the same amount of grain as ten coins last year. Beowulf has not lost anything by not having these ten coins sit in his treasure chest all year.

Now let us go forward to the year 1540. Carlos usually invests his excess money in partnerships that are exploring South America and trading with the populations there. He lends ten coins to Alfonso for a year. When he gets back ten coins in a year, Carlos realizes that they have lost 10 percent of their purchasing power due to a massive influx of gold from Ecuador. Also, if he had invested those ten coins with the Niña, Pinta, and Santa Maria Company he would have received two gold coins in profit. Carlos is clearly worse off by having made the loan. Many Catholic thinkers realized that to ask Alfonso to compensate for these real losses was not asking for gain. The problem they found was that real examples were much more complicated and difficult to calculate. Some suggested that the parties might estimate in advance the likely amount of these losses and agree in advance an amount of compensation. Again, there were practical disagreements among faithful Catholics on how to compute these new types of losses; but disagreement on this level does not involve a change to the basic teaching. Time and again theologians and canonists would insist that if the lender would prefer to

68. Debasement means adding some amount of non-precious metal to coins. This has the effect of causing two coins of the same weight to have different gold contents and hence different intrinsic values.

loan out his money and keep interest accruing it was likely he was looking to gain and not merely cover his losses.

Due to all of these debates about application of the usury teaching, Benedict XIV issued *Vix Pervenit* to clarify the situation. He restated the perennial teaching on this subject:

> The nature of the sin called usury has its proper place and origin in a loan contract. This financial contract between consenting parties demands, by its very nature, that one return to another only as much as he has received. The sin rests on the fact that sometimes the creditor desires more than he has given. Therefore he contends some gain is owed him beyond that which he loaned, but any gain which exceeds the amount he gave is illicit and usurious.[69]

The Holy Father went on to explain,

> By these remarks, however, We do not deny that at times together with the loan contract certain other titles—which are not at all intrinsic to the contract—may run parallel with it. From these other titles, entirely just and legitimate reasons arise to demand something over and above the amount due on the contract [i.e., claims to interest (meaning compensation)]. Nor is it denied that it is very often possible for someone, by means of contracts differing entirely from loans, to spend and invest money legitimately either to provide oneself with an annual income or to engage in legitimate trade and business [i.e., a *societas* or *census*]. From these types of contracts honest gain may be made.[70]

He acknowledges that it is often difficult to discern whether a particular transaction is a usurious loan or another just title. As to some specific contracts referred to him, he did not give a verdict, as there was still disagreement among theologians and canonists. Yet Benedict XIV warned those who would attempt to exploit the situation by engaging in transactions clearly usurious but using the false pretext of a different other title that did not in reality apply:

> [S]ome will falsely and rashly persuade themselves—and such people can be found anywhere—that together with loan contracts there are other legitimate titles or, excepting loan contracts, they

69. Benedict XIV, *Vix Pervenit*, no. 3, I.
70. Ibid., no. 3, III.

> might convince themselves that other just contracts exist, for which it is permissible to receive a moderate amount of interest [here he uses the term in the modern sense of pure payment on a loan not connected to a loss]. Should any one think like this, he will oppose not only the judgment of the Catholic Church on usury, but also common human sense and natural reason.[71]

Simply because the application of moral principles may be difficult and opportunities for cloaked evasion exist, this does not justify immoral behavior or the rejection of the moral norm.

Now, what does all of this mean for our world in the first half of the twenty-first century? If application of usury teaching was difficult in the sixteenth and eighteenth centuries, it is certainly more so today. One might speculate that the usurers who bleed our nation dry have designed this complexity to hide their ill-gotten gains. Money has become much more susceptible to manipulation and volatility. The dollar bills in our wallets are called "fiat" currency. This means they are worth only what the government says they are worth. They have no intrinsic value. They are made of mere paper, which if you read the fine print entitles you to the dubious right to receive another identical piece of paper in exchange. That is right; a dollar represents the right to trade in a dollar bill for another dollar bill. Even a child can see the circularity of this system. On top of that, the amount of money in the economy is not limited by anything fixing its value. At least in the sixteenth century it was limited by the amount of gold extractable from the ground. Now banks can just create money out of thin air. For example, if a bank has $1000 in assets, you might think they would be limited to lending no more than they have or $1000. This is not true; banks can lend money they do not have by just writing an entry in their books. This is called fractional reserve banking.[72] There is really no natural con-

71. Ibid., no. 3, V.

72. Fractional reserve banking is one reason Fr. Bernard Dempsey saw our monetary system as inundated with usury. One reason the Church has explained that God forbade usury is that one is charging for something he does not sell since the money lent is returned. How much more so is this true when the bank is not even lending money that it has? It only invents the money to lend it. What loss could a bank experience by lending money it does not even have?

trol on how much money will be pumped into the economy by banks inventing money and then lending it to people and thus diluting the value of money in supply.

So what does all of this mean? First, we need to be aware of how far the world's entire monetary system has strayed from Catholic principles. Money has lost all meaning. Banks are charging people large gains on loans of money the banks do not even have. Lending institutions are some of the most profitable companies in our country. Lenders are charging people amounts clearly constituting gain on loans of money to be used to buy things like cars, vacations, and houses (rather than invest in production). As proof of this, credit card companies have calculated exactly how many months of minimum payments they need so as to have made such a large profit they do not even care if the borrower ever pays back the original advance. An economy flooded with the sin of usury cannot bear good fruits over time. We need change quickly and desperately.

On the personal level, we need to discern what we are doing with our money. If we are investing it in something productive, we are entitled to a share of the profits. This applies even if our investment is labeled by modern business language a "loan" or "debt." Yet we must really be investing in a productive venture, not a ponzi scheme or some virtual or synthetic business. (Also other moral principles may restrict our ability to invest. For example, we cannot invest in a business that produces pornography, notwithstanding the Knights of Columbus and the US Bishops seeing no problem doing so.)[73] If we are truly lending money to someone for them to spend (to buy a car, to buy food, etc.), we may charge them interest to compensate for the inevitable decline in value of our fiat money over the period of the loan. Since we live in a monetary system much more unstable than even the sixteenth century, the payment of $100 next year is certainly worth less than $100 today. With a monetary system that creates more money out of thin air and with the government constantly changing the components of the consumer price index, we have really no accurate method to estimate this decline in value. In

73. See Thomas Strobhar, "Holy Porn," *New Oxford Review* (February 2008), available online at https://www.newoxfordreview.org/article.jsp?did=.

such a situation of factual uncertainty we can only do our best at estimating, and given the seriousness of the issue err on the side of conservatively estimating this loss.

I have only scratched the surface of this issue.[74] It is a very complicated and difficult subject. Is not such a situation exactly why our Lord appointed bishops to rule over us? They are supposed to help guide us in morally uncertain territory. They are there to preserve and remind us of moral principles and help us make difficult applications. Why then are our pastors so silent about usury? Why does the topic only get passing references in the Compendium of the Social Teaching of the Catholic Church (I could find only two pages in the entire book that even mentioned it)? Given its complexity and its pervasiveness, should it not be dealt with extensively in such a document? I obviously don't have the answers to these questions. I can only wonder if the reason has something to do with our pastors possibly becoming hirelings to the usurers. Maybe reasons lie in the covered-up Vatican bank scandals of the past several decades?

In conclusion, we have seen that, in accordance with the many injunctions of sacred Scripture, the Church has taught that charging usury on a loan of money is morally wrong. Despite the puzzling silence of our current hierarchy, this is and will remain so. As economic circumstances have changed, the application of this truth has become complicated. The changing nature of money and the terms used to describe financial transactions have caused much confusion. The principles remain simple. If a loan is involved, no more can be asked than the return of the lender to his original position. If an investment of capital arises, usury is not present. The devil, as they say, is in the details, and we live in an economy infiltrated with demonic details. To morally navigate through this sea of usury is difficult, yet we need not be led to despair. In the absence of clear assistance from our pastors, we can attempt to order our own financial dealings in accord with the perennial teaching of the Church by applying the principles as best we can. As to the larger

74. For a more comprehensive treatment of the topic, see my book *The Church and the Usurers: Unprofitable Lending for the Modern Economy* (Washington, DC: Sapientia Press, 2013).

monetary and financial system rife with institutional usury, it is so far advanced it is likely that only an act of divine intervention can reverse it.

The Only Bailout of Finance: Capitalism that Will Work—Catholicism

The politicians, pundits, and media gurus seemed to be in a contest to outdo one another with hyperbole during the heady days of the financial collapse of 2008. I heard the financial crisis described as "catastrophic," "Armageddon," "nuclear," and other colorful phrases. What are we to make of the whole saga? We need look no further than the Church, which holds all the answers to our woes.

Saint Thomas Aquinas predicted such a collapse of an economic system like the one under which we have been toiling. In Lecture IX on the *Ethics* of Aristotle, he commented that eventually all exchange transactions will cease in a society that continually violates the principles of commutative justice in economic exchange transactions. The economic philosophy our society has come to embrace is permeated with habitual violations of Catholic principles of economic morality. In this chapter, we will only dwell on the major aspects that have led directly to the financial "Armageddon" that has politicians and bankers in a state of apoplexy.

First, the system for allocating housing resources in this country is based on a violation of the divine and natural law against the taking of usury, which we already addressed in the previous chapter. In this section, I will focus on aspects of the usury doctrine applicable to the housing market.

As we have already noted, the charging of a profit or gain in consideration for the making of a loan of money (as distinguished from the investment of capital in a business) is a violation of natural justice. Since money in itself is barren (it can produce nothing), merely to lend it to someone for a time and to require more than the amount lent plus compensation for expenses is to charge for something one does not own: time. Even non-Catholic philosophers like Aristotle and Islamic thinkers can observe this truth in the natural order. At the root of the current financial crisis is the systemic trend developed from World War I onward of having to borrow large sums of money and repay even larger sums in order to procure one of the most basic necessities of life: housing. We have already considered the following chart from the perspective of the Just Price Doctrine. It also demonstrates the injustice of at least some home mortgages according to the usury doctrine. The chart demonstrates that illicit profit (*turpe lucrum*) made on a home mortgage at various rates that are all well below the higher end sub-prime rates charged (often after a short period of a lower deceptive teaser rate). I treat all amounts as profit, as the lenders also typically require the consumers to reimburse the lender for all the costs of making the loan. I have also included a 1 percent origination fee, which is typical for mortgage transactions. All calculations are for a $100,000 loan.

Annual Fixed Interest Rate	Years of Amortization	Total Payments to Lender	Equivalent Percentage Increase of Total Payments over Original Price of the House
6%	30	$216,850	116.9%
6%	15	$152,890	52.9%
10%	30	$316,930	316.9%
10%	15	$194,425	94.4%

Assuming that the lender also charges a fee to cover the costs of origination, such loans appear to extract a significant profit for making the loan. This practice violates the natural and divine law forbidding usury.

Yet when these loans are made by banks, the usurious nature of the loans is often masked by the complexity of our monetary system based on fractional reserve banking not backed by any commodity form of currency. As the pre-eminent theologian and economist Fr. Bernard Dempsey pointed out in the mid-twentieth century, these banks are worse than the usurers of the past so clearly condemned by the likes of St. Thomas Aquinas and St. Bernardino of Siena. For at least in the Middle Ages, the usurers did lend real money. In the fiat money system of fractional reserve banking of modern times, the banks lend money that doesn't exist, and charge interest for the use of money the bank does not even possess. We all know the child's fairy tale of the emperor's new clothes. This would be like charging someone for borrowing imaginary clothes. Such an observation led Fr. Dempsey to observe in the 1930s that the individual sin of usury had become a societal institutional sin of usury. If it is unjust to charge a profit for the use of real money, then it is obviously unjust to charge for the use of money people do not even own. Many may respond that the risks the banks take in lending money justify the profit. In raising such an objection I would like to hear someone explain how one is at risk of loss if someone fails to repay money that did not even exist before the loan was made? Put another way, but for the loan itself the funds would not even exist. How can one claim to have lost something that never existed in reality? We need look no further than such a shell game to find a central cause of the current crisis. Hard-working Americans have been losing their homes because they could not pay enough of the wages they earned from doing real work to repay loans made by banks that never had the money to lend in the first place.

The other major cause of the 2008 economic depression, whose effects remain even today, lies in the speculative derivatives and credit default swaps that permeated the real estate finance markets. To understand the problem we need to know how the mortgage financing market worked (or more accurately didn't work). Contrary to what many Americans believe, they do not repay their mortgage to the bank that lent them the money they borrowed. For decades, almost all mortgages that originated in America were immediately sold by the bank and then repackaged and spliced and combined with other mortgages and then placed in a new entity that sold securities to the capital markets. These indirect purchases of pools of mortgages were then traded for profit. Beyond this trading of interests in pools of mortgages, many institutions entered into credit default swaps. These contracts were in substance no different from placing a bet at a virtual horse track. They were promises to pay the counter-party in the event that identified mortgage securities declined in value. Now, it is possible that a similar type of transaction could be morally licit as a form of insurance. For example, it is morally licit to enter into an insurance contract whereby the insurer agrees to pay you a specified amount if your car is destroyed (assuming the pricing of the premium charged is just). But these credit default swaps were routinely entered into by parties that owned no mortgage securities. In other words, they were not insuring against existing risks, but the contracts themselves were actually creating new financial risks. Here is a simple illustration of why this is so. If I own a car worth $10,000, I face a risk that I will lose the value of $10,000 if my car is destroyed. I can transfer that risk to an insurer for a premium. Now there is still only a $10,000 risk that exists. The only difference is that risk is borne by the insurer and not by me. If the insurer sells a contract with five different people whereby those people agree to pay the insurer $10,000 if my car is destroyed, there is now a risk of $50,000 related to the same $10,000 car. (Five different people might have to pay $10,000 each.) This is exactly what happens when parties who do not actually face risk of loss from mortgages entered into credit default swaps. Rather than just transferring pre-existing risks to different people, the transactions themselves create financial risk. This fact answers the question many people are asking: If only about 12 percent of all mortgages in the country defaulted, why was the financial crisis so large? For every $1 of mortgage loans, there are multiple dollars at risk through the creation of additional risk by these contracts that are no better than mere gambling contracts.

Aside from the practical effect of exacerbating an economic crisis, this financial system is immoral. The Church has long taught that although it is morally licit to be in business, to be an artisan or a merchant, it is illicit to be a mere speculator. Saint Thomas Aquinas explains in Question 77 of the Second Part of the Second Part of the *Summa* that one who makes a profit from trading but in no way creates or adds value to the thing traded makes an illicit profit. Someone who buys wood and carves it into tools is justified in making a profit because he has improved the value of the wood by his labor. One who buys goods manufactured in another city and transports them is justified in making a profit as he has added the value of bringing the goods to where they are needed. A mere speculator, one who buys and sells without adding value and merely seeks to make a gain on trading, is violating natural justice. Gratian includes a similar condemnation of mere speculation by Pope Julius in his *Decretum*.[75] On top of the unjust usury and unjust prices being charged in the housing finance market, financial institutions have been multiplying risks by engaging in speculative (as opposed to true risk-shifting) financial bets.

Once this mountain of unjust economic activity is erupting volcano-like, the federal government claimed to be riding in on a white horse to save the day. The federal government and the shadow governmental entities, the Federal Reserve Banks and the Federal Deposit Insurance Corporation, had two solutions. First, bail out the system with $700 billion (or more) of newly created fictitious money (through the sale of treasury bills to the Federal Reserve Banks, which will invent the money with which to buy them). Second, "facilitate" the purchase of troubled banks by other banks. We are witnessing proof of the apt description of the spirit of finance capitalism by Amintore Fanfani in his seminal work *Catholicism, Protestantism, and Capitalism*,[76] a book all Catholics should read to make sense of current events. Fanfani explains that the spirit of capitalism is concerned only with advancing its two fundamental principles: increasing wealth and decreasing the cost of attaining that wealth, both of which are to be attained through the use of all possible means. The spirit of finance capitalism, says Fanfani, "regards wealth as the best means for an ever more complete satisfaction of every conceivable need."[77] This ever-increasing wealth is to be sought "with whatever means seem best."

This utilitarian spirit of capitalism views politics and the state in a completely opportunistic and utilitarian fashion. It adopts whatever political philosophy serves these two goals. Thus, in the age of

75. Gratian, *Decretum*, Causa 14, q. 4, C. IX.

76. Amintore Fanfani, *Catholicism, Protestantism, and Capitalism* (Norfolk, VA: IHS Press, 2002).

77. Ibid., 57.

mercantilism (sixteenth through the middle of the eighteenth century), when capitalism saw the ability to profit through state intervention in and intense regulation of the economy, it favored an interventionist state. When capitalism estimated that more gain was to be had from a non-interfering state, it advocated *laissez-faire* policies (mid-eighteenth century through the twentieth century). Now capitalism sees that it can again prosper through an alliance with the state, so financiers cajoled the state into becoming their insurers of profit. The formerly *laissez-faire* government is now to be the partner of finance capitalists, buying all their failed investments from them (the Bailout). The second part of the plan is a use of state power to effect the longed for consolidation of the financial industry into the hands of a small elite. The dream of the Rothschilds, Rockefellers, and Morgans for centuries has been to own the entire banking system. Witness the reported comment of Mayer A. Rothschild: "Permit me to issue and control the money of a nation and I care not who makes its laws."[78] They are now using the coercive power of the state to achieve their goal at bargain prices. Take, for example, the purchase of Washington Mutual Bank by JP Morgan. For years, JP Morgan had publicly made it known it needed to acquire a network of branches in the lucrative Florida market. Now it has done so at a bargain basement price thanks to the exercise of the power of the state. This was not a "free market" sale of the Washington Mutual Bank at an arms-length negotiated price. On one night the state acting through the FDIC seized control of Washington Mutual and then forced it to sell all of its $307 billion of assets (not its liabilities) to JP Morgan for $1.9 billion. That is right—the Office of Thrift Supervision of the FDIC seized control and sold over $300 billion of assets without an auction, without free market negotiating with other candidates, without a vote of the shareholders, and apparently without even the knowledge of its board of directors, for $1.9 billion. To be fair, that $307 billion of assets includes an estimated $34 billion in bad loans. JP Morgan need not

78. Gertrude M. Coogan, *Money Creators: Who Creates Money? Who Should Create It?* (1935), 170. http://www.scribd.com/doc/22393130/GM-Coogan-Money-Creators-Who-Creates-Money-Who-Should-Create-It-1935.

worry about those, however, because a few days after this shotgun sale the Congress voted to buy those bad loans in the Bailout. Just as Fanfani observed more than sixty years ago, when capitalism can do well without the government it is for free market *laissez-faire* government action. Yet when finance capitalists see that they can use the government to make a great deal, *laissez-faire* is jettisoned for a massive coerced fire sale and a free give-away of $700 billion at public expense. Capitalism is not synonymous with a "free market" but only advocates a free market when it is to its benefit. When more can be made from an interventionist state forcing shotgun sales, then finance capitalism is in favor of bailouts and intervention.

This phenomenon is understandable because as great Catholic economic thinkers like Fanfani and Fr. Dempsey knew, finance capitalism (as opposed to those really advocating a free market) as a philosophical system is immoral. It places the quest for gain and profit as its only moral ends. It rejects the moral constraints of the natural law as preserved and taught by the Church as limits on unbridled profiteering and unrestrained means. As Fanfani stated,

> But at bottom the true and deep-seated reason for the conflict between Catholic and capitalistic ethics, lies—let us repeat—in the diverse manner of correlating human actions in general and economic action in particular to God. The Catholic, as we have said, appraised the legality of every action by the criteria of Revelation. The capitalist does not doubt the lawfulness of any act that fully corresponds to what he considers the exigencies of the human reason. The Catholic order is a supernatural order, the capitalistic order is a rational order in the sense of the Enlightenment.[79]

It is important to note that Fanfani is talking about the philosophical system of finance capitalism rooted in usury not the freedom of individuals to pursue their own economic welfare through morally licit means.

Thus this expensive bailout passed by the Congress has not bailed out anything. Its entire goal was to prop up and preserve the very economic spirit that produced this crisis. It is just another rational

79. Fanfani, *Catholicism, Protestantism, and Capitalism*, 117–18.

means to keep making illicit usury and unjust profits. Where will we find a real bailout? Where we find the answers to all questions: the Church. The details of this real bailout, letting the ship of capitalism sink and jumping in the lifeboat of Catholic economic teaching, is right there before us. Where do we find it? Fanfani tells us:

> The Catholic ideal of economic life finds condensed expression in the principles of the Gospels, which were elaborated successively by St. Paul, the Fathers and the Doctors till, in the age of the *Summa* and of Scholasticism, St. Thomas Aquinas, prince of Catholic philosophers, grafted Catholic principles on to the old, all but forgotten, trunk of Aristotelianism, scattering through his works a series of maxims, which taken as a whole, enable us to attain an accurate and complete vision of economic life according to Catholic ideals.[80]

As St. Augustine was prompted to conversion by the children's words *tolle legit* (take and read), so too let us be converted by reading the principles for the true bailout from our Catholic forebears.

80. Ibid., 106.

5

What Are Catholics to Do? Practical Advice for Surviving an Immoral Economy

THE PRIOR CHAPTER has demonstrated that the current economic model is flawed at the level of principle. Our money system is based on a shell game. The banking system manufactures money and permits the foxes (banks) to regulate the raiding of the henhouse (the money supply). Transactions fly through the economy without concern for setting just prices or evaluating the justice of charges related to finance. Unjust prices and usurious charges permeate the system. Even for those who accept Catholic principles, the injustice is virtually undetectable, having been camouflaged by an elastic and ever changing money supply. Yet God has allowed us to be born at such a time and into such a system. What are we to do? How can we manage the household entrusted to us in the midst of such problems? Clearly we must do what is possible proper to our state in life to advance the triumph of the Kingdom of Christ over the kingdom of debt. We must make Catholic principles known to the world. Yet until the day that Christ once again reigns, how do we navigate such a contingent economy?

Before beginning to answer these questions, I want to preface my arguments with the teaching of St. Thomas Aquinas. He explains that the first precepts of the natural law are universal, immutable, and knowable by all men. The proximate conclusions drawn from those precepts, however, are less absolute and more difficult to discern. Finally, the application of the precepts of natural law and the proximate conclusions drawn from them are more contingent. Due to different circumstances, the precepts of the natural law may lead to different practical conclusions. There is also more room for good faith disagreement among men about the results of applying the natural law in varied contexts. Thus, my conclusions are formed by my own application of these natural law principles (guided by historical precedents, where they exist, of analogous situations) to the complex economic situation in which we find ourselves. As such, my arguments may not universally hold for all times and circumstances and they are certainly fallible.

Avoiding the Debt Trap

As I argued in the prior chapter, our economic system is saturated with usurious transactions from the federal government down to the local department store charge account. Some contact with usury is almost inevitable. I want to assuage any scrupulous consciences that we need not fear culpability for sin if our involvement in usury is that of borrower. The Church has taught for centuries that the guilty party is the usurer, not the one paying usuries. The incurrence of excessive debt may have been imprudent, even culpably, on a borrower's part, but he is not guilty of the sin of usury. Those paying usurious gain on home, car, or school loans are not due punishment but rather are entitled to restitution. Although the borrower who has contracted for a usurious loan is not culpable for the sin of usury, the implication is that we should not borrow at usury. The virtue of prudence dictates that we should avoid incurring usurious debt obligations to the extent possible. The reason is that, as Pope Innocent IV pointed out in his commentary on the Decretals, the borrower is always harmed by paying usury in that he suffers a transfer of future wealth to the usurer, which has the effect of impoverishing him. It is therefore prudent to avoid borrowing at usury if at all possible. One should follow the advice of St. Bernardino of Siena and in lieu of taking out a usurious loan, forgo any unnecessary consumption, sell assets to raise the necessary cash, or accept charity. In some circumstances, recourse to a usurious loan may be the only option to obtain something necessary, such as housing, transportation, medical treatment, or required education for our profession. In fact, the economic system that developed in the twentieth century with inflated housing prices, rising higher education costs, skyrocketing medical costs, and a drastic reduction in charitable institutions (i.e., free hospitals and schools), produces an unprecedented amount of unavoidable borrowing by families of average wealth. On top of this, the legal and financial regime of finance capitalism and its various deceptive shell games often make imprudent usurious loans difficult to detect and therefore difficult to avoid.

If one finds himself surrounded by a mountain of usurious debt and sinking further and further into financial stress, what is to be done? The first step is to pray hard. Ask God to enlighten your mind with the knowledge of what to do to improve the situation and to fortify your resolve to do it. Each situation is different, so I cannot offer specific advice for someone caught in the all-too-typical American debt spiral. In general, try to get a handle on your complete financial picture. Create a list of all debt and debt service payments. Try to work out a long-term plan to reduce the debt burden, starting with the most expensive loans. If there is just not enough income and no hope of increased future income to ever get out of the debt hole, investigate the possibility of using a bankruptcy proceeding to discharge debt (eliminate it) or reschedule or modify its terms. Thanks to the deceptively named Bankruptcy Reform and Consumer Protection Act of 2005, bankruptcy has become more expensive and less helpful to consumers (more types of debt are now ineligible for discharge). A more accurate title for the statute would have been the Bankruptcy Corruption and Usurer Protection Act of 2005.

Many people, despite being in a situation that could be helped by a personal bankruptcy filing, refuse to consider it as an option. It is too often viewed as humiliating and involving a social stigma. These feelings are a product of the false Protestant ethic that dominates American culture. This ethic made financial prosperity the arbiter of worth rather than spiritual prosperity and a sign of a falsely conceived predestination. Financial distress was equated to and in fact replaced moral failure. The vast majority of Americans who are in the vice grip of excessive debt are not there because they are lazy or shiftless. They are there because they have been victimized by a financial elite that has enriched itself on the back of their labor.

That same elite fosters this Protestant stigma attached to bankruptcy in order to protect its own *turpe lucrum* (illicit profit). Let me repeat: the Church has clearly taught that those who have suffered from usury are entitled to restitution of the usury paid. Our post-Christian legal system does not require such restitution once mandated by every kingdom in Christendom. Thus, a bankruptcy filing may be a way to obtain at least some restitution or at least to reduce the amount of usury paid in the future. Any social embarrassment should be prayerfully accepted in the true Catholic spirit of humility as a sacrifice for the common good of one's family. I am not at all suggesting that everyone with a mortgage or credit card debt go out and file bankruptcy (the new restrictive laws passed by a Democrat-controlled Congress often rule it out as an option anyway). But in severe financial circumstances it should not be ruled out due to embarrassment.

Let us flip to the other side of the usury question. What if one has been involved in the making of usurious loans? The Church again is clear: all illicit gain from usury must be restored to the borrower if possible, but if not possible it must be given to the needy generally. Before someone jumps to the conclusion that everyone who has ever made a loan at interest has to disgorge the interest, please reread the prior discussion of usury and its varied distinctions. Remember that not every loan charging interest is an instance of usury. If the loan was in substance the investment in a business venture or other wealth-producing asset, it likely did not involve a usurious loan even if called a loan at interest in our modern parlance. Even if a loan was made to someone for consumption purposes, not all interest payments constitute usury. Recall that a lender is justified in requiring the borrower to return the borrowed money plus pay compensation for loss. One of the most difficult aspects of applying the prohibition on usury to our economic situation is the fiat currency system that we are forced to use. Dollar bills do not have any stable value. The value of our money is constantly being manipulated by the inflationary financial system, headed by the Federal Reserve Banks, so that there is great uncertainty as to the real value of a dollar bill at any future time. Thus, interest payments on a loan may in many cases merely represent the equalization of the value of the dollars used in repayment to the value of dollars originally lent. Although there is no consistent, transparent methodology for measuring the constant decline in the value of our currency, we all can tell that dollars lose value over time. Would your salary of ten years ago if unchanged today represent an equal amount of wealth in 2008?

Yet if one has made a loan at such a high rate of interest that it is likely to exceed a reasonable estimate of the decline in value of the amount originally lent, I would suggest bringing the matter to the internal forum. Seek out a holy priest who is knowledgeable about Catholic moral teaching and lay the facts into the hands of his judgment. (I recognize this may be difficult advice to follow given the crisis in the Church.)

Given that most people do not go around making interest-bearing loans to people for consumption, I want to address one scenario that is more common and over which some good Catholics have expressed concern—depositing money in interest-bearing accounts with banks. Is it morally licit to deposit our money in banks for safekeeping and collect interest on our savings accounts? In general, I would argue it is. First of all, it is likely that any interest paid on a typical savings or checking account (currently less than 2.5%) is well below a rate necessary to compensate for the decline in value of the dollars deposited over time due to the inflationary monetary policy of our government and the extra-governmental Federal Reserve Banks. Thus, I think it is a safe conclusion that we are not receiving usury on our deposit accounts under current conditions; in fact, we are likely losing value over time. It is perfectly legitimate to place money in a bank to protect it from physical loss or theft (although subjecting it to the risk of loss in a banking system collapse) and to take advantage of the convenience of the payment methods possible only with a bank account (checks, debit cards, etc.). Thus, one may out of prudence want to reduce deposits in a banking system that is crumbling. Remember, the bank does not keep your money in a safe (unless you have a safe deposit box); it owes you and all of its other creditors that money that it likely does not have on hand. If the music stops, your bank account may be without a chair to sit on. Beyond this prudential decision, we need not be scrupulous over whether we are committing the sin of usury by having an interest-bearing checking or savings account. I recognize some Catholics may still have concerns about placing money on deposit since they know banks and other financial institutions are engaged in usury. Likely the moral principle of double effect is useful to answer this concern. As long as your intention for depositing money in a bank is good, i.e., to safeguard it and access the payment systems, and not to assist the economic immorality of the system, the harm caused by your personal deposit is likely proportionate and thus a permitted unintended double effect.

In conclusion, prudence dictates that we avoid usurious borrowing as much as possible, although for many trying to survive in our corrupt system, this may be impossible. The borrower is not culpable for the sin of usury, however, and is entitled in justice to restitution of every penny of usury extracted from him. Given our perverse legal system that denies the existence of usury, bankruptcy may be the only legal recourse to approximate a claim for such restitution. If one is trapped in a sea of usurious debt, there are likely no easy answers. Pray for the virtues of prudence and fortitude and seek counsel from a trustworthy source. If one has made a clearly usurious loan, restitution may be necessary—but remember that usury is very difficult to detect in our surreal monetary system. Seek confessional guidance if you are concerned. We live in trying times on a number of fronts. Navigating an unjust financial system is not easy. With the grace of God we can steer our way through and keep alive hope for the restoration of an economic system that is rooted in the moral precepts of the natural law and is subject to Christ the King.

Avoiding Usury

As already noted in the previous chapter, translating Catholic moral teaching on economics to practical advice is a most difficult task because we make a transition for the realm of principles of reason to contingent matters, the facts to which the principles must be applied. As St. Thomas explains, the first principles of the natural law (do good and avoid evil) are self-evident and easily understood by the soul through synderesis. The next level of general principles can, with the use of right reason, be deduced from the first principles and we can obtain certainty as to these secondary principles when they accord with divine revelation. That usury is an evil we are obligated to avoid is a clear principle of the natural and divine laws. These truths are discovered through the use of theoretical reason (our faculty for discerning the truth). The application of these known truths to particular and varied factual situations involves the use of our practical reason. We cannot be as certain of the determinations of the practical reason as it is applied to what St. Thomas calls "contingent matters." Thus, we can know the natural law with a reasonable degree of certainty, but depending on the complexity of particular contingent situations we may experience difficulties in reaching clear conclusions in practical applications.

There is nothing more contingent in my mind than our economy. Primarily we lack a basic measuring device for even collecting factual data. Money, which is meant to be the fixed measure of economic activities, has become a shadowy, ever-changing, and manipulable measuring device. Thus, as Fr. Dempsey pointed out over a half-century ago (before the gold standard was completely scrapped), detecting usury has become nearly impossible in our current monetary system. This cloak of obscurity has allowed those who control the manipulation of the money supply to spread usury throughout the entire economy. In light of these difficulties, any practical conclusions must be arrived at and adhered to with great caution. We see in these economic shadows less clearly than the cavemen in Plato's cave. Thus, our practical reason has very contingent matter to work with.

That being said, we can apply Catholic moral principles to arrive at some conclusions. We know, as Fr. Dempsey observed, that usury pervades the economy; we cannot escape it completely. As social and political animals we also cannot avoid society completely. What we can do is avoid directly lending money in a way that is clearly usurious. We can also strive to avoid as much as possible indirect involvement in what appear, with a high degree of moral certainty, to be usurious transactions.

I would therefore conclude that it would be morally impermissible to work for a payday lender. These pernicious enterprises lend to consumers with jobs at rates of several hundred percent per annum against future paychecks. They will lend $500 against the next paycheck at a rate of something like 350 percent per annum. Even Congress has taken note of their immoral preying on members of our military and has restricted (to some extent) their ability to sell their schemes to armed forces personnel and their family. Clearly all of their loans are for consumption, and whatever numbers you want to use for inflation, they are charging in excess of their costs. To assist these lenders directly is to be materially complicit in usury. So much for the "easy case," but now we must turn to more difficult cases.

What about someone who has a job with a more "mainstream" commercial bank. As discussed in the previous chapters on usury, it is very difficult to distinguish usurious loans from loans charging merely just compensation for loss in our monetary system. Although we can conclude that it is morally certain that commercial banks are engaging in at least some usurious loans, it is difficult to determine if any individual loan is in fact in violation of the prohibition on usury. Again we lack a clear measuring rod of cost in a world of a variable money supply. A hypothetical person (Mr. Cratchit) who is merely an employee of a bank (say First Scrooge Bank) is not necessarily guilty of sin (particularly if Mr. Cratchit is not working as a loan officer on consumer loans but rather as a teller) just because Scrooge Bank is engaged in some usurious loans. Under these facts, Mr. Cratchit is not directly implicated in any commission of the sin of usury. Although we might conclude that Mr. Cratchit is indirectly involved in First Scrooge Bank's usurious dealings (by working for the entity and thus making their entire business possible), we need to consider the implications of the Catholic moral principle of the double effect. If Cratchit is working at this job to support his family, and if Cratchit would put his family in danger of not meeting the necessities of life by quitting his job at First Scrooge Bank, any effect his work might have on the ability of the bank to profit from usurious lending appears to be a double effect of his intention of working to support his family. The case would be different if Cratchit went and got the job so that he could ensure there was a usurer in town to whom he could direct his enemies so that they could be harmed by borrowing at usury. Assuming the absence of such malicious intent, Cratchit need not have scruples over the unintended potential effect of his working for Scrooge. It certainly would be morally preferable (more perfect) to avoid working for such a company altogether. If Cratchit were offered a job with Fred's Restaurant Operations, a company not involved in lending in any way, and this job involved no serious risk to the support of his family, it would be morally preferable to accept this other job. If there is no such alternative, Cratchit should continue in the Scrooge job. In fact, quitting the job and putting his family into a state of poverty could be seen as a morally unsound choice if doing so would likely result in the poverty of Cratchit's family.

If Cratchit's case can be accepted, we can then conclude along the same lines as to even more indirect involvement in the usurious banking system. Mr. Calculus, an accountant with an auditing firm, is not morally complicit in usury simply because his firm audits the financial statements of banks like First Scrooge Bank.

One of the effects (perhaps even intentional) of globalization is to mix everything up. This further spreads covert usury. As a result, it is likely many people work at jobs that have some indirect causal relationship to usury. Car manufacturers run financial arms that likely deal in usurious loans. This is the consequence of living in a corrupted *and* intermingled global economic system. Again, we are forced to be *in* this world to some extent to live, but we must work not to be *of* this corrupt globalized world. The Catholic virtue of prudence is necessary to distinguish the clear cases where we must absent ourselves and those involving an unintended double effect.

I wish to make clear I am not going soft on usury or Catholic moral teaching. The pervasive violation by our economic and financial system of the divine and natural law is a grave problem for America and the world at large. Our society's continual flouting of these principles will only end in our country's economic, but more importantly moral, ruination. We must as part of our efforts to restore all things in Christ and establish the Social Reign of Christ the King oppose the anti-Catholic economic ordering of our society. This is why I have spent a considerable amount of my professional research effort in exposing the moral flaws in our financial system and arguing for their reform. Yet we need to be guided by the cardinal virtue of prudence in applying these matters to our individual lives prior to the restoration of Christ the King and the attendant economic restoration. We therefore need to distinguish whether our current employment is directly and materially complicit in certain usury. If so, we need to make a change. If we are merely indirectly, to one extent or another, involved in the pervasive covert system of usury, we need, consistent with our duties towards the support of our families, to be open to opportunities to earn our daily bread in a way that requires less involvement with potentially usurious situations. In tandem with this discernment, we must work towards the establishment of a truly Catholic social order by doing what we can, consistent with our abilities and station in life, to promote awareness of the problems and the ingredients of a restoration. Such a nuanced and balanced program will likely not sit well with fiery idealists, but, in my humble opinion, the twentieth century saw far too much of such utopianism. Catholicism is not utopian. It has and always will be rooted in Truth as discerned by our speculative reason. Catholicism has always balanced this undying loyalty to Truth with a prudent recognition of the limitation of decisions of our practical reason in putting these known truths to work in our individual and contingent lives. Unlike non-Catholics of good will who at least discern these truths of the natural law (and are, as St. Paul says, a law unto themselves), we have supernatural forces to aid us in navigating these practical applications. We have the sacraments, prayer, the saints, the sacramental—all the channels of grace. This realization should give us much hope, a virtue much needed to avoid despair in these difficult times. *Ad regnum Christi!*

Contributing to the Support of the Church in an Economic and Ecclesiastical Crisis

In Chapter 3 when we considered the Catholic understanding of wealth, we emphasized that charity—the use of wealth to support others—is an obligation in justice. We noted that the Church has left to the determination of individuals the particular recipients of charity out of superabundance, although insisting that the performance of works of charity in general is obligatory. There is one exception to the freedom of determination as to the direction of superabundance: there is an obligation to contribute to the support of the Church. How do we fulfill this general duty in the context of a collapsing economy? The answer is complicated by the phenomenon of contributing to the Church at a time when much of its human element is collapsing into modernism and liberalism.

When preparing for our First Holy Communion, we should have learned the precepts, or laws, of the Church. These six rules involve particular determinations of our general obligations towards God and his Church, one of which is to contribute to the support of the Church. In the flood of solicitations for all sorts of causes that stream across our lives every day, we should not forget about our serious obligations to give to our Mother, the Church. Giving to the support of the Church is not something optional, like giving jars of Christmas jam to our neighbors. It is an obligation. But what is the nature of the obligation? How much ought we to give? And in which manner should we give?

First, it is clear that Catholics are obligated by law to give financial support to the Church. The obligation predates the precept of the Church. It is a precept of the natural law. Saint Thomas explains: "natural reason dictates that the people should administer the necessaries of life to those who minister the divine worship for the welfare of the whole people even as it is the people's duty to provide a livelihood for their rulers and soldiers and so forth."[1]

But how much is one required to give in support of the Church? Unfortunately, some Catholics are under the impression (and in fact even some priests have falsely taught, in imitation of Protestant preachers) that Catholics are obligated by the Mosaic Law to tithe, i.e., to give one tenth of one's income or produce per year.[2] As St. Thomas teaches, the Mosaic or Old Law contains three types of precepts: moral precepts, ceremonial precepts, and judicial precepts. Following the proclamation of the New Law by Christ Our Lord, the ceremonial and judicial precepts have been revoked. These were not eternal and immutable laws but were laws given for a time only—from the time of the establishment of the Old Covenant with

1. Aquinas, *Summa*, II–II, Q. 87, art. 1.
2. See, e.g., Leviticus 27:30, 32.

Moses until the coming of the Redeemer.[3] Saint Thomas explains that "the precept about the paying of tithes was partly moral and instilled in the natural reason; and partly judicial, deriving its force from its divine institution."[4] The moral precepts included in the natural law remain in force after the coming of the Redeemer, not by virtue of their having been included in the Mosaic Law but by virtue of their prior inclusion in natural law. The ceremonial and judicial precepts were abrogated by the promulgation of the New Law.[5] For example, the Ten Commandments are moral precepts of the Old Law and remain binding today as they did in the time before the coming of Christ. The obligation to refrain from eating pork was not a moral precept and thus no longer binds the conscience even though it did bind the Jews before the coming of Christ. So if you have been misinformed that the judicial or ceremonial precepts of the Mosaic Law bind you in conscience, you have been fed theological error. If you have been told that you should observe the ceremonial or judicial precepts of the Mosaic Law because it is superior to—by virtue of being older than—the New Law, you have been fed error. The New Law perfects or fulfills the Old Mosaic Law. By definition, that which perfects something is greater than that which it perfects.

The general obligation to contribute to providing a livelihood for those dedicated exclusively to divine worship is a dictate of natural reason as an obligation of justice and thus a binding moral precept. Saint Thomas explains,

> But the fixing of the proportion to be offered to the ministers of divine worship does not belong to the natural law, but was determined by divine institution, in accordance with the condition of that people to whom the law was being given. For they were divided into twelve tribes, and the twelfth tribe, namely that of Levi, was engaged exclusively in the divine ministry and had no possessions whence to derive a livelihood: and so it was becomingly ordained that the remaining eleven tribes should give one-tenth part of their

3. See *Summa*, I–II, Q. 98–105.
4. Ibid., II–II, Q. 87, art. 1.
5. Ibid., I–II, Q. 98–105.

> revenues to the Levites that the latter might live respectably; and also because some, through negligence, would disregard this precept. *Hence, so far as the tenth part was fixed, the precept was judicial,* since all institutions established among this people for the special purpose of preserving equality among men, in accordance with this people's condition, are called judicial precepts.[6]

To misinform a Catholic that he is obligated to tithe (as defined by the Old Testament) is equivalent to telling him that he is forbidden to eat a ham sandwich.

Even though the judicial precept of the tithe has been revoked by Christ, the natural law obligation to support the Church's ministers remains. The Church is also free to supplement this natural law obligation with a more precise human-made law. In past centuries and for certain peoples, the Church has done so. Some dioceses still establish particular laws about the percentage of weekly collections that are to be paid to the diocese by pastors. Yet at the present time there is no particular law of the Church fixing any amount or percentage of income as obligatory on Catholics to fulfill the natural law other than the general precept to contribute to the support of the Church.

The Church has been prudent in not fixing a specific percentage or amount for Catholics in our time. The financial and monetary system it is our lot in life to struggle to live in is filled with complexity and injustice, which makes it impossible to establish justly a universal percentage. The concept of a fixed percentage works well in an economic society when most people actually produce wealth that can be reliably measured by a stable monetary standard. As Hilaire Belloc observed almost a century ago, the modern economy is populated not by people who own their own means of production and generate new wealth but by wage slaves. Most people do not receive newly produced wealth for their labors but payment in money for the time they spend producing for others. Thus, a tithing system rooted in the sharing of a fixed percentage of fruits of work produced does not easily translate to a system where most people do not produce or receive new wealth but merely receive monetary

6. Ibid., II–II, Q. 87, art. 1.

income. Secondly, the value of the monetary income received is difficult to calculate, as our money is unstable and its value is constantly being manipulated. This makes calculating the amount of anyone's wealth virtually impossible for purposes of finding a percentage of it. It is like trying to determine 10 percent of the perimeter of a room while using a ruler whose unit of measure is constantly changing.

Finally, we live in a radically unjust and usurious governmental and economic system. In the West, the average person has anywhere from 30–70 percent of his wages taken by the government (when all sales taxes—both the explicit and hidden forms, including state, local, real estate, and federal—are aggregated, to say nothing of the new healthcare and carbon taxes). Secondly, a usurious housing finance system mandates that most people pay about 25 percent of their gross annual income to usurious home mortgage lenders just for the privilege of continuing to live in the house they are told they "own." Taking these factors into account, the Church prudently recognizes that in our time, when most people lose between 55 and 95 percent of their income to taxes and usurious home loans, to require generally the giving of 10 percent of one's gross income to the support of the Church would not only be unjust but frankly impossible for most people. Thus, if you earn $50,000 gross income and someone has attempted to make you feel scrupulous because you have not given $5,000 to the Church, it is the person falsely accusing you that should feel guilty and not you. At a 30 percent aggregated tax rate, and if you have a typical mortgage, $5,000 represents 22 percent of the income the government and the mortgage usurers allow you to keep to feed and clothe your family!

So if the Church has in prudence not fixed an amount that must be given to fulfill her precept to support the Church but left it to particular determinations, what principles determine how much one should give? The principles of the law of grace, the New Law, provide the answer. Unlike the Jews of the Old Law, we live in the law of liberty, as St. Paul calls the New Law. As supported by grace, we strive to fulfill the moral precepts liberally.[7] Grace inspires us to

7. Ibid., I–II, Q. 106–108.

want not to do the minimum the moral law requires but to desire to live perfectly as our heavenly Father is perfect. As to charitable giving, we are obligated to give generously out of our surplus, our superabundance.

Saint Thomas explains, "people are obligated in justice to give whatever they have in superabundance."[8] Thus, each man is obligated to give alms from the amount of wealth he possesses above and beyond abundance. What is abundance? Enough to sustain oneself, to perform pious works, to make reasonable provision for future emergencies, or to support offspring constitutes abundance.[9] As can be seen, the exact amount constituting abundance for determining superabundance varies from situation to situation. The amount constituting abundance will differ greatly between a bachelor whose parents are deceased and who owns his home free of debt and a wage-earning father of seven children who does not really "own" his own home (i.e., he can retain his home as long as he makes his usurious payments). The principle is therefore clear: whatever we earn beyond what constitutes abundance we are obligated to give generously to the support of the poor and to support the Church. But the precise calculation of this amount varies dramatically and should be determined in honesty and frankness and preferably with the assistance of a good spiritual director well versed in moral and practical principles. In working through this issue, we must remember that God will not be mocked, and we must be honest in assessing our actual situation and obligations. We should strive to give liberally and generously and with love not grudgingly and minimally.

We also must be on guard against an opposite extreme tendency to give out of proportion to our actual superabundance. As St. Thomas explains, "Yet it would be inordinate to deprive oneself of one's own, in order to give to others to such an extent that the residue would be insufficient for one to live in keeping with one's station and the ordinary occurrences of life: for no man ought to live unbe-

8. Ibid., II–II, Q. 66, art. 7.

9. See Henry of Hesse, *De contractibus*, in Gerson, *Opera omnia*, 4, cap. 12, fol. 191ra.

comingly."[10] To give so much in support of the Church that we cannot feed our children anymore is a vice not a virtue. As with all moral issues, the correct way is a balance against two opposite extremes. Here it is a median between unjustly hording our superabundance and giving more than justice and prudence require.

Now that we have considered the difficult question of how much, we turn to an issue particularly relevant in our time. What if the resources we give are used for immoral ends or for moral ends but through immoral means? In such a situation, we face a conflict of two moral requirements: we are obligated to support the Church, and we are obligated not to assist in another's sin. We cannot resolve this conflict by choosing to obey one moral requirement and disregard the other. We must determine a course of action consistent with both obligations. Thus, it is morally unacceptable either simply to retain what we are obligated to give in support of the Church as well as simply to give to support those we know are using such funds immorally. Several bishops, members of the United States Conference of Catholic Bishops, have publicly confirmed that this moral conflict is real. They have shown that the funds raised by many dioceses and the USCCB have been used to support the immoral activities of groups such as the IAF and AACORN. In particular, the bishops' Campaign for Human Development has such a scandalous history that several bishops have instructed the faithful and their own chanceries to provide no support whatsoever to it.

We must recall that we are culpable for assisting in the sin of another only if we were aware that our activity was so assisting. There is therefore no need to agonize over money given in the past in ignorance. But if we are aware that our local geographic parish or bishop is not using the funds entrusted to them for the support of sacred ministers and consecrated souls but rather to pursue immoral or destructive activities, we cannot simply give and close our eyes. Neither can we just keep our money. We are obligated to find another morally licit means to support the Church. Fortunately, the Church is universal and we can find ways to fulfill our obligation to support the Church and avoid assisting in sin. There

10. Aquinas, *Summa*, II–II, Q. 32, art. 6.

are a number of Traditional orders, monasteries, convents, and other communities working every day to restore all things in Christ through moral means. Seminarians need funding, convents and monasteries need building, missionaries bringing the Traditional Mass and sacraments to foreign lands need resources. If we find ourselves in such a moral conflict and there is no way to give to our geographic parish or diocese without moral compromise, we must make the extra effort to find other ways to support the Church. To neglect to do so is a neglect of the natural law and the fundamental positive law of the Church. True, it was easier in an age when one could simply drop a donation in the local parish collection and not have to concern oneself with how it would be spent; but God is calling our generation to make sacrifices. It was also easier when one could just walk to the local parish and be virtually certain to find a valid, doctrinally correct, reverent, and edifying Mass. Rather than bemoan the trials God has given us for our sanctification, we should joyfully accept the fact that we have to think more and work more than other generations to fulfill our obligations, remembering that God will give us the grace to see through our trials.

So how do we give to the Church? We must give generously out of our superabundance to support the Church. The precise amount to give is a matter of particular determination in light of specific facts which must be assessed in honesty and charity. We also must give morally. We must not knowingly assist in the furthering of immoral ends or means. We must work to reconcile these obligations so as to fulfill both. In short, we must give generously and give well.

6

Politics: Life of the Perfect Society

THOUSANDS OF YEARS AGO, the Greek philosopher Aristotle observed that man was by nature a social and political animal. As Aristotle's monumental work on ethics indicates, if politics and society are natural to man, good politics and a good society are not necessarily naturally given. Although we cannot help but be political, we can help being bad at politics. History is littered with failures to live well politically and socially. Living well is not something attained once and for all in this life; it requires continual work and vigilance. From Greece to Rome to Christendom, history likewise evidences the fall of once good and virtuous polities and societies.

At the dawn of the twenty-first century, American politics and society seem in a spiraling free fall. The radical separation of civil society from the Church examined in Chapter 1 is reaping its bitter fruits. We have already seen the consequences in the sphere of the household and the economy. The Supreme Court of the United States equates unnatural acts with the natural state of marriage. Economic liberalism and its injustices dominate the economy. The effects of the radical separation of the Church from politics and civil life has forced the Church into the status of a mere private association. The Church lacks the necessary liberty to proclaim the Kingdom of Christ throughout the public square. This chapter examines in more detail the Catholic understanding of politics developed in Chapter 1 and contrasts it with our broken system. Like the early Christians living in a Roman empire in a similar state of free-fall, we have been born into this time. God wants us to live in, although not becoming of, this time in history. We can be tempted to two equally dangerous extremes. We can become seduced by corrupt politics and social life and simply conform to the corruption and consequently lose our souls. Alternatively, we can attempt to deny our nature. We can say we opt out of being political and social and attempt to live as an island unto ourselves. But Aristotle unwittingly agreed with God, who declared, "It is not good for the man to be alone." Dropping out of society is as much not the right choice as is throwing virtue to the wind and joining the degeneration. We are called to walk a very fine line. We must avoid being corrupted by the world but must not abandon our duty in justice to the society in which we live. As with the crisis in the Church, we cannot opt for the apparent ease of sedevacantism and just drop out of the Church, nor can we embrace the novelties of the crisis and lose the faith. In civil society we must avoid both extremes. This section explores the principles supporting this difficult process of navigating the proper medium in our time. Although there are many problems and dangers associated with contemporary society, we must not allow these facts to draw us into the error of despair. We must face the reality of the world no matter how bleak but maintain the real joy that only the Lord can give in the midst of it.

Magna Carta and the Continuing Battle for the Liberty of the Church and Natural and Divine Justice in the Increasingly Secular Commonwealth

As Richard Weaver noted in the first half of the twentieth century, ideas have consequences. The imprisoning of the Church behind the wall of separation (even if most Churchmen have acquiesced to accept their gilded cage) has consequences. This imprisonment marks a victory in a centuries-old struggle of civil government to imprison the Church, which seems constantly to get in the way of the aggrandizement of powermongers. From Henry II and St. Thomas Becket to King John and Innocent III, temporal leaders have all hoped to restrict the liberty of action of the Church. Those who value the true liberty accorded to human action have seen this danger and have enshrined in the Anglo legal tradition, of which America is offspring, the principle of the liberty of the Church. This chapter examines the importance of this principle for Anglo-American law as enshrined in the *Magna Carta*.

The evil decision of the Obama Administration to mandate that all employers, including Catholic institutions, provide medical insurance covering contraception and abortifacients has evoked strong language in the media. Mark Steyn compared President Obama to the English King Henry VIII who plundered the Catholic Church in England.[1] Similarly, Cardinal George wrote that the Church is being despoiled of her institutions through an act of theft.[2] Clearly both lay and clerical commentators realize something important is happening to the Church at this moment.

It is something large but not something new. For her entire history the Church has been at war with ungodly civil rulers defending her divine and natural rights to liberty of action as a perfect society. This battle has at times abated with centuries of truce and, for a few centuries in the Middle Ages, a real peace. Yet the battle is as old as the Church. Since she is a divinely instituted society with universal jurisdiction, power-hungry temporal rulers have always realized the Church represents a check and curb on their megalomaniac designs. The solution: despoil her of the means of fulfilling her mission. Recall the Prefect of Rome demanded that St. Lawrence surrender to him the "great treasures of the Church." What is at stake goes even beyond the Church. Since this attack on the Church involves an attack on divine and natural law itself, the just treatment and liberties of all men are at stake. To the extent that the Church's liberty is unjustly compromised, the liberty of all is at risk.

At times of intensity in this battle in the English world, references to a document have been uttered. The document is the *Magna Carta*, the "Great Charter." Saint Thomas More invoked the *Magna Carta* in his famous defense at his trial (another round in this ongoing war). "That Law [declaring the King the supreme head of the Church] was, even contrary to the Laws and Statutes of the Kingdom yet unrepealed, as might evidently be seen by *Magna Charta*,

1. Mark Steyn, "Obama goes Henry VIII on the church," *Orange County Register*, February 10, 2012, available at http://www.ocregister.com/articles/church-339789-one-catholic.html.

2. Cardinal George, "What are You Going to Give up This Lent," *Catholic New World*, February 26, 2012, available at http://www.catholicnewworld.com/cnwonline/.

wherein are these Words: *Ecclesia Anglicana libera sit, & habet omnia jura integra, & libertates suas illesas. . . .*" These original Latin words of one of the oldest surviving laws of England can be rendered in English, "May the English Church be free and have all her just rights entire and her liberties inviolate." To understand the meaning of these words we need to consider somewhat the history of *Magna Carta.*

Like all attempts of mere human beings (as opposed to the divinely guided Church) who struggle to maintain a purity of intention, *Magna Carta* presents an admixture of the universal and the human particular. It states true universal principles yet is also comprised of and born out of practical political issues. Notwithstanding its shortcomings, the points of contact with universal Truth continue to echo down the centuries to our own time.

The story of the *Magna Carta* begins decades before the famous version of the document accepted by King John at Runnymede in 1215. King John's father, Henry II, also went to battle with the Church and his old friend St. Thomas Becket over this very issue, the liberty of the Church. Henry II had nominated Becket to be Archbishop of Canterbury expecting his old friend and ally, then Chancellor of England and second in command to the King, to do his bidding within the Church. However, something happened to Becket. That something was grace. He took on the responsibility of being the primate of England with full vigor. He gave his life as a martyr to defend the right of the Church to have complete jurisdiction over her clergy. An English priest had been accused of murder. The king demanded that the Church turn over the priest to his courts for trial. Becket defended the jurisdiction of the Church and insisted that the priest be tried for his alleged crimes by a Church court. For this resistance to his friend the King, he gave his life. Yet Becket and the Church prevailed in the end. Henry was forced to come to Canterbury as a penitent to atone for his sin and to acknowledge the liberty of the Church as a perfect society to have jurisdiction over her clergy.

Like Father like son; King John had his own war with the Church. For centuries the Church had accommodated the desire of temporal rulers to be involved in the appointment of Church authorities.

Since bishops often served both ecclesiastical and lay functions working in both spheres, this involvement was tolerated by the Church as a *modus vivendi* with a variety of temporal powers. This practice, however, was only a tolerated accommodation. The great reform movement led by Pope Gregory VII had as one of its central tenets to curb this practice, which had come over time to harm the Church. When abused, it facilitated the appointment of unworthy men to high Church office because of the hoped-for political benefit to the monarch. Playing on the temptation to human respect, it could make weak men feel the pressure of being beholden to the king who wrought their appointment. As with Becket, this process could backfire on the king, but Becket is the exception that proves the general rule. The Gregorian Reform movement, which had as its motto *Libertas Ecclesiae* (Freedom of the Church), fought throughout the eleventh and twelfth centuries to limit the influence of temporal rulers to appoint and invest Church authorities. Part of this struggle involved reasserting the supreme jurisdiction of the pope over the Church, which had been obscured by centuries of accommodation in practice to temporal lords.

In 1205, ten years before the Runnymede *Magna Carta*, the See of Canterbury became vacant. King John, the cathedral chapter of Canterbury, and the other bishops of the Canterbury province disagreed over whom should fill the vacancy. Pope Innocent III settled the dispute by selecting Stephen Langton, the choice of none of these partisans, as the new archbishop. While maintaining his supreme jurisdiction to appoint bishops, Innocent acknowledged the longstanding custom of the king of England to be involved in the selection process and so presented Langton's appointment to the king for his consent. John refused. Innocent then asserted his supreme authority and appointed Langton to the office anyway. John retaliated by forbidding Langton to enter England and seizing control of all papal property (including seizing all revenues). The plan was to bring the papacy to heel by despoiling her of her temporal goods and so blackmail her into submission. Yet John did not appreciate the strength of character of Innocent III. The pope placed England under interdict (forbidding the celebration of Mass and the sacraments other than baptism to infants and absolution to the dying). As the controversy raged on, he later excommunicated John. Eventually John relented. In 1213, a reconciliation was achieved whereby John surrendered the kingdom to the pope and received it back as a feudal fief, making the king of England a vassal of the pope. John also compensated the Church for the property stolen during the crisis. The interdict and excommunication were lifted. As a loving father, Innocent III truly forgave John and in fact became a strong defender of King John in future temporal disputes with France and John's own barons.

Two years later and in the midst of a rebellion of his own barons, John agreed to the terms of the *Magna Carta* at Runnymede in 1215, of which the article quoted by St. Thomas More is the first. When the document was drawn up to set down on paper the ancient principles of justice that were to be respected as the core of English law, the first matter affirmed is the freedom of the Church from undue interference by the government. Understanding the history of the recent conflict with Innocent III makes the lines following the one quoted by St. Thomas More comprehensible:

> which [referring to the liberty of the Church] is apparent from this that the freedom of elections, which is reckoned most important and very essential to the English church, we, of our pure and unconstrained will [a statement those at the time would see ironic given the interdict and excommunication], did grant, and did by our charter confirm and did obtain the ratification of the same from our lord, Pope Innocent III, [acknowledging the vassalage under which the king now held the kingdom], before the quarrel arose between us and our barons: and this we will observe, and our will is that it be observed in good faith by our heirs forever.[3]

The remainder of the charter then goes on to discuss the principles of justice applicable to the temporal subjects of the kingdom.

It is important to note that this first article of the document so clearly affirms the liberty of the Church defended by St. Thomas Becket and Innocent III when this issue had nothing to do with the dispute between John and his barons that led to the charter. Notwithstanding it is placed as the first article of the charter, showing

3. *Magna Carta*, art. 1. http://www.constitution.org/eng/magnacar.htm.

its importance in the mind of John and his subjects, who it will be recalled suffered the severe effects of the interdict used to defend the principle of divine and natural justice, the liberty of the Church.

The rest of the charter continues to list a mixture of general principles and more particular rules relevant to the specific political feudal constitution of England. It is also important to note that many of the articles treat of the justice and protection of the king due to the weaker members of the realm: widows, under-age inheritors of property, and those indebted to the Jews exacting usury. With respect to the last of these, the charter proclaims that if those debts fall into the hands of the king, he will not collect any usury on these loans and that the dower property of widows may not be touched by the usurers in attempting to collect payment. Many of the other provisions of the charter speak of particular details of the organization of the kingdom. What can be abstracted from these provisions, however, is an important principle of justice: the ancient customs of the country should be respected and preserved and not circumvented for political gain. By listing these particular rules the king acknowledges the limits of authority. His authority is limited in that it must be exercised in a way not to contravene ancient customs including principles of natural and divine law.

Like Article 1, however, several articles do contain more universal principles of justice that remained critically important for the development of the English, and later American, legal system. Articles 39 and 40, for example, read: "39. No freeman shall be taken or imprisoned or disseised or exiled or in any way destroyed, nor will we go upon him nor send upon him, except by the lawful judgment of his peers or by the law of the land. 40. To no one will we sell, to no one will we refuse or delay, right or justice."[4]

These two articles sum up the core principle of justice: citizens should be given their due according to justice (*suum jus*) not according to the self-interest of the powerful. Thus Articles 1, 39, and 40 represent a general summary of justice in that the Church and the members of civil society must be guaranteed the protection of the rulers due to them in justice.

4. Ibid., arts. 39, 40.

Interestingly, Pope Innocent III condemned the *Magna Carta* and declared it non-binding on John. This fact may seem an enigma. Yet if we delve into the pope's reasons, the answer to the enigma is obvious. Innocent condemned *Magna Carta* not because of errors in its stated articles[5] but because of the method of its adoption. Innocent condemned the method of exacting agreement from the king by violent rebellion. In a sense, Innocent's condemnation shows a greater respect for the principles of justice embodied in the charter. The liberty of the Church is not something given by a king under duress or the threat of force. It exists in the fabric of the universe as a tenet of divine and natural law. To tie such an important principle to a document signed at the point of a sword is to diminish the principle and to imply that it has been created or granted by an earthly king and not by the King of the universe. Future kings of England acknowledged the principles of the *Magna Carta* by issuing later versions of the document or signing acknowledgements of the validity of its principles. These later restatements, not obtained under threat of force, were accepted by the papacy and the Church. As St. Thomas More remarked at his trial, the principle of the liberty of the Church in her government and in her just powers and possessions was reconfirmed in the coronation oath uttered by none other than Henry VIII.

The case of Henry VIII shows us the beginning of the abandonment of the principles of the *Magna Carta*, which culminates in the decision of President Obama's administration pursuant to the Affordable Care Act to require Catholic hospitals to provide immoral contraceptive paraphernalia or close Catholic hospitals. Notwithstanding Article 1 of the *Magna Carta* and his own oath, Henry VIII eliminated the liberty of the Church in England and subjected it to his supreme headship. This Act of Supremacy was, like King John, followed by a theft of her temporal goods through

5. Innocent may have taken issue with Article 69, which established a committee of barons to watch over the king. This responsibility to supervise the highest temporal authority through an indirect power falls under the jurisdiction of the spiritual authority not the lesser authorities. This article was eliminated from later versions of the charter.

the dissolution and confiscation of the monasteries and religious houses. Henry VIII understood keenly that his was a move in a long war. One of the first religious shrines he ordered destroyed was the grand shrine to none other than St. Thomas Becket, that great defender of the liberty of the Church. Henry could bear no reminder of the defeat of his predecessor and namesake in attempting to subjugate the Church.

The articles of *Magna Carta* remained entrenched within English law until the nineteenth century. That great century of destruction of the old order saw the first legal attack on the Great Charter. In 1829, Article 26 (dealing with the just settlement of the debts of a deceased according to due process) was repealed by the new supreme ruler of England: Parliament, which through two revolutions (one involving a bloody civil war) usurped the authority of the king and made that institution into a puppet of Parliament. It should come as no surprise that a body that had cast off the ancient customs and rules of the kingdom by aggregating to itself the power of the king would have little respect for a document premised on respect for ancient custom.

Today only three articles of the original charter of 1215 remain on the law books of England: Article 1 (Liberty of the Church), Article 13 (Ancient Liberties of the City of London), and Article 39 (Due Process). The fact that Article 1 on the liberty of the Church in England can remain on the books five centuries after the Church has been subjected to the supreme headship of the government (then the king, now Parliament) shows that the principles of the *Magna Carta* have lost all their substance and become mere historical relics.

Every provision of *Magna Carta* still held force in English law when the American colonies adopted the common law of England to govern the newly formed states of the United States. *Magna Carta* thus was the basis of American law and justice from the beginning. Just like her former mother country, America, however, has repealed the principles of the charter and treats its provisions as mere words. The bishops' unjust and immoral cover-ups of the sexual abuse scandal has sapped all moral authority from a defense of the Church's right to judge her own clerics. The principle for which St.

Thomas Becket died has been squandered by the cover-ups of the past few decades so that when the state demanded sole jurisdiction over the clerical perpetrators the Church meekly complied. The Obama Administration now holds the temporal institutions of the Church—schools, hospitals, universities—hostage and demands their relinquishment unless the Church bow down and worship his New World Order by agreeing to facilitate the sins of contraception and abortion. Like King John's confiscation of papal property to pressure Innocent III, President Obama does likewise.

The Church is not alone in the vacuum created by the abandonment of universal rules of justice and ancient customs. As often happens, the unjust treatment of citizens often corresponds to the level of unjust treatment of the Church. The due process principles embodied in Article 39 of the Great Charter have been cast aside by the American government at an accelerated pace since September 11, 2011—casting people into offshore prison camps, inflicting torture on suspects, suspending the ancient custom of *habeas corpus*, subjecting innocent citizens to invasive full body scans and other invasive provisions of the misnamed Patriot Act. The concept of due process has all but been emptied of its contents as has the liberty of the Church to govern herself and to hold her powers and possessions inviolate.

Yes, this issue is about much more than a technical regulation of the Department of Health and Human Services. It is another full-out advance in the battle of ungodly and power-hungry men against the Church of Christ and the divine and natural laws of which she is the guardian.

Nullification Nonsense: The Wrong Solution to a Real Problem: *The Great Façade of American Law and Politics*

As the federal government continues to grow ever more bloated, occupying more space and leaving less space to ordinary Americans, people are becoming angry at the loss. The Tea Party and Occupy Movements, although different in philosophy, both represent a reaction to the loss of space by ordinary people in the face of a growing leviathan. Throughout history, it has been the power of the other sword, the spiritual power of the Church, that has acted as the true check and balance on the power hungry. Yet, while the power of governments rises to levels never dreamt of, the Church cowers behind the wall of separation between Church and state. With the Church locked within its gilded cage holding the key of her own escape but refusing to turn the lock, many search for alternate solutions. Forgetting that Christ the King is the only way, they attempt to craft solutions that are the mere work of human hands. A darling particularly of the Tea Party crowd born of their legitimate frustration with government imperialism is nullification. Thomas E. Woods, Senior Fellow at the Ludwig von Mises Institute, published an entire book on the subject: *Nullification: How to Resist Federal Tyranny in the 21st Century*. As a professor of law with a particular interest in Catholic legal theory, I purchased the book to see what suggestions Mr. Woods has to offer for the current crisis of government.

Mr. Woods and the other Tea Party luminaries are correct in identifying a deep crisis in civil society that has been progressing in tandem with the crisis in the Church these past decades. Government, whose teleological end is to promote the common good, has done nothing of the sort for far too long. The laws passed by our governmental entities have promoted and protected some of the worst evils in history: the slaughter of millions of unborn, the subsidization of contraception, divorce, sex education in the public schools that corrupts our youth, and so-called same-sex "marriage."

This tyranny of evil must be resisted by all Catholics just as vigorously as the tyranny of modernism in the Church. Our government must be recalled to its divinely instituted purpose of promoting, rather than destroying, the common good.

Here was an author who had contributed to one of the greatest books diagnosing the crisis in the Church, *The Great Façade*, so I thought perhaps his book on nullification would just as skillfully diagnose the problems in civil society.

The Constitutional Convention and Vatican II: The Search for the Original Spirit of the Convention

If you thought along the same lines, you will be sorely disappointed. Rather than diagnosing the true crisis in government as a departure from Catholic teaching on law and the state, the book is a call to embrace the same flawed Enlightenment philosophy that led to the current crisis. Ironically, for a Catholic who could write so eloquently about the misguided attempts of "conservative" Catholics to defend the ambiguities of the Second Vatican Council, which have been injected like viruses into the Body of Christ, Woods defends the Constitutional Convention and the document it produced with the same zeal.

Woods argues that the "real intention" of the drafters of the Constitution and the state conventions that ratified it was to create a limited federal government and promote a federated alliance of sovereign states. The essence of *Nullification* lies in what Woods calls the "axiomatic point that a federal law that violates the Constitution is no law at all."[6] The phrase "no law at all" is, as we shall see shortly, an inaccurate borrowing from the principle of Catholic teaching enunciated by St. Augustine and St. Thomas Aquinas, and even by Martin Luther King in his Letter from the Birmingham Jail—but not a teaching enunciated, very conspicuously, by Woods. I mean the principle that a law contrary to *eternal, divine, or natural law* is "no law at all."

According to Woods, however, if the federal government passes a purported law that exceeds the authority granted in the Constitution, such law is void and should be nullified by the sovereign states. The two recurring, and thus most prominent, examples in contemporary political life that Woods uses in the book are the federal criminalization of the use (including medical use) of marijuana and the federal mandate to buy healthcare insurance. To maintain his argument requires Woods to prove that these acts are not provided for in the Constitution.

But the problem is that the Constitution—like *Dignitatis Humanae*, *Sancrosanctum Concilium*, and other documents of Vatican II—contains time bombs in the form of ambiguous, equivocal, open-ended clauses clearly inserted by a liberal cabal in the process of drafting and approval by a committee in a setting where no unified

6. Thomas E. Woods, Jr., *Nullification: How to Resist Federal Tyranny in the 21st Century* (Washington, DC: Regnery Publishing, 2010), 3.

intention or interpretation existed at the time. These time bombs were worked into the give-and-take of group negotiation so as to be exploded later in order to justify the Hobbesian/Lockean state the Federalists desired.

The General Welfare Clause, the Commerce Clause, and the Necessary and Proper Clause are some of the most prominent examples of constitutional time bombs Woods addresses in his book. Just like the dogged defenders of the ambiguities of Vatican II, however, Woods defends these time bombs by arguing that they must be interpreted according to the "original intent" and the "spirit" of the Constitution.

He writes: "For it is they whose interpretation of the Constitution—and in particular, the precise nature of what they believed they were getting into—is of ultimate importance."[7] Finding this evasive original interpretation of the Constitution is an exercise as futile as searching for the original intention of the Vatican II Fathers. Woods quotes extensively from Madison, Hamilton, and Jefferson as well as numerous passages from the polemical Federalist Papers claiming these clauses were meant to have a narrow and limited meaning. All of these arguments sound just like those of the defenses of the Vatican II novelties. "*Dignitatis Humanae* stated that it left intact traditional Catholic teaching on social obligations of states to Christ the King." Likewise, Woods quotes President Madison as saying, "It exceeds the possibility of belief that supporters of limited government 'should have silently permitted the introduction of words or phrases in a sense rendering fruitless the restrictions & definitions elaborated by them.'"[8]

Does it really exceed the possibility of belief? That is like saying it is inconceivable that Vatican II would quietly insert words in *Dignitatis Humanae* that would undermine Catholic Social Teaching on Christ the King when stating in the opening lines that they were not changing such teaching.

Defending a restricted reading of the Commerce Clause, for example, by appealing to "the understanding that informed the

7. Ibid., 104.
8. Ibid., 24.

decisions of the ratifying conventions"[9] is like appealing to the understanding of the Council Fathers who voted for *Dignitatis Humanae*. What the past forty years have shown in the Church is that appeals to an elusive understanding of a vast group of Fathers is no real bulwark against what these men actually did by their vote—promulgate a document that had a life of its own once issued.

The Constitution is no different. It cannot be saved by appeals to an original understanding, which in any event we have two centuries of litigation to show can never be proven conclusively. Given any desired interpretation of a clause in the Constitution, any half-decent researcher can find some off-hand comment of some Founding Father or other to prove it accords with the "original intent." To claim that the "state ratifying conventions are full of assurances about the innocuous nature of the clause"[10] is analogous to asserting that the records of the Council are full of assurances of the innocuous nature of the ambiguous clauses that have caused so many problems in the Church.

The Federalist Framers acted no differently from the liberal Council Fathers and *periti* at Vatican II, who vehemently denied they were introducing anything radical or novel into Catholic life and teaching at the time of the Council, only to explode all the time bombs they left in the documents for the next four decades to justify doing just that. Woods admits as much with respect to Alexander Hamilton, even if he seems blind to the same conduct by other Federalist "fathers" at the "council" in Philadelphia:

> For one thing, prior to New York's ratification of the Constitution, Hamilton noted in Federalist #17 and #34 that the [Commerce] clause did not mean that an area like agriculture would come under the purview of the federal government. But having given the people that assurance, Hamilton then declared, several years after the Constitution was ratified, that the clause *did mean* agriculture could be directed by the federal government.[11]

9. Ibid., 26.
10. Ibid., 29.
11. Ibid., 25.

Although Woods views Hamilton as the exception that supposedly proves the rule that the *other* Founding Fathers were consistent in their "original intention," history shows otherwise. Madison and Jefferson are used as examples throughout the book of those upright Founders who consistently maintained the "true" spirit of the Convention and fought against unauthorized elastic interpretations of the ambiguous clauses. James Madison is quoted extensively in the book as an example of a Founding Father defending the compact theory of the Constitution and the right of states to disregard federal law, and the limited scope of clauses such as the General Welfare and Commerce Clauses.[12] Madison is presented as a most compelling historical proof that these ideas embody the spirit of the Constitutional Convention because he was, after all, a Federalist and thus more in favor of a centralized government than the Republicans.

Yet, as with Alexander Hamilton, Madison's earlier protestations of delimited federal powers and states' rights quoted by Woods are contradicted not only by his actual actions as President but even by his own words. Not quoted by Woods, for example, are statements by Madison such as the following, in which he denounced as one of many "strange doctrines and misconceptions" the thinking of those who deny

> the nature of the Constitutional compact, *as precluding a right in any one of the parties to renounce it at will*, by giving to all an equal right to judge of its obligations; and, as the obligations are mutual, a right to enforce correlative with a right to dissolve them [which would] make manifest the impossibility as well as injustice, of executing the laws of the Union, particularly the laws of commerce, *if even a single State be exempt from their operation*. . . .[13]

Decades after the Constitutional Convention, Madison denounced the very idea of nullification of federal law by individual states as

12. Ibid., 22.

13. James Madison to Mathew Carey, Letter, July 27, 1831. http://memory.loc.gov/cgi-bin/query/r?ammem/mjmtext:@field(DOCID+@lit(jm090131)).

> this *preposterous & anarchical pretension* [of which] there is not a shadow of countenance in the Constitn. [sic] and well that there is not; for it is certain that with such a deadly poison in it, no Constn. [sic] could be sure of lasting a year; there having scarcely been a year, since ours was formed, without a discontent in some one or other of the States which might have availed itself of the nullifying prerogative.[14]

As for Jefferson, a single chapter provides insufficient space to demonstrate that his actions as president repudiated all his high-sounding ideas about liberty. He expanded the power of the presidency even more than his Federalist predecessors. Even Woods includes in his book the letter of a citizen denouncing Jefferson as a fraud and calling him "one of the greatest tyrants in history."[15]

The Viruses of Enlightenment Liberalism

The ultimate problem with the remedy of nullification is that it depends on the very document that is the root cause of our government's going haywire. The Constitution is a product of the errors of Enlightenment liberalism just as *Dignitatis Humanae* can be viewed as a product of neo-modernism. Pointing to a few traditional-sounding phrases or holdover concepts from the Catholic past—the borrowed capital that has been keeping our nation afloat these past 200 years—does not inoculate the body politic against these Enlightenment viruses.

Unfortunately, in arguing the case for nullification, Woods demonstrates that some of these viruses have infected his own political philosophy. The most deadly viruses are the following:

- That sovereignty comes from the people and is delegated to the government by them;
- The limitation of an appeal against federal authority to some other form of positive law rather than to the higher law; and
- An ultimate acceptance of the majoritarian fallacy.

14. James Madison to Nicholas P. Trist, Letter, December 1831. http://memory.loc.gov/cgi-bin/query/D?mjm:16:./temp/~ammem_m7q8::.
15. *Nullification*, 61–62.

The "Sovereignty of the People"

The Constitution and Woods's defense of it are rooted in a false notion of sovereignty, which is the authority to govern the *res publica* or civil polity. According to Woods, "In the American System the sovereigns are the peoples of the various states."[16] Wrong! The only sovereign in *any* political system is Christ the King.

In the encyclical letter *Quas Primas*, Pius XI confirms the constant teaching of the Church that all authority comes from God. Sovereignty over the world has been delegated not by man but by God the Father to his Son:

> Moreover, Christ Himself speaks of His own kingly authority; . . . after His resurrection, when giving to His Apostles the mission of teaching and baptizing all nations, He took the opportunity to call Himself king, [Matt. 25:31–40] confirming the title publicly [John 18:37], and solemnly proclaimed that all power was given Him in Heaven and on earth [Matt. 28:18]. These words can only be taken to indicate the greatness of his power, the infinite extent of His kingdom. What wonder, then, that He Whom St. John calls the "prince of the kings of the earth" [Apoc. 1:5] appears in the Apostle's vision of the future as He Who "hath on His garment and on His thigh written 'King of kings and Lord of lords!'" [Apoc. 19:16]. It is Christ Whom the Father "hath appointed heir of all things" [Heb. 1:2].[17]

Pius XI had already explained that the world had gone haywire precisely because men had inverted the order of delegation from the Father to the Son and the Son to constituted political authorities, to one where it was delegated from the people upwards. Pius XI stated in his first encyclical:

> [W]ith authority derived not from God but from man, the very basis of that authority has been taken away, because the chief reason of the distinction between ruler and subject has been eliminated. The result is that human society is tottering to its fall, because it has no longer a secure and solid foundation.[18]

16. *Nullification*, 36.
17. Pius XI, *Quas Primas*, no. 11.
18. Pius XI, *Ubi Arcano*, quoted in *Quas Primas*, no. 18.

Catholic teaching has always allowed for a multiplicity of means for designating which individuals will exercise, as viceroy for Christ the King, his sovereignty in a particular country or territory. The designation of the one to hold this office can be, and has been, by hereditary succession, election by a group of hereditary electors or by the entire people as a whole (as is currently the practice in America today). The most appropriate means of designating the one who holds the office of exercising Christ's sovereignty are a subject for legitimate debate among Catholics—and the Church has always allowed such debate to occur unencumbered. What is not up for debate is the proposition that he who is designated receives the authority to govern—sovereignty—from those who selected him. The only sovereign—he who has a right to rule—is Christ. Therefore, he is the only one with the power to confer a portion of his unlimited sovereignty to particular political leaders. Leo XIII explained brilliantly in his encyclical *Immortale Dei* the reasons for Christ's unique claim to universal sovereignty. Christ's claim is twofold. First, by his divine nature, as creator and sustainer of the whole universe, he is sovereign by right. If he is the only one bringing the universe into being and maintaining it from slipping into nothingness, Christ as God has the sole claim to be sovereign of that which he keeps in existence. Secondly, Christ in his human nature has merited to be sovereign of the whole world by the act of his redemption. Christ's passion and death saved and redeemed the entire world. As the Savior of the world, without whom the world could only promise death, Christ is entitled to his position as Sovereign of the world. For this reason St. Paul declares: "That in the name of Jesus every knee should bow, of those that are in heaven, on earth, and under the earth" (Phil. 2:10). Presidents or kings or prime ministers may exercise governing powers after their designation by some or all of the people, but one truth remains: these powers come not from those designating them but from Christ the King. To hold otherwise, to claim a sovereignty coming from the people is tantamount to refusing to bow one's knee to Christ.

Woods appears throughout his book to be steeped in the Enlightenment rejection of this Catholic understanding of sovereignty. He speaks repeatedly of sovereignty coming not from Christ but from the states or the people. Woods spends the entire fourth chapter of his book arguing vigorously that the US government received its authority "from an agreement among states and the various peoples thereof" rather than "from a single sovereign people."[19] Regardless of whether his historical argument is correct about which of these constitutional theories was held by early Americans, it is a distinction without a difference. The government of the United States derives its authority neither from the states and peoples nor from a single sovereign people, but from Christ the King, the one, true, and only sovereign. Woods's entire constitutional law theory, from which he derives the nullification remedy, is rooted in the false contractual or compact theory of government taught by Grotius, Hobbes, Locke, and their fellow travelers.

Catholic teaching, which perfected Aristotelian natural philosophy, has always held that government is not a product of some humanly created contract in the false political creation story invented in the eighteenth century. Political authority is part of the natural social order created by God in the Garden of Eden, not by man in the jungle of the state of nature. Man is by nature a social and political animal, as even Aristotle could see. Political authority is not some haggled-over concession by "naturally free" men as a necessary evil. It is part of God's plan.

As Pius XI noted almost a hundred years ago, the theory of the contractarian "sovereignty of the people" is why the world is "tottering to its fall."[20] Thus, nullification, whose justification lies in this false notion of political sovereignty, cannot be the cure to our woes since its use involves acceptance of an unCatholic political philosophy.

The Need for Higher Law

Woods's final plea for nullification consists in the question: What alternative exists? He plays on the fact that Catholics and non-Catholics alike in increasing numbers are realizing that our government is spiraling out of control. He advises, as the only alternative, a

19. *Nullification*, 88.
20. Pius IX, *Quas Primas*, no. 18.

return to the original principles that set us on this spiral course: popular sovereignty and contractual government. But there is another alternative, Mr. Woods: the constant teaching of the Catholic Church.

According to the Church, the check on tyrannical and oppressive government that Woods wants to find in state nullification is not some Newtonian gravitational system of contracting agents competing with the federal government for power. It is the entire legal order created by God—the eternal, natural, and divine laws, which, as St. Thomas demonstrates in the *Summa Theologica*, are real laws binding on all men, including those who govern civil society.[21] All human law is subject to and restrained by these higher laws.[22]

Suffice it to say that this higher law was the bulwark against tyranny, oppression, and injustice until the Protestant revolutionaries and their Enlightenment offspring discredited and dismantled it and argued for the substitution of a contractual government of competing interests and "separated powers" that Woods embraces as the answer to our self-inflicted woes. John Dickinson summarizes the role of this higher law in his introduction to the classic twelfth-century Catholic political work, *The Policraticus*:

> It has become a historical commonplace that mediaeval thought was dominated by the conception of a body of law existing independently of the authority of any government and to which all positive law must conform and to which government no less than individuals owed obedience. Rulers were thought of as bound by a higher law . . . which accordingly made it possible to apply to their acts another criterion of legality or illegality. In the words of the *Policraticus*, "between a tyrant and the true prince there is this single or chief difference: that the latter obeys the law and rules the people by its dictates. A tyrant is one who oppresses the people by rulership based upon force while he who rules in accordance with

21. Aquinas, *Summa*, I–II, Q. 90, et seq.

22. See Brian M. McCall, "The Architecture of Law: Building Law on a Solid Foundation: The Eternal and Natural Law," *Vera Lex* 10 (2009): 47; Brian M. McCall, "Consulting the Architect when Problems Arise: The Divine Law," *Georgetown Journal of Law and Public Policy* 9 (2011): 103. I plan to integrate these articles into a comprehensive treatment of the Catholic understanding of law.

> the laws is a prince." "There are certain precepts of the law which have a perpetual necessity having the force of law among all nations.... And not only do I withdraw from the hands of rulers the power of dispensing with the law, but in my opinion those laws which carry a perpetual injunction are not subject at all to their pleasure."[23]

It was the "conception of a higher law" in Christendom that "tended to retard the organization of effective government,"[24] not some populist appeal to a contractual document like the Constitution under the false notion of a sovereignty derived from the people.

It is the appeal to the higher law in which real nullification of evil human laws consists, not in the notion of nullification by contracting states or peoples. True nullification of invalid laws is not a product of Thomas Jefferson, James Madison, or the Virginia and Kentucky resolutions. It is the product, rather, of Catholic teaching on true liberty. Saint Thomas Aquinas provides a concise explanation of *Catholic* nullification—which, incidentally, is referenced nowhere in Woods's book:

> [L]aws may be unjust in two ways: first, by being contrary to human good, through being opposed to the things mentioned above—either in respect of the end, as when an authority imposes on his subjects burdensome laws, conducive, not to the common good, but rather to his own cupidity or vainglory—or in respect of the author, as when a man makes a law that goes beyond the power committed to him or in respect of the form, as when burdens are imposed unequally on the community, although with a view to the common good. The like are acts of violence rather than laws; because, as Augustine says (De Lib. Arb. i, 5), "*a* law *that is not* just, *seems to be no* law *at all*." Wherefore such laws do not bind in conscience, except perhaps in order to avoid scandal or disturbance, for which cause a man should even yield his right, according to Matthew: "If a man ... take away thy coat, let go thy cloak also unto him; and whosoever will force thee one mile, go with him other two...."

23. Dickinson, *The Statesman's Book of John of Salisbury*, xxviii.
24. Ibid.

> Secondly, laws may be unjust through being opposed to the Divine good: such are the laws of tyrants inducing to idolatry, or to anything else contrary to the Divine law: *and laws of this kind must nowise be observed*, because, as stated in Acts, "we ought to obey God rather than man."[25]

This is the true statement of the grounds for nullification of human law, misquoted by Woods, as mentioned above. It is not that a law contrary to the *Constitution* is no law at all, but rather that a law *contrary to the higher law*—which establishes the good and ends of man—is no law at all. The test of legality or illegality (nullification) is not the varying interpretations of a piece of paper haggled over in Philadelphia more than 200 years ago, but the higher laws of God: eternal, divine, and natural. Nullification occurs when a political ruler exceeds the sovereign power committed to him *by God*, not the interpretation of the power committed to him by men either in convention in Philadelphia or in the most recent election.

We do not have time to explore this teaching in detail here, but at least note that St. Thomas's teaching on nullification is laced with Catholic prudence. Even when a ruler exceeds the power committed to him by God, nullification is not always justified. It involves a complex moral decision depending on what aspect of higher law has been violated in light of the common good. Yet when human law violates a fundamental precept of divine law—like the Fifth Commandment ("Thou shalt not kill") by abortion laws—it must be deemed nullified and must in nowise be observed. This is true nullification in the Catholic sense.

The Majoritarian Fallacy

The omission of Catholic grounds for nullification and the substitution of a compact theory of government ultimately lead Woods to fall into the majoritarian fallacy. This consists in relying on public opinion, or majority opinion, to determine what is right or legal. Once the objective standard of the higher law is abrogated in favor of a negotiated contractual relationship embodied in a documentary work of human hands, subjectivity is ultimately the result.

25. Aquinas, *Summa*, I–II, Q. 96, art. 4 (emphasis added).

Notwithstanding Woods's protestations that nullification is not simply the states refusing to enforce "laws the states do not like,"[26] that is exactly what nullification turns into without the objective standard of the higher law. The Constitution is *not* an objective standard. It is an ambiguous statement of a political compromise achieved through ambiguous generalities and concepts that work in tension with one another—again just as we see in certain of the Vatican II documents. Since the constitutional standard of the meaning of the contracting parties is itself open-ended and subjective, all that is left as a standard for nullification is majority opinion.

And that, indeed, is precisely where Woods's argument ends up. He writes, "Are we surprised when a government on this scale, so remote from popular control and oversight, routinely acts in such open defiance of *public opinion*?"[27] The history of the Kentucky and Virginia Resolutions that Woods expertly summarizes in his book demonstrates the very point. A number of states did not support the nullification of the Alien and Sedition Acts by Virginia and Kentucky because they did not think those acts violated the Constitution. This very example of nullification demonstrates that the only standard for determining constitutionality for nullification purposes *is public opinion in each state* as to the interpretation of a humanly crafted document. Nullification as proposed by Woods is a slave to majority opinion.

This fatal defect in Woods's case is brought home by his own recent answer to a question on a radio show discussing his book.[28] A caller inquired whether nullification should be used to put an end to the unjust and tyrannical decision in *Roe v. Wade* without reference to popular opinion:

> Do you believe that state officials, governors for instance, should interpose themselves between the US Supreme Court and the unborn? And the second part is: Do you think it should be necessary for there to be some sort of groundswell in order for a governor to do that? In other words, should he stick his finger up in the

26. *Nullification*, 16.
27. Ibid., 18.
28. Kerby Anderson's "Point of View," Monday, July 19, 2010.

> wind and make sure he has popular support before he defends the unborn, or should he go ahead and place himself between an unjust, tyrannical law and the unborn regardless of his popular support?

Here is Woods's reply:

> Uh, here we have to distinguish between, uh, you know, between, what's morally right and what's likely to work. Because I mean, I could, I could try all kinds of things that would just wind me up in jail and accomplish nothing. So, the point is that I wanna' think about what is likely to work. Now, of course, morally I believe a governor or anyone who is in the government, any human being, oughta' stand up in between the federal government and *Roe v. Wade*. I, I absolutely believe that because it's morally wrong, and we have to obey God rather than men. So, there's no question there's a moral obligation to do this. The reason I would be concerned about using nullification for this purpose is not that I doubt the moral rectitude of that position—not at all. But it would be this: that nullification has really only started to be talked about really in the past year, and we've got a big uphill battle just to get this concept accepted as it is. So if we were to come out swinging with probably the most controversial issue in America, I'm afraid it would take nullification down with it and we would be no better off than we were before. I would rather ease into this by starting with areas in which there is a *general consensus* that the federal government has overreached, so that if we get to a point where nullification becomes an acceptable part of the constitutional landscape, then we can stick our necks out a little more and move into areas where there's gonna' be more controversy. But as I say, because nullification itself is a source of controversy, I think we need to be more modest about what we can expect from it, and then perhaps try more conventional approaches with more intractable issues like abortion.[29]

It is hard to think of human law today more opposed to the divine law than *Roe v. Wade* and all the statutory laws flowing from it. Should these be nullified as "no law at all" and declared the "acts of violence" they really are? Not according to Woods, who says its "too

29. Ibid.

controversial" and not part of the "general consensus." In other words, he is personally morally opposed to abortion, but only willing to use nullification for causes everyone can agree on—like legalizing marijuana or preventing the government from issuing real IDs. Meanwhile, the slaughter of the unborn continues, because, according to the Woods, that "issue" is "intractable."

Do not misinterpret my argument. I am absolutely no supporter of Barack Obama or George Bush or Nancy Pelosi or any of the other rulers of our country, who, drunk on the intoxicating idea that sovereignty comes from people, have been overreaching their authority delegated from God and pushing our nation ever further on the path of destruction. A whole host of statutes, regulations and court decisions range, in their errors, from flagrant violations of the divine and natural law to poorly thought out, wasteful, and imprudent. The solution, however, is not to nullify whatever law for which we can muster a general consensus in favor of nullification. The answer is the same as it has been since the tyranny of liberalism first reared its ugly head: perennial Catholic legal and political teaching.

Our faith in the illusory "original intent" behind a piece of paper written by deistic and anti-Catholic liberals in 1789 needs to give way to our submission to the true Sovereign: Christ the King. Until the political authorities of our country renounce the idea that their power originates in the people and acknowledge the sovereignty of God, including *his* nullification of their unjust laws, the American regime will continue to go, as Woods puts it, "haywire." Resorting to a compact theory borrowed from the toolkit of Enlightenment liberalism is like treating a heart attack victim with Band Aids.

So let's dispense with nullification—the latest liberal cure for liberal ills. Let us instead recognize for what it is the ungodly legal and political order that has weighed for too long on the Western world. Let us call on our nation to take up instead the easy yoke of Christ the King. "What is the alternative to nullification?" Woods might ask. Here is the answer from Pope Pius XI—and it is the *only* answer that can save us now:

> Thus the empire of our Redeemer embraces all men. To use the words of Our immortal predecessor, Pope Leo XIII: "His empire

> includes not only Catholic nations, not only baptized persons who, though of right belonging to the Church, have been led astray by error, or have been cut off from her by schism, but also all those who are outside the Christian faith; so that truly the whole of mankind is subject to the power of Jesus Christ." [*Annum Sacrum*, May 25, 1899]. Nor is there any difference in this matter between the individual and the family or the State; for all men, whether collectively or individually, are under the dominion of Christ. In him is the salvation of the individual, in him is the salvation of society. "Neither is there salvation in any other, for there is no other name under Heaven given to men whereby we must be saved" (Acts 4:12). He is the author of happiness and true prosperity for every man and for every nation.... *If, therefore, the rulers of nations wish to preserve their authority, to promote and increase the prosperity of their countries, they will not neglect the public duty of reverence and obedience to the rule of Christ.*[30]

God Save the King!

If Christ is King, are all obliged to institute a monarchy as a form of government? Often those proclaiming and defending the Church's doctrine on Christ the King are heckled with the name "monarchists," a term that has for some become synonymous with un-American. What is the relationship, if any, between Catholic political philosophy and monarchy?

To begin, we have to define some terms. Often this discussion is short-circuited by people using the term "monarchy" to mean different things. As I use the term, it merely means a form of government where some or all of the governing authority is vested in a single person (monarch) who rules the kingdom for the remainder of his natural life or abdication (i.e., he is not subject to constant elections). Often the term is conflated with a hereditary right of succession or the principle of inheritance known as primogeniture. These aspects of transmission of authority may be coupled with a monarchy in particular periods of history but are not essential to its definition. The Holy Father is a monarch, but his position is not inherited but obtained by election through the College of Cardinals.

30. Pius XI, *Quas Primas*, no. 18.

The Holy Roman Emperor was elected by a collection of German princes (although for many centuries it became customary for the electors to make their choice from one particular family, the Hapsburgs, but without necessarily being bound to primogeniture). Abbots and abbesses are monarchs elected by their communities. Some monarchies have been hereditary (for example the kings of France and England, etc.). What is important to note is that some people's purported objection to monarchy is actually an objection to hereditary succession, which is really a separate and distinct issue.

Now that we have established that a monarchy need not involve inheritance, we can turn directly to Catholic political philosophy. Catholic thought in this area does not judge a particular governing system merely on the form of government employed. Rather, the touchstone of Catholic political philosophy is the common good. The essential test of any system is whether or not the governing authorities govern the civil society in accordance with the common good or only a private good. The concept of the common good is a rich philosophical topic that could occupy, and has occupied, entire books. For our purposes, I merely wish to note that both elements of the term are essential to its definition. First, the government must in its legislative, executive, and judicial acts really be pursuing something that constitutes a "good." Saint Thomas defines the "good" as "that which all things desire."[31] A "good" is a perfection of something's nature, an end that it seeks. Thus, knowledge of God, knowledge of Truth, procreation and rearing of children, preservation of life and beauty are all examples of "good."

Secondly, the good must be common to the members of the community as opposed to merely oriented towards the personal good of the ruler. A ruler who pursues the increase of knowledge among the people of his kingdom pursues the common good. A ruler who pursues public policies that merely increase his own personal wealth pursues a personal good. The common good can thus be seen as being in opposition to both a mere personal good and an evil.

With this framework we can see how Catholic philosophers such as St. Thomas categorized different forms of government not only

31. *Summa Theologica*, I Q. 5, Art. 4.

by the method of governing but also by the type of end pursued by the ruler. Thus, when a community is ruled by one person who pursues the common good of the community, it is called a monarchy. When the one ruler pursues his own personal good or an evil, it is called a tyranny. A community ruled by a small group of virtuous men pursuing the common good is called an aristocracy. A community ruled by a small group of powerful men pursuing their own personal good (personal wealth or power) or ends constituting evil (such as unjust conquests) rather than the common good is called an oligarchy. A community ruled by many of the members of the community who govern the community in the interest of the common good is called a polity, whereas a government run by the many that pursues evil ends (such as debauchery or depravity or economic injustice) is called democracy. Obviously as with many categorizations, actual communities can exhibit aspects of several of the above descriptions. Just as with personality types, a person may have a dominant character but still have some elements of the other characters (in their good or bad aspects).

To help make the discussion more concrete I will give some examples of communities that have exhibited primarily one of these forms. A monarchy would be France under the reign of St. Louis as he pursued the common good and primarily ruled France by his own authority. A tyranny would be Henry VIII, for he pursued not only private goods (mostly of sensuality) but also evil, heresy, and schism. Although the English parliament existed, it played little role other than rubber stamping the will of Henry (likely out of fear of the scaffold). An aristocracy could be seen in some periods of ancient Israel when it was ruled by a council of elders. At the time of Our Lord, it was essentially an oligarchy (in Judah at least where Herod had no power) ruled by the powerful Sanhedrin, which worked against the common good of salvation brought by the Messiah, our Lord, as well as pursuing their own personal good of maintaining wealth and power. An example close to a polity would be some periods of the Roman Republic where the city was governed by representatives of the patricians in the Senate and the plebeians through plebiscites and tribunes and when their policies pursued the common good of the Roman city. An example of a perversion of polity—democracy—would be contemporary America. We are ruled by vast numbers of people; look at the size of the federal government alone. Our government promotes common vice not virtue (I think I need not rattle off the list of these) and a staggeringly large proportion of those in power govern for their own personal good—wealth and power (again I think it unnecessary to name names).

Now since any of the three forms of organization (one, few, and many) possess the potential to be (and throughout different points in history, have in actuality been) oriented either to the common good or to its perversion, none of the three can be declared *per se* the only or best form. In this sense, the Church has never said that a community is obligated to establish a monarchy or aristocracy or a polity in the same sense that she has required every community to acknowledge Christ the King. Catholic perfection of a civil community is possible, in theory, under any of the three. At the same time, the Church throughout history has certainly shown a tendency to favor monarchy. This can be seen both in the realm of ideas and in the realm of praxis. First, thinkers like Aquinas argue that although virtue is possible in any of the three forms, if a choice is possible, monarchy is preferable. Several reasons can be given. First, it has the potential to be more effective in promoting the common good because a monarchy by its nature is more capable of unified and coherent action. With one ruler the will of the ruling authority possesses a greater degree of unity (although not perfect, as the human will suffers from the effects of original sin, one of which is inconstancy). A monarch who governs oriented to the common good has greater potential to do so more effectively than a group of people requiring coordination. Yet, as St. Thomas points out, this very effectiveness can lead to the perversion of monarchy: tyranny. A tyranny is more effective in pursuing an antithesis of the common good. Thus, monarchy is capable of being the best but also one of the most dangerous forms of government.

Beyond effectiveness in pursuing the common good, monarchy as a government of unity tends to accord more to the supernatural order established by God. One God rules the visible and invisible worlds and a monarchy more perfectly reflects this order. One might object that this one God contains three divine Persons, which is more akin to aristocracy; but if we consider the matter, the Trinity is more like a human monarchy. The Trinity, despite being comprised of really distinct Persons, possesses a complete unity of attributes, perfections, desire, will, and purpose. Such unity on the human level is not possible and more similar to a single person.

On the level of praxis, a plenitude of prayers of the Church (before the Bugnini "Wreckovation" of the liturgy) echo images and vocabulary of monarchy. Again, in the interests of time, I will not prove this assertion with detailed examples. Anyone following a Traditional Mass Missal for any period of time should see this as obvious. I will just note that before the Americanist-leaning Abp. Carroll penned his novel prayer for the generic term "government" in the early nineteenth century, it was for centuries customary after a High Mass to chant a "Prayer for the King [or Queen]," the *Domine Salvam Fac.*

Such considerations have led many Catholic thinkers (including in one place St. Thomas) to consider that although monarchy represents in theory the best choice, it may be prudent to temper this form with elements of the others as a safeguard against a potential tyranny. With some role in governing for the virtuous few and the common citizens, the ability of a future tyrant may be restrained. This precaution comes with a price. A true monarch may be less effective in realizing the common good than he otherwise would have been.

Some contemporary thinkers have latched onto this idea of a tempered form of government (or what St. Thomas calls in one place a mixed form) as justification for (or even explanation of) the American constitutional system. Such a comparison is inaccurate on many levels. Most importantly, the idea of a monarchy in a government is much more than a central executive figure such as a president. One of the benefits of a monarch is that his governing power is more obviously seen as proceeding from God. He is not beholden to an electoral cycle or constant change of office. One of the main roles a monarch can play in a mixed form of government is to be a conscience standing outside the realm of electoral politics who can act as a guardian of the divine and natural law when the few or the many may attempt to pervert the common good. The presidency of the United States is not and has never been a monarchy thus understood. America may at some point in its history been close to an aristocracy or a polity (although personally I think it has mostly been an oligarchy or a democracy), but it has never been a monarchy in any way. That does not mean the United States has a unique place in history among governments opposed to the common good. History is littered with many tyrannies, oligarchies, and democracies. Yet the United States constitutional system is also not the utopian and mystical perfect form of government that many Americans, including some traditional Catholics, pretend it to be.

Recognizing that the United States is not a real mixed form of government (as there is no element of monarchy present), a reaction that anything in praise of monarchy is un-American may not be an inaccurate statement. Yet a visceral reaction against monarchy is certainly un-Catholic. First, as we have seen, the Church has held all three forms (monarchy, aristocracy, and polity) to be acceptable forms of government. Secondly, for almost all of its history, the Church has exhibited in thought and words a preference for monarchy, although particular circumstances have not always made it possible or even prudentially advisable. I did not set out in this chapter to unveil a plan for reformulating the US governmental system along Catholic lines. I do believe it needs serious reforming as we have long toiled under a government not oriented to the common good. My more modest objective was to argue first that a government oriented to the common good is the most important priority in any such reconstitution, and secondly to argue that monarchy should not be jettisoned from the table as unacceptable *per se*. What is certainly clear is that the standard of the common good needs to be the prominent litmus test of any government, whether a monarchy or not. On this litmus test, the United States has for a long time not measured up to that standard. For this reason we need to implore *Christus Rex, miserere et salva nos!*

The Final Curtain: Exit Stage Left, Grand Duke Henri of Luxembourg

In the prior chapter we considered the position of monarchy within Catholic political thought. One benefit of a monarch not subject to electoral politics was identified as the ability to serve as a fixed conscience for the political community. When electoral winds blow in favor of policies or laws contrary to the divine or natural law, the monarch has the ability to rise above the tempest and defend hard truths. Such a role is why revolutionaries universally seek to do away with monarchs. They are an obstacle to shortcutting the divine and natural law.

The last act of the French Revolution came to a close on March 12, 2009, but hardly anyone was watching. The demonic forces unleashed more than 200 years ago took on the aim of destroying all monarchial authority in Europe. The rulers of the once Christian nations of Europe, or at least their governing authority, had all been executed, except for the tiny nation of Luxembourg. On March 12, without much fanfare, the parliament of the Grand Duchy of Luxembourg voted to end government of their small nation by the Grand Duke.

Luxembourg was the last European nation to be governed by a real monarch—not just a figurehead but a monarch who could actually govern. Although the tiny nation has had a parliamentary chamber, that body functioned as parliaments were originally designed to function. It was an advisory body to the Grand Duke. After the Chamber of Deputies voted on new legislation, Article 34 of the Constitution stated, "The Grand Duke sanctions and promulgates the laws. He makes his resolve known within three months of the vote in the Chamber." This provision permitted the Grand Duke to perform the proper function of a monarch in a mixed form of government. He served as a check on the potential excesses of political parties legislating when they encroached on the principles of the natural law. As a hereditary ruler for life, the Grand Duke is immune from elector politics. He can thus serve as an outside supervisor of the results of the legislative process. This is exactly what he did last year in an act that precipitated the March 12 vote.

In 2008, the Chamber of Deputies voted to approve a law that authorized the intentional killing of human beings, commonly referred to by its morbid proponents as euthanasia. Such a law is contrary to the natural law. For, as St. Thomas observed in his

Summa, the civil law cannot always punish everything that the natural law forbids, but it may never sanction such evil. Now we know both by reason and divine authority that euthanasia is prescribed. It violates the first principle of the natural law: self-preservation. The Church has confirmed this deduction of reason on several occasions by pronouncing euthanasia to be immoral. Even the *sensus Catholicus* of this overwhelming Catholic nation was clear; the populace of Luxembourg opposed the bill pushed through by the Socialist and Green parties.

Henri, the current Grand Duke, fulfilled his moral obligation as a good Catholic monarch and refused to sanction this evil legislative act. As a reward for doing the right thing, the so-called "conservative" Prime Minister, Jean-Claude Juncker, called for an amendment to the Constitution stripping the Grand Duke of his authority to sanction laws passed by the Chamber of Deputies. The March 12 vote approved the removal of the word "sanctions" from Article 34. Prime Minister Juncker made clear the intention was to remove the right of the Grand Duke to approve of or reject laws. According to Juncker, he must be required to promulgate all acts passed by the Chamber. The Luxembourg monarchy has thus entered the realm of Walt Disney monarchs inhabited by the remaining figureheads of Europe such as England, Spain, and Belgium. They can parade around for tourists in quaint costumes and live in nice palaces, but they have no authority to protect and defend their nation by governing it.

The old sly tactics of the spirit of liberalism were visible in the way this final act unfolded. The press and politicians called the Grand Duke's prevention of this immoral euthanasia legislation a "constitutional crisis." Now a constitutional crisis occurs when an official violates the norms and rules constituting the mode of government of a civil society. In this case the Grand Duke did not violate a single provision of the existing written constitution. He merely exercised his legitimate and rightful authority to withhold his sanction from a proposed civil law contrary to the natural law. And the reaction of liberalism to the exercise of his legitimate right—strip him of that right! Liberalism has always been willing to grant freedom and rights so long as the recipients only exercise that freedom in accordance with the wishes of liberalism. Post-French Revolutionary liberalism claims to stand for the "rule of law," a phrase that purports to mean that rules are not to be changed merely to reach a desired outcome. The established rules of the game, liberalism claims, are sacrosanct. In reality, the rules are changed whenever liberalism does not get its way. Like a spoiled child, it picks up its toys, which it previously claimed to have given away, and goes home. A few years ago after several nations clearly voted to reject the proposed European Constitution, the forces of liberalism decided that the right to vote on the proposed Constitution was no longer necessary. The Constitution was repackaged as a treaty needing only the approval of the governments of the member states, not a vote of the population at large. Ireland stood as the only exception and allowed the Irish people to vote, and they said no. Even this vote did not stop the forces of Liberalism, who vowed to find another way. Likewise, when Grand Duke Henri uses his legal right to withhold his sanction from a law, the right he thought liberalism had conceded to his ancestors in the modern constitution is seen for the illusion it is. He has the right for only as long as he does not actually use it.

This pattern of give and take rights is as old as the French Revolution, which began by proclaiming liberty for all and then proceeded to guillotine those who did not use that liberty in the way the Committee for Public Safety thought they should (i.e., by apostatizing from the Faith). Liberalism means the right to be liberal (as defined and redefined by the reigning generation of liberals).

Fortunately for Grand Duke Henri, his confrontation with the old enemy cost him only his legitimate governing authority and not his head. Some liberals have at least learned that the messy business of liberally severing heads always seems to turn on them, literally. Still, the Grand Duke is to be commended for his fortitude. One can only imagine the subtle voices of temptation that were poured into his ears by the Machiavellian politicos. "Just sanction the euthanasia law and avoid a 'constitutional crisis' and conserve your rights"; "You can compromise by expressing your personal disapproval but still promulgate the bill as the 'will of the legislature'"; "This is not an issue worth losing your privileges and rights over." But Grand

Duke Henri's Catholic conscience was too well formed for these deceits. He refused and was duly reprimanded. Again, in an absurdity of contradiction, the new "liberal" Article 34 will prevent the Grand Duke from acting in accordance with his conscience. Its terms require him to promulgate all laws, even those that violate his well-formed conscience—so much for "freedom of conscience"!

In lieu of tossing flowers to the Grand Duke as he makes his final bow on the decaying ruins of the theater of Christendom, I suggest readers instead offer a rosary for his Highness that God, whose divine law leaves no good deed unrewarded and no evil deed unpunished, will bless him for his courage. While you are doing that, perhaps you can utter a prayer for the tiny population of Luxembourg who are now defenseless against the enactment of euthanasia laws and all the other gruesome ordinances of twenty-first-century liberalism. These will all be possible now despite the will of their Grand Duke and even, as in this case, even their own overwhelming sentiments. *Libera nos ab potestate tyrannico liberalismi, Christus Rex.*

Big Brother Is Recording: Some Reflections from Within Our Made-in-China Cage

All authority has been swept away in the name of liberty. Yet this liberty bought at the price of so many wars since the eighteenth century has turned out to be an illusion. We live under more restriction and regulation and constraint than a medieval peasant could even imagine possible. We all seem aware of the massive expansion of government control over our lives. Big Brother is everywhere. Government operatives are manhandling us in the airport or taking pictures of us (which despite early denials TSA now admits can be saved). Our phone and email conversations are constantly monitored and recorded. Computer programs pore over our recorded conversations with algorithms to detect "suspicious behavior." As we drive about doing our Christmas shopping, we are likely being recorded by omnipresent cameras on street corners, in stores, schools, and offices. Some cities have cameras on every intersection. Banks, brokers, and other financial intermediaries have become outsourced government informants with a dizzying array of "reporting obligations." Try to cash a check over a certain level, buy some gold, wire some money with Western Union, and the details of your transaction are required under severe sanctions to be reported to Big Brother, to be filed away for use against you whenever the time seems expedient. Every tyrant from Nero to Diocletian to Robespierre to Napoleon to Hitler could not have imagined amassing so much information about the general populace to be even within the realm of fantasy. Raise factual questions about privileged "historical" events or quote unpopular condemnations from the Bible, and you might be hauled off to jail for "hate speech" by the thought police. The myth of the "Land of the Free" is fading faster than the daylight in this darkest time of the year. Rather, we are the "Land of the Monitored."

Ironically, as our publicly supervised day care (commonly called public schools—another method of Big Brother control) drones on about the oppression of the serfs during the big bad "Dark Ages," we blithely go about enduring a level of control and supervision that would have been unimaginable to any "serf" across Europe for centuries. It was easier for a serf to obtain his severance from the land (not that most even wanted to do this) by remaining in a town for a year and a day, than for any of us to be severed from the surveillance and control mechanisms of the modern state. There are no "free towns" to hide out in for a year and a day! The government has annexed them all. The consolation for our modern imprisonment is that we are consigned to a gilded cage. Don't get too excited, for it is a cage gilded with gold-colored plastic covered with lead-based paint made in China. So what do the jailors want us to do? Play with all the gadgets and gizmos you want. They do not care which you choose; they are monitoring all of them just in case you utter some newly defined "hate" speech. Eat the soy bean, high fructose food of your choice selected from among the different artificially colored varieties imported from China and graciously permitted to be consumed by the Food Police (the FDA). But don't reach your hand out of your cage to buy some real food—cheese made from a cow next door that has not had his fix of vaccines—and you might just find yourself fined or thrown in a prison whose bars you can see. You are also free to choose your own healthcare from among the preapproved options selected for you by the government or its outsourced healthcare regulatory partner, the insurance companies. If you want to travel out of the country, you are free to do so if you can get a government-issued passport and visa (documents that were non-existent in those oppressive "Dark Ages"). Of course even with these you might be quarantined at the airport by the TSA. If you want to expatriate out of the gilded cage and find some (actually non-existent) part of the planet where you can have some unsupervised liberty, like hunting an animal to feed your family any time of the year, you are pretty much stuck with your US citizenship (or at least the cost of it—federal taxes). That is just how things work here in the Land of the Free!

As we survey our electronic and paper prison, can we identify the philosophical source of the tyranny to which we have become numbly indifferent due to its omnipresence? It lies in a rejection of a Catholic understanding of civil society and the laws it creates. Traditionally, civil society was considered one of two self-contained societies, the other being the Church. The end of civil society is the peaceful and orderly attainment of man's natural end: natural happiness. Natural happiness consists in the fulfillment of the natural ends of man, which can be summarized as the preservation of life, the procreation and education of new life, and the pursuit of knowledge and wisdom in a social community. The end of the Church is the salvation of men by attainment of the Beatific Vision. Although both are self-contained in that they each have their own ultimate end and their own self-contained means to that end, there should be no wall between them but rather a porous membrane. The civil society's end is subordinated to that of the Church, since her end is supernatural. By subordinated, I do not mean unimportant but merely a lower plane, the natural. The civil society and Church are meant to pursue their own ends in tandem. The idea of a conflict between them is rare since the natural end of man is encompassed within his supernatural end. The pursuit of life, families, knowledge, and social communion all are consistent with and in fact oriented towards the ultimate end. A conflict only arises when we try to make one of these natural ends an ultimate end in itself. In such a conflict the supernatural must be reasserted over the natural.

This cosmological view puts a dramatic limit on the expansion of the governing authorities of the civil society. Government is not a necessary evil as the Enlightenment liberals proclaim. It is a necessary part of the fulfillment of man's social nature. Yet the activities and scope of government action are limited, not by some written constitution, but by the supernatural end of the supernatural society, the Church. Governments do not have free reign over the governed, body and soul. The body and soul can and should be guided towards natural virtue, but all attempts in this area should be subordinated to the Church and its supernatural end.

Remove the governing authorities of the Church as the other sun in the universe (to use an image from Dante) and the only remaining institution, civil government, will expand like a gas to fill the vacuum left in the universe. The separation of Church and state really means the relegation of the Church to a secondary and subordinate association within the state, with her light blotted out. This ultimately removes any check on the domain of the state. Once this "wall of separation" (to use Thomas Jefferson's phrase) went up and quarantined the Church in its little walled cage, the road to our current prison was chosen.

The other limit on oppressive government expansion in the Age of Faith was the hierarchy of law. Human-made laws (whether made by a legislator in Church or state) were on the bottom rung of this hierarchy. All human laws were subject to the higher laws, the eternal law, the natural law, and the divine law. Each of these higher laws carved off a limited jurisdiction for human law to make necessary determinations for practical human decisions. Yet this jurisdiction was not plenary; it was limited by the universal jurisdiction of these higher forms of law.

In summary, the eternal law is God's providential plan for the universe and all creatures. Eternal law establishes the particular end of each creature by integrating its end into the end of the universe, God himself. The natural law is the rational participation of man in this eternal law. The natural law consists of the principles of reason that can be deduced from the nature of man as created by God. Finally, the divine law represents specific principles and rules revealed by God that either make clear the contents of the natural law or supplement the natural law with material beyond its scope, rules relating exclusively to the supernatural end of man.

The scope of human lawmaking authority is limited by all these forms of higher law. A human law that violates any of these is "no law at all" (to quote St. Augustine and St. Thomas), but rather a violence done to law. One of the principles of natural law consistently identified by the Catholic jurists (see Gratian's *Decretum*, for example) is the "common liberty of all men." In essence, this principle establishes that as a rational creature, man must be at *liberty to pursue his natural and supernatural ends.* Note this was never understood as a liberty to do as one chose or to do evil. It was liberty to pursue the end of man established by the eternal law. A bloated, tyrannical Big Brother state violates this end of man. Human laws were in the Age of Faith (which we might call the Age of Liberty) subject to judicial review of a very different sort from what we have today. Today our mountains of human laws are only reviewable in light of themselves. The Constitution is itself a human-made law. Thus, the ultimate law recognized by our legal system is still the bottom tier of law: human-made law. We entrust judges to review the laws we make by the very standards we make and change at will for ourselves. Is it any wonder our government has grown without any serious check on the expansion of its power? It is its own keeper.

Even the pagan stoic philosopher Cicero could understand the grave danger of leaving human laws to their own devices. He warned, "the greater the human law, the greater the injury." Yet we have so imbibed the lie that freedom from the Church has meant more liberty that we cannot see the exact opposite has happened. Since the false principles of 1789 have taken hold of the world (and after the Second Vatican Council, the Church), only one thing has had its scope of activity enlarged: secular atheistic (or at its best agnostic) government. The growth of its power and jurisdiction has been at the expense of individual liberty of action. The poorest peasant in rural France of the thirteenth century would likely collapse in horror if he were to be shown the extent of secular government power today. Not brainwashed by the myths of liberals, he would see the bars and balls and chains weighing us down that appear invisible to most due to being trained not to see them. A true student of history would be able to see this contrast.

Modern liberal philosophy withdraws nothing from "the hands of rulers" to make, break, and dissolve any laws they want. The notion of a higher law, says historian John Dickinson, "tended to retard the organization of effective government."[32] Yet with the higher law declared dead and tossed over the wall of separation into the private associations of religions, there is nothing left to retard this growth of effective government. And grown it has—to put shackles on our feet and electronic devices to monitor us. The only power in the universe capable of slaying this man-made Leviathan is the hierarchy of law and its faithful guardian, the Catholic Church. The abdication of her God-given authority in the Vatican II declaration *Dignitatis Humanae* in favor of the revolutionary idea of religious liberty has severe consequences. As simply one of many equally tolerated private religious organizations, the Church poses no real obstacle to the monitoring and controlling of everyone. All the cackling and protesting and whining about the pat-downs and other trappings of the police state are impotent to break the bonds of our chains until we knock down the wall of separation put up by Jefferson and his fellow travelers that keeps our country safely away from our Mother, the Church, the guardian of true liberty.

The Fruits of Poor Political Theory: Case Study, The Unaffordable Care Act, and Obama's Healthcare Debacle

What Is Healthcare Reform?

The flagship issue of the Obama administration's first term was Healthcare Reform. If you are like me, you are probably confused about what was actually done to reform healthcare. Did this legislation change the way healthcare is provided and paid for? Was it reforming regulation of insurance? Is government going to be running the healthcare system? All of these have been asked about this massive law the size of a phone book.

32. Dickinson, *The Statesman's Book of John of Salisbury*, xxx.

The confusion lies beyond the recent legislative activity in the transformation of health insurance. Health insurance has become conflated with paying for healthcare. Insurance describes when many people share a similar risk, the consequences of which are large but of low probability (e.g., a house burning down). If the event occurs, an individual is unable to shoulder the economic consequences, but all sharing the risk could afford collectively to pay for it. Insurance facilitates the transaction. Each person at risk pays a fractional portion of the recovery cost to an insurer that retains these payments (and invests them) until the event occurs. The insurer pays the funds collected to the victim who now can absorb the loss. Thus, no person bears the entire loss.

This is how healthcare insurance started. Most people paid for their ordinary healthcare services. Everyone knew they were at risk for a cataclysmic health event, a serious car accident, a rare and expensive disease. In addition to paying for their routine doctor visits, they paid a small sum to an insurer and were entitled to payment if one of these extraordinary losses occurred.

Insurance companies have long been regulated by government. They are monitored to make sure they retain and prudently invest the premiums pending payment of claims. The contracts they enter into are reviewed for fairness.

In the late twentieth century, health insurance companies gradually migrated their products from true insurance to a method of paying for all forms of healthcare. Americans now pay vast sums each month (often more than $1200) and have all aspects of their healthcare (and not just cataclysmic events) paid for (routine doctor visits and medicines). Whereas payouts from true insurance are rare, we expect to receive routine payouts from healthcare "insurance." We think of our payments more as prepayments of health expenses. Insurance companies are not set up or regulated to deal with this model. Rather than claims being few and far between, they are processed by the thousands each day. Health "insurers" have really become the masters of the health sector, deciding what routine health services should be paid for and when. Tests and treatments must be preauthorized with the guardians of the system. Despite many Americans expressing fears over a government-run healthcare system, what we have now is really not so different. A small group of international conglomerate companies control the provision of health services to most Americans. A transition to the government would merely replace one health czar for another.

Although all the implications of ObamaCare have yet to be seen (it is like a Vatican II document in that it will take years to unpack), I am uncertain it in no way addresses this fundamental reality. The legislation still leaves the legal regime of insurance law regulating what has long ceased to be insurance. Unless this fundamental legal reality is addressed, nothing will really change for the better.

Healthcare and Taxation

There has certainly been much debate about the ObamaCare overhaul. It was considered one of the major causes of the Republican victories in the Congressional elections of 2010. Access to care, death panels, forced coverage of contraceptives have been on the lips of many since the law was first introduced. I wish to focus on only one, and perhaps not the most important aspect of the debate. The healthcare package contains many new or expanded taxes, or as the politicians prefer, revenue increases.

The healthcare legislation marks another stage in a long history of expanding the sources (often obscured) of taxing authority. It is interesting to recall that America is a nation that launched its rebellion against the then existing governing authority in large part over the institution of new taxation. The Stamp Act was a catalyst igniting the Revolution. In terms of size, the amounts were quite modest. A few pennies or shillings had to be paid to make a written legal document valid. Newspapers were taxed about a penny a page. The largest tax was a £10 tax on obtaining a lawyer's license. Who can really object to taxing lawyers!

More than 200 years later, Americans are subject to a dizzying array of taxes (federal income, Social Security, Medicare, estate and gift, customs duties, state income, local property, and sales tax, just to name the most well-known). Now healthcare has introduced a new array of taxes. The Joint Committee on Taxation estimates over the next nine years the legislation will produce an additional $370 billion in revenue. I do not deny that in justice citizens are obligated to bear an equitable share of the costs of administering the civil affairs of government. I also do not deny that something has to be done about the social problems connected to payment for healthcare. Yet I cannot help but ponder the irony that our forefathers rebelled against a lawful government for a tax of mere pennies when we have now become accustomed to paying taxes as a part of every aspect of our lives. Estimates vary widely, but it is probably fair to say that anywhere from a quarter to a half of our annual income goes to pay taxes and government fees of one kind or another. American colonists were paying single-digit percentages of their income in taxes in the time before the Revolution. As far as I can see there is no serious revolution in the offing today as a result of this astronomical increase from the times of King George. Our founders also did not dispute the necessity of taxation; they demanded taxation together with representation. We have obtained representation through a dizzying array of what feels like never-ending campaigns and elections—but what has all this representation produced? More, not less, taxation. I mean more not just in terms of absolute dollars but also in types and manners of taxation. One mistake the English Parliament seems to have made was to make the tax too visible. With every contract, land transfer, or newspaper, a tax was present. Our "parliament" has corrected this mistake by a counterintuitive approach. The more types of taxes and the greater the number of hands reaching for them, the harder it seems to see any one of them. Ask the average American how much he pays in total taxes and he is unlikely to be able even to begin to calculate it. He might be able to tell you his effective federal income tax rate, but this is only a piece of the taxing pie. So a war was fought to end small taxation without representation to replace it with much taxation with representation.

Healthcare and VAT Taxes

The Obama administration's fascination with the post-war socialist initiatives of European countries seems alive and well. Every European country that has adopted a form of national healthcare (as has now happened here) has also adopted a large money-making tax known as a value-added tax (VAT). France obtains over half of its revenue from an approximately 20 percent VAT.

The VAT tax is hidden and disproportionately burdensome to the poor. It is a tax paid by the seller of goods or services on the gross margin of all sales. Non-consumers claim a credit for the amount of VAT already paid through the supply chain. The amount of VAT the retail seller will have to pay is built into the price on the tag in the store, so most consumers are unaware of how much tax they are paying. This is one of the reasons why goods seem to cost so much more in Europe than in America. The price includes a 15 or 25 percent mark-up to cover the seller's VAT liability.

The VAT is oppressive to the poor. It makes the cost of consumption higher. Since poorer people spend a higher percentage of their income (rather than investing), they bear a disproportionate share of the VAT as a portion of their income. For example, assume a 20 percent VAT. A person who earns $200,000 a year and spends half of their income ($100,000) will have paid $20,000 in VAT or 10 percent of their income. A person only earning $50,000 who spends their entire income will have paid $10,000 in VAT or 20 percent of their income. The effective rate on the poor person is double that of the wealthy person! It is obvious that the poorer one is, the higher percentage of his income is spent and not saved.

Remember this VAT tax would be on top of income, Social Security, Medicare, and estate taxes, not to mention state income, property, *and sales taxes.* While living for seven years in England, I realized that almost 70 percent of our income went to taxes (including a 17.5 percent VAT). Most people do not realize this since there is neither a tax return to file nor any addition to the receipt for VAT. People just get used to goods being priced higher than otherwise.

There is nothing original in much of the Obama plan for change. He is just following the play book of the Labor and Socialist-leaning governments of Western Europe in the post-World War II period. First down: establish national health care; second down: pay for it with a VAT.

The idea of a federal VAT was first floated in a PBS interview in October 2011 with House Speaker Pelosi, who said, "Somewhere along the way, a value-added tax plays into this.... Of course, we want to take down the healthcare cost, that's one part of it. But in the scheme of things, I think it's fair to look at a value-added tax as well."

Despite denials by White House aides, during the discussion of the Affordable Care Act, President Obama did not rule out a VAT tax in a CNBC interview but rather indicated it was under consideration.[33]

Healthcare Exchanges

In April 2011, Oklahoma's Governor Mary Fallin made national headlines by reversing her earlier decision to accept $54 million from the federal government made pursuant to ObamaCare. It is certainly possible this reversal of the decision to accept the money was a product of politicking, but there is a core principle of government necessary to the evaluation of such a decision. Subsidiarity is an ancient principle of political philosophy indispensable to a federated, or multi-level, form of government. Yet the principle has become so obscured in our day that the spell check program on my computer does not even recognize it as a correctly spelled word. How far (or low) our governing political philosophy has come in the past few centuries!

The principle of subsidiarity is that the lowest level authority ought to be left by higher orders of authority to make any decisions or perform any actions which it is capable of doing. Put negatively, more remote or higher levels of government should refrain from interfering with the work of lower orders unless the lower order lacks the necessary means to complete the required action. The reason for the principle is simple. Political decisions are prudential matters which need to take account of all the contingent matters relevant to choosing the most prudent course of action. A governing authority of a smaller or lower order within the governing hierarchy will be closer to the facts on the ground and thus more capable of taking them into account in making a prudential decision. The lower order is also better placed to responding to changes in the facts on the ground. Now, some activities involve such vast resources, defending a country's borders for example, that a lower order may not possess the resources to accomplish the task. Only in such circumstances should the higher order intervene.

33. See http://cnsnews.com/news/article/obama-won-t-rule-out-value-added-tax.

Applying these principles to the healthcare insurance exchange Oklahoma is in the process of building, it would seem that the involvement of the federal government with its $54 million dollars and the related regulation and red-tape attached to it seems unnecessary to establish a healthcare insurance exchange. The exchange under construction is an internet based information portal where insurance customers can obtain transparent pricing and other information. It would seem that building a website, albeit a well-designed and complex one, for Oklahomans could be achieved within the fiscal resources of Oklahoma. Put another way I think our state could build a lot more than a website for $54 million! In fact, House Speaker Kris Steele told reporters that it will cost "a whole lot less" than $54 million to build a system for Oklahoma. Rejecting the big fat $54 million carrot seems to be a positive way to resist the federal entanglement that the carrot will bring and leave to those governing Oklahoma the full authority to build a healthcare insurance exchange for Oklahomans. Perhaps, such concerns were not what swayed Governor Fallin, but they should have been.

In the End the Supremes Decide about Obamacare

On November 14, 2012, the Supreme Court announced that it would hear a series of cases challenging the constitutionality of certain aspects of the Obama healthcare law. The French political commentator Alexis de Tocqueville commented, "Scarcely any political question arises in the United States that is not resolved, sooner or later, into a judicial question."[34] His observation is as true today as it was in the early days of the Republic. It also presents a clear example of the double standard of American political philosophy. American rhetoric extols the moral weight of "democratic elections" and "majority votes" while fighting wars to impose these slogans all around the world. As de Tocqueville observed, Americans think votes are fine as long as they agree with the victors. When they do not, they head for the courthouse to use any legal tool to overturn the results of "democratic elections."

34. Alexis de Tocqueville, *Democracy in America*, Bk I, ch. 16. http://www.gutenberg.org/files/815/815-h/815-h.htm.

Let me say up front: Obamacare is wrong. It violates important moral principles. The Supreme Court should have struck it down on many grounds, but none of these were actually argued in the failed attempt. Obamacare is not wrong for the reasons advanced by the plaintiffs in the cases decided by the Supreme Court. These cases are mere political events staged to score points to influence the next "free" election; they are not about moral principles.

The appeal, which was heard in an unusually long oral argument (five and a half hours), combined three cases and a host of legal issues. At the core of the controversy was whether the healthcare law that requires all Americans to buy insurance or face a penalty is constitutional. Twenty-six states joined, at great cost to their taxpayers, claiming that the mandate is outside the power granted to the federal government.

This argument is the old drum beaten by libertarians and others who harbor a fantasized version of American history and law. They spin the myth that the American republic was created as a limited federal government. They desire to contrast this modest limited government with the purported tyrannical government of preRevolutionary England. Yet this limited government tale is nothing more than a myth employed by the Federalists at the time of the drafting, ratification, and adoption of the Constitution to lull the American people into accepting a liberal government of unprecedented power and scope. Within a generation and before the third president had completed his term of office, the federal government had already flexed its constitutional muscles showing its true strength by suppressing the Whiskey Rebellion, authorizing naval attacks in North African seas, and buying the Louisiana Territory from Napoleon. English monarchs would have loved to be conferred the broad enumerated powers showered on the US federal government.

Like a Vatican II document, the Constitution was purposefully laden with time bombs that have been exploded over the past 200 years to increase the power of the government over the lives of Americans. The "Commerce Clause," which featured prominently in the Obamacare decision, is one such time bomb. The clause grants Congress the power to regulate commerce "among the several states," which the Supreme Court has interpreted for almost a century to allow any law that applies to activity that impacts or affects interstate commerce. Notwithstanding the complaint of libertarians that this interpretation goes beyond the Constitution, the language is what it is. Like many of the sweeping statements of the documents of Vatican II, this clause is broad and general in its scope. It sits in the Constitution waiting for the continued integration of economic activities foreseeable even in the late eighteenth century. It provides for the gradual expansion of federal power as commerce (itself a broad term) becomes more interconnected. Not surprising to anyone even generally familiar with Commerce Clause cases over the past century, a majority of the Supreme Court found the Obamacare law within the vast scope permitted to regulate commerce.

If this is not enough of a virtually blank check, the Commerce Clause, along with the other enumerated powers, is supplemented by a sweeping authorization of power to enact other laws "necessary and proper for carrying into Execution the foregoing Powers *and all other Powers vested by this Constitution in the Government of the United States.*"[35] To argue that the vast powers accumulated by the federal government over our nation's history are unconstitutional is about as logically impossible as arguing that the hermeneutic of continuity shows that Vatican II is reconcilable with Tradition. The Vatican II documents are just too ambiguous to *require* a Traditional doctrine. In the same manner, the Constitution is intentionally worded with equal breadth so as to preclude a restrictive interpretation of mere limited powers.

Now, do not misunderstand or misquote my argument. I am neither defending the virtually totalitarian power grab by our federal (and state) government nor the radically unjust and imprudent Obamacare law. Both are morally and legally illegitimate. Yet the liberal Enlightenment Constitution written in the spirit of John Locke is not the bulwark that will reverse such problems. *Adjutorium nostrum non in nomine Constitutionis sed in nomine Domini!*

35. This latter grant was used to invoke the general power of "sovereignty" of a national government to force government debt currency and fiat currency on its citizens in the Greenback legal tender cases following the Civil War.

"Our help is not in the name of the Constitution, but in the name of the Lord!" The continual accretion of power and the Obamacare law emblematic of it are wrong because they violate the constitution of creation, the eternal law, not a man-made substitute for it.

God is the source of all authority and law. Human positive laws, like the Constitution and Obamacare, have only the character of law to the extent they conform to the eternal law. One aspect of the divine constitution of creation that is violated by both is the moral principle of subsidiarity. Rooted in the fact that God desires rational creatures to participate in the eternal law through the use of their reason and free will (unlike animals that participate by instinct), God requires that human laws work toward the free and knowing obedience to the natural law by men. Where there is compulsion there is a defect of the capacity to freely participate in the eternal law through rational choice. Yet the coordination of human actions in society requires there be some level of compulsion by law. We must drive on the right side of the road in this country because order and safety require a decision be made by an authority. The Catholic understanding of authority neither despises authority nor exalts it excessively. The proper exercise of authority lies in the tension between rational coordination by rules and scope for the exercise of the reasonable will of individual men. Subsidiarity is the keystone of this tension. The principle requires that any authority only make rules with respect to actions that can only be addressed by that authority, leaving matters that can be competently dealt with by lesser authorities or individuals to their determination. God provided for this form of trickle-down authority throughout human history. He makes laws for Adam, who makes laws for Eve. God instructs Moses who rules the people of Israel through the seventy-two elders selected from the twelve smaller tribes. Christ establishes a Church that transmits authority from himself to Peter, to the Apostles, to the disciples and so on down to the properly formed human conscience. God's rule is one of graduated authority flowing from God down to the lowest level.

Applying this principle to medical care, we see that medical treatment operates directly on the health of individuals. Although the health of an individual usually has only an indirect effect on the common good of a larger national community, it always has a direct effect on the individual and therefore is a matter best dealt with as closely to the individual level as possible. This means that healthcare decisions should be regulated by the individual, the family, or the immediate local community. There are exceptions. A massive, highly contagious epidemic may shift the balance to directly affect the common good of a larger community. In such a case, a larger level of government may have to enact laws (such as quarantines) to safeguard the common good of the larger community. Nevertheless, routine healthcare is best decided and regulated as closely to the individuals affected as possible.

The problem with our nation's healthcare system is precisely that it already, before Obamacare, did not work that way. It should not be a *national system*, but it had become such long before the Obamacare law was introduced in Congress. Healthcare decisions are taken and regulated far from the *specific* patient and *his* doctor. These decisions are taken by the massive national insurance companies from their desks hundreds of feet above sea level and often thousands of miles away. Decisions on which medicines should be used or tests run are dictated by rules made in the board rooms of these superpowers. Medical care has been nationalized and removed from the local decision-making level in a process beginning around the end of World War II.

Most who object to Obamacare as "national" healthcare do not realize that we have national healthcare already. They object on the grounds that it is unconstitutional for the federal government to nationalize healthcare but have no objection to massive corporations or even large state governments doing the same things. As a case in point, I attended a lecture by the Oklahoma Attorney General in which he described his decision to join the lawsuit currently before the Supreme Court. He made quite clear that he did not actually object to the substance of the Obamacare mandatory insurance requirement but only to the federal government's invocation of the Commerce Clause to implement it. He repeatedly stated that he would have no objection if Oklahoma had passed the same law for its state or even, in fact, if the federal government had done so under a different enumerated power (such as the taxing power).

Such objections appear unprincipled in light of Catholic doctrine on subsidiarity. It is not the exercise of legislative power at a too-distant level that is being argued, but rather a legal technicality over which organ of distant conglomerate power should do so: the state, the federal, or the corporate.

As I predicted, after millions of taxpayer dollars (that neither the federal government nor the twenty-six states possess) were spent, the Supreme Court did not strike down Obamacare as unconstitutional. It really cannot do so as long as the Constitution is in place. The reason is that the Constitution not only includes broad and ambiguous grants of power to the federal government, it specifically *excludes* the principles of law that are the only real protection against tyranny: the law of God. The Constitution arrogantly declares itself to "be the supreme Law of the Land," to which the Prince of the heavenly hosts would reply, *Quis ut Deus?* There is only one Supreme Law of the Land, and that is the law promulgated by the only Supreme Being. The Constitution defiantly rejects the law of God and then imprisons it behind a man-made wall of separation of Church and state. The law of God is to be separate from and irrelevant to the Supreme Law of the Land. The only true check on human totalitarian authority, whether exercised by a state, the federal government, or a massive corporation, has been reduced to irrelevance. The true defense against unjust exercises of authority is the eternal, natural, and divine law of the Creator of the universe, Christ the King. Squabbling over strained interpretations of flawed liberal documents composed "in the bright morning of liberal thought" (to use the phrase of one of America's most pre-eminent constitutional scholars) will not reverse the problems facing our nation.[36] Only a return to the acceptance of Christ the King, and all the political and legal restraints on the abuse of authority that such acceptance provides, will.

36. Rebecca L. Brown, "How Constitutional Theory Found Its Soul: The Contributions of Ronald Dworkin," in *Exploring Law's Empire: The Jurisprudence of Ronald Dworkin*, ed. Scott Hershovitz (Oxford: Oxford University Press, 2006), 51.

To Love Our Country; To Reject Its Errors: Teaching American Political History to Our Children

At this point in this section on politics, you might be feeling a bit overwhelmed or discouraged. The prior chapters have focused on identifying many of the philosophical errors underlying the political organization of our country and some of the practical consequences flowing from them. You might be wondering: "In light of these problems, can we still love our country?" The answer to this question is definitely yes, as long as we properly understand what we mean by loving our country. Second, the conclusions of the prior chapters may lead educators, in schools and at home, to wonder how we approach teaching our children about the history of our country while avoiding the Scylla of false admiration for error as well as the Charybdis of contempt for the good aspects of our nation and its history. This chapter will explore answers to these concerns.

Pope St. Pius X warned us against the dangers of modernism more than 100 years ago. One of the most dangerous aspects of this heresy is its insidiousness. Since the Modernist mixes truth with a degree of error, it is difficult to repel his inroads. Yet as the late Fr. Hugh Thwaites, SJ, often warned, if someone makes a cake and laces it with poison, it might be 90 percent good ingredients and only 10 percent poison, but the poison will kill you anyway.

It is this subtle technique we must be on guard against in our school curricula, be they traditional Catholic schools or home school programs. If we are going to all the effort to run a home school or start and support a traditional Catholic school, we need to be careful not to waste these heroic efforts by letting the smoke of Satan enter through a fissure. We are likely vigilant with our catechism texts and lessons, being careful to root out any heterodoxy. Yet there is a hidden danger in other subjects that need to be watched with equal vigor. Let us focus on history. History, and American history in particular, can present difficult questions with regard to what information to present when and in what manner so as to cultivate in our children a proper understanding and love for our country, but without coaxing them to drink of the stream of nationalism and Americanism.

This involves a fine line that must be walked with care. We need to avoid turning our children into bitter anti-Americans just as much as we need to avoid the danger of raising nationalists steeped in the errors of Americanism condemned by Leo XIII in *Testem Benevolentiae Nostrae.* The fine line rests on the virtue of patriotism. You might be asking: What is the distinction? Is not nationalism a synonym of patriotism? They are related words but actually distinct concepts. The Oxford English Dictionary defines patriotism as "love of or devotion to one's country." Nationalism is defined as either "[a]dvocacy of or support for the interests of one's own nation, especially to the exclusion or detriment of the interests of other nations" or "[t]he doctrine that certain nations (as contrasted with individuals) are the object of divine election." The following comment under nationalism in the OED is helpful to draw out the distinction: "Whereas patriotism usually refers to a general sentiment, nationalism now usually refers to a specific ideology, especially one expressed through political activism." The etymology of patriotism comes from the Greek for love of one's father or clan, whereas nation is derived from the Latin for race or gentiles. Fathers or clan has a more personal connotation, linking the individual to a close familial association, whereas race or gentiles are more generic and impersonal (think of a family reunion as opposed to a committee meeting of a federal government agency).

As can be seen from the definitions, patriotism involves love of the country (natural beauty and resources) and family ties and history that God has given us to aid in our path of salvation. Nationalism involves an advocacy of a nation with respect to other nations, advocacy of the interests of one nation as opposed to another. To support this inherently competitive uncharitable zeal, the makers of nationalism need to create myths and legends that will arouse the passions. A patriotic person can be honest about history—good and bad—of his region of the world, for he loves it not for what makes it better than other countries but for what it is, much in the same way a parent can love his child without denying his faults. A nationalist must engage in glorification of the nation to maintain the impulse of manifest destiny.

How does this understanding of patriotism and nationalism

affect our history curriculum? We need to devise a strategy for presenting the facts of the discovery, formation, and establishment of the United States in a way that does not promote uncritical bias towards the form of government produced but at the same time instills a love of country and people. How do we discuss the Masonic liberal and revolutionary ideas, actions, and policies of a Thomas Jefferson, George Washington, or Patrick Henry? If we allow our children to imbibe the myths of these purported patriarchs that are more or less pervasive in nearly every school history textbook, only later to deflate them with the truth of history, we risk diminishing our own credibility with our children (were all those stories about the saints equally untrue?) as well as cultivating an unhealthy level of cynicism in our young. Yet, are our six- or eight-year-olds capable of being told all of the heresy and immoral strategy and tactics of these men when first presented with their history? This is the challenge of a country like ours with such an ambiguous prehistory and founding directly opposed to the historical principles of Christendom. America was a great source of new vigor and opportunity and of zeal for the spread of the faith to millions of God's creatures. The now much maligned phrase "gold, glory, and Gospel" is apt. Yet this glory was co-opted and diverted by the Masonic and liberal forces of the eighteenth and nineteenth centuries to spread the poison of anti-Catholicism, anti-monarchism, and the false "rights" of man. Ambiguity is difficult for adults to live with; even more so for children.

The situation is analogous to the dilemma of modern Christmas, or as the world now calls it, "Holiday [of your choice] Season." How do we teach our children to love the great feast of Christmas while explaining and combating the vices of materialism, greed, consumerism at the heart of the Santa Claus festival of getting? To bury our heads and pretend this sewer is not all around us is insufficient, but to rant and condemn Santa and Rudolph unceasingly will destroy the joy. Likewise, to utterly ignore the facts of our country's past does a disservice to our children, but to overindulge in the critique runs the risk of strangling the feelings of devotion to history and familial ties we need nurture to arrive at a balanced Catholic worldview.

If you were expecting precise directions for walking this fine line,

I apologize that this is beyond my ability. The specific path must vary from grade level to grade level and even from school to school. We must first start by recognizing the precipice we walk on so we can carefully scrutinize the books used and prepare in advance of, and not in reaction to, the hard questions they will ask. "So Dad, was George Washington a good guy?" or "If America was part of England, why could it just leave?" They will ask these and we must be prepared to give a balanced answer that avoids the untruthful glorification of ambiguity as well as the wholesale rejection of it. In short, we must inspire patriotism while discouraging nationalism. We must encourage love of the goodness of our country—how its vast natural resources reflect the providence of God, and how resourceful and enthusiastic Americans have been over the years—while not unduly glorifying the political model promoted and implemented by Freemasons in Philadelphia—the promotion of the idea that sovereignty comes from the people and not God, the separation of the Church from the State, and the glorification of unbridled liberty. Thank God we believe that nothing is impossible with God! Our Lady of Guadalupe, Empress of the Americas, pray for us and inspire us!

Toward the Common Good: Voting Obligations When Trapped Between Scylla and Charybdis

As we noted in the previous section of this chapter, we must walk a fine line between embracing the errors of our liberal political system and abandoning our political nature through despair. In a nation where public elections serve as a means for designating those who should govern society under the eternal law through the natural law. What principles should inform a Catholic's interest in and perspective on elections? The most recent presidential election presented a very difficult choice to Catholics. On one side there was a rabidly liberal president who was clearly in favor of all the goals of the City of Man. He continues to work at the destruction of family, economy, and nation. The Republicans could only put forward a moderate liberal who at most would simply delay much of the evil proposed by President Obama. What was a committed Catholic to do faced with such a choice? This section of the chapter will take a deeper and more long-term view of the election choices than merely squabbling over electoral strategizing. Although you will not find any candidate or party endorsements, you will find some negative endorsements.

The first principle of Catholic political teaching is that, in accordance with man's social nature, we have an obligation in legal justice to work for the common good. In pursuing our own individual good we must do so in harmony with the common good of society. One of the most unfortunate consequences of the modern pluralist society in which we find ourselves is that the reigning cultural ethos runs completely contrary to this principle. To most people, politics is a big marketplace where we engage in attempting to get the most for our votes. Politicians and the mass media play on this false inclination constantly. The refrain from the Reagan era is typical: "Are *you* better off than *you* were four years ago?" (emphasis added). The Catholic perspective is, rather, is *society* more virtuous than four years ago? Americans are taught from an early age effectively to sell their vote to the highest bidder who can promise the most personal gain. It is this phenomenon that led a majority of nominally Catholic Americans voting for President Obama both elections arguing that, although he advocated intrinsically evil actions, he would fix the economy and improve *my* economic prospects. This electoral shopping for individual benefit is completely alien to Catholic political teaching. It is for this reason that no Catholic can morally vote for a candidate like President Obama. Even if his promises to bring prosperity to the economy were true, no Catholic could accept his Faustian bargain. From increasing government subsidies for abortion and contraception to promoting and rewarding unnatural aping of marriages, etc., the president made clear that he would ruthlessly continue to pursue the enactment of laws and policies directly opposed to the divine and natural laws. He is not merely suggesting a prudent toleration of some evils but rather the governmentally funded promotion of them as well as mandates that all must participate in sin (e.g., the administration's mandate to provide contraceptive coverage in insurance). No matter how many chickens he promised in every pot, that is a bargain no Catholic could accept.

With easy cases like President Obama off the table, what principles should inform Catholic voting decisions for candidates who are not blatantly pursuing evil? Again, the starting point is the obligation to pursue the common good. Although this is an absolute principle (meaning that one can never intentionally act contrary to the common good for the sake of individual aggrandizement), the means of acting in accordance with this principle are not always identical. What acts are required by a commitment to the common good vary across time and geography. In the context of electoral politics, we can examine another easy case, the mirror image of the Obama case. If hypothetically speaking there were a candidate for public office who espoused a completely Catholic governing program and whom we could with moral certainty believe was honestly committed to such an agenda (i.e., it was not merely empty rhetoric targeted at securing the Catholic vote), then a Catholic would be obligated to vote for such a candidate. To fulfill the requirements of such obligations, such a candidate must not merely be a nominal Catholic nor even advocate some laws favorable to the Catholic position. He must stand for nothing less than the establishment in all institutions of our society of the Kingship of Christ. There has not been a candidate of either major party (or even the nationally known minor parties) who meets this standard of being integrally Catholic in living memory, if ever. Any candidate who not only accepts but applauds the current secular anti-Christian pluralist organization of our country no matter how many good policies he supports is an integrally Catholic candidate. Not even a candidate who would claim to personally believe in the Social Reign of Christ the King but oppose its public implementation can be considered integrally Catholic. Thus, any person, be he priest, bishop, or lay person, who tries to tell you that you are morally obliged under pain of sin to vote in conscience for any of the type of candidate on offer lately is wrong. This is the second negative endorsement: no candidate currently capable of being placed on a national ticket can garner mandatory Catholic support.

Given that Catholics are prohibited morally from voting for a candidate such as President Obama and that no integrally Catholic candidate on the national scale has run or is likely to run for president in the near future, what are Catholics to do in fulfilling their obligation to work for the common good? We have reached a point where there are no definitive answers. The extremes of President Obama and a hypothetical integrally Catholic candidate require specific reactions. The cases in between these two poles are more complex and require a more nuanced analysis. This task is to be governed by the virtue of prudence, which is the virtue by which we apply principles to variable and contingent factual situations. Where there is no obviously clear moral obligation that the will can easily choose, our will must be guided by an informed intellect acting with the virtue of prudence to select the most appropriate morally permissible option.

To engage in this analysis we must understand the Catholic principle of double effect. This principle has been articulated by Catholic moral theologians as a guide to assist us in making difficult choices not involving simple moral/immoral distinctions. When we are presented with a course of action that will accomplish some good but will also cause some evil, we must use these rules to guide our prudent evaluation. The rules demonstrate when it is morally permissible to do an action to accomplish some good but that will cause some evil. The three requirements are:

1. The specific act being done must not be intrinsically evil, that is, an act that in itself is contrary to the divine and natural laws and can never be done without sin (mortal or venial).

2. We must only intend (meaning we desire or wish) the good outcome of the action not the evil consequences.

3. There must be a due proportion between the good achieved and the evil consequences.

These three rules can be more easily understood in the context of an example. There is a doctor in a rural remote location treating two patients with a fatal snake bite. He has only one dose of anti-venom. By the time an additional dose arrives it will be beyond any doubt too late. The choice the doctor must make is to whom to administer the only dose of anti-venom. He knows that if he gives it to one patient, the other patient will certainly die. The death of a patient is an evil outcome. The doctor hesitates, fearing that by choosing one to receive the dose he is causing the death of the other. The rules of double effect help to resolve his scruple. First, the action he contemplates is not intrinsically evil. His action is the administration of a medicine that is a morally neutral action (one capable of being good or bad depending on the circumstances). Secondly, he does not intend or wish the death of the patient not receiving the venom; he merely knows it will occur without intending it. To understand this better, it would be immoral for him to make the choice if it were based on the fact that one of the two patients was the doctor's enemy and he gave the medicine to the one patient so that his enemy would die. Such a hypothetical illustrates the failure of the second rule in that this doctor actually intends the death of his enemy. Thus, the ability to choose an action carrying with it an evil effect is that the evil effect not be intended.

The third rule requires proportionality among the effects. By giving the medicine to one patient and not the other, one person will be saved and one will die, which—absent other facts—are proportional outcomes.

You may ask: Accepting that he can morally choose one patient and assuming the doctor does not want one of the two men to die, how does he make a choice as to which he gives the anti-venom? The second rule does not require a particular method of choice but merely eliminates an impermissible method, i.e., desiring the death of one. Some permissible reasons for making the choice, depending on the circumstances, might include the following. One patient is in better health and thus has a higher chance of responding to the medicine. One man has a large family to support and the other has no dependents. One man volunteers to forgo the medicine. Finally, if there appears no rational basis to choose between the two, the doctor could select one at random. Any of these methods would be morally acceptable. What is important is that the analysis is one of proportionality.

Before continuing we must distinguish the principle of double effect from the immoral principle of choosing the lesser of two evils, which is sometimes confused with it.[37] The principle of the lesser of

37. Occasionally some people unversed in moral philosophy mistakenly use the phrase the "lesser of two evils" to refer to the principle of double effect. This is a failure of language and meaning, but given the evil nature of the false principle, it can lead to confusion in those who hear the false theory advocated accidentally.

two evils advocated by some forms of utilitarianism states that one may choose to do an evil or immoral act if that act will accomplish a lesser evil than its alternative. In a certain sense the lesser of two evils principle is a mutated form of the principle of double effect. The mutation consists in omitting the first rule: one can never choose an intrinsically evil act. An example of a lesser of two evils analysis can assist in seeing the difference. A medical student is told that in order to graduate he must either perform five abortions or perform one abortion and write a twenty-page report about the one abortion. The student chooses the second option because the first will definitely result in the death of five innocent children but the second will kill only one and thus represents the lesser of two evils. His choice is morally wrong. The act of abortion (deliberately killing a person in gestation) is intrinsically evil. Even if choosing option two can be seen as avoiding killing four additional lives, the act itself is immoral and thus under the first rule of double effect cannot be done. Catholics may never choose to do a wholly evil action simply because a more evil option is an alternate possibility. In the described example the medical student must refuse both choices. Applying the lesser of two evils analysis to electoral politics would result in an immoral choice if one were deciding between two wholly bad candidates. Thus hypothetically, if Hitler were running against Stalin and one knew all the facts about what they would do, one could not vote for Stalin even if he honestly believed Stalin would do less evil than Hitler. Both are completely evil choices and thus the only moral choice is to choose neither.

Now let us apply this understanding to electoral politics. Can a Catholic vote for a candidate who will do some good (perhaps restrict the number of legal abortions) but also some evil (fund contraception, for example). This is a situation calling for double effect analysis. Voting is not in and of itself good or evil; it is morally neutral. Its morality depends on the circumstances (for whom do you vote and for what intention?). Thus, the choice—voting for a certain candidate—is not intrinsically evil and thus passes the first rule. Secondly, the voter must not intend or wish the evil that the candidate will bring about. For example, if the Catholic wants to engage in the immoral use of contraception and votes for the candidate so that his immoral contracepting will be paid for by the government, he may not vote for the candidate. Assuming the voter definitely does not vote for the candidate for the intention of advancing the evil the candidate will do, the second rule is satisfied. Finally, we come to the third rule, which is the most difficult to apply in this context. It requires a prudential analysis of the proportionality between the intended good and unintended evil outcomes. Is the good of reducing the number of abortions proportionately greater than the evil of making the use of contraceptives (which may be abortifacients) more widely available and affordable? This is an evaluation on which we may have legitimate differences of opinion. In fact, the analysis is even more difficult because we are dealing with predictions about what elected officials will in fact do. Even if the candidate promises to reduce abortions, we may doubt his sincerity (based on his prior record) or the ability to actually do what he promises even if honestly desired by the candidate. Since we are dealing with predictions about future actions and possibilities, it is possible to have different morally acceptable evaluations of those possibilities. For example, given the prior hypothetical of a candidate promising fewer abortions but more free contraceptives, one might conclude the candidates' ability to actually pass a law reducing abortions through a Congress dominated by abortion fanatics is very slim, but his ability to pass a law funding contraception is very strong. Thus, on balance it seems more likely than not that his evil position (funding contraceptives) will succeed and his good position (limiting abortion) will not. If one reached such a conclusion, the third rule would prohibit so voting.

The application of the proportionality analysis is also further complicated because the election of a candidate is likely to have many more consequences than just two (as in our prior example). It is more often a large matrix of consequences that must be considered. An important consideration for Catholics often omitted in this analysis, however, is also the support of a morally flawed system. If the entire electoral system is based on false metaphysical and moral principles, participation in the system by voting may unintentionally further the legitimization of the false system. Again let me give an example. If one were in communist Russia, a government system based on evil principles of atheistic communism, and were permitted to vote in an election between two candidates, one of whom, as unlikely as it may seem, was not integrally evil, and this candidate actually proposed some good (perhaps reversing some gravely evil laws of the regime), one could conclude that even if some good would be done by this candidate, one would cause proportionally more evil by participating in the election and thereby supporting the operation of an immoral Communist form of government. Put another way, the short-term gains of this hypothetical candidate's good might be disproportionate to the long-term harm of delaying the collapse of this immoral form of government. This moral concern is legitimate and would need to be factored into the decision of whether or not to vote for this morally mixed candidate.

The American political order is not as pervasively evil as a communist state but is more of a mixed system. Notwithstanding some good principles, such as a commitment to procedural justice, the American political system is based on some erroneous principles of Enlightenment liberalism, such as authority coming from the people and not God, and the separation of the true Church and the state. Thus, one of the factors of unintended consequences that should be weighed in the proportionality analysis is the implicit support of false systemic principles by voting. By this I do not mean that a Catholic could never vote in our current system. Under double effect, voting for an integrally Catholic candidate proposing to correct the erroneous aspects of the system could be morally permissible notwithstanding that participating in the election might have some legitimizing influence on the unreformed system. The good the integrally Catholic candidate would do if successful would be proportionately greater than the temporary legitimization of the flawed system.

As we concluded, the virtue of prudence is necessary to survive the contingent economy. We must navigate the financial and banking system guided by Catholic principles, neither embracing and intentionally profiting from its injustices nor throwing up our hands and letting our family starve because of the confusing mess. Likewise, we cannot embrace the errors of popular sovereignty, liberalism, and choosing the lesser of two evils to get a better deal for ourselves. Yet we cannot neglect our duties in legal justice to work for the common good. Even if all we can do to advance the common good is refuse to vote for any unacceptable candidates, we must intentionally make some choice for the common good. What that choice will be in any circumstance or election will be a matter of prudentially evaluating the circumstances. Our political system is dominated by liberalism and a rejection of Christ the King, but that does not mean all political systems must be that way. Despair and presumption about politics are both opposed to prudence.

Conclusion

Our survey of the commonwealth from the foundation of the family to the heights of politics has shown that the City of Man is currently dominating the City of God on all levels. The constitution, essence, and authority structure of the family is under assault. In response, Catholics must not only speak the truth about the nature of marriage and the real differences between men and women but also must live according to those principles. A family is founded on the marriage of a husband and wife for the primary purpose of begetting, rearing, and educating children. All other ends of marriage and the marital act must support in some way this primary end of marriage. The education of children must form the whole child—physically, intellectually, and spiritually. The parents bear a God-given responsibility and authority to form the fruits of their union in the ways of truth, goodness, and beauty. An abstract intellectualism must be avoided as much as a pagan obsession with sports or puritanical repression of beauty and art.

In the marketplace, false conceptions of the very basic tools of economic activity are in wide circulation. Money, wealth, and property are distorted and corrupted by an economic liberalism that falsely presents this basic human activity as lacking moral dimensions. Economic liberalism rationalizes greed for filthy lucre by denying human choice in household management, purporting to substitute fixed scientific laws to which we are merely slavish pawns. For the Western tradition from Aristotle to modern Catholic Social Doctrine, the art, not science, of managing the temporal affairs of our households is a fully human activity subject to the divine and natural law and their principles of justice. Our economy is falling apart primarily because our households are not well managed. Generations have been formed in a way not founded on the Kingship of Christ and his laws. Usury and unjust pricing dominate our economy and are papered over by an obscuring paper-based system of debt money created in exchange for healthy profits by a government banking cartel that regulates itself.

If families and the marketplace have rejected the Kingship of Christ, it is no surprise that His Reign is also rejected in the governance of the perfect society of the commonwealth. All political parties reject the Kingship of Christ and for many years offer at best a candidate who may be tolerated under the moral principle of double effect. All authority is seen to rest on the will of the masses rather than on God. If a political ruler attempts to resist laws that offend God's natural and divine law, the people simply nullify the authority they falsely claim to have conferred. The most that can be achieved by exercising any vote in such a system is some marginal improvement on one issue at the expense of toleration of a proportionate evil. The political community is built on the family, the household, and economic associations. The whole is not greater than its parts. If liberty is claimed to redefine marriage and pursue wealth without restraint, obviously such domestic and economic liberalism will emerge as political liberalism. If Christ's law is rejected by the component communities of the commonwealth, it is not surprising that a fundamental agreement on the nature of justice necessary for the survival of a commonwealth is atrophied to the point of the dissolution we see around us. Once again, the liberals come forth offering to inoculate the real problem by injecting vaccines cultured in liberalism. Nullification of federal law is not demanded because that law violates the natural and divine law. Rather, it is promoted in the name of a false liberty rooted in popular sovereignty, a liberty that was merely a myth tolerated to ensure submission to a Constitution that explicitly denied the supremacy of states' rights.

At every level there is a crisis of authority because the source of authority has been under attack for too long. As Pope Leo XIII observed as early as 1881, the power of authority

> resides solely in God, the Creator and Legislator of all things; and it is necessary that those who exercise it should do it as having received it from God.... And this is clearly seen in every kind of power. [T]he authority of fathers of families preserves a certain

> impressed image and form of the authority which is in God, of Whom all paternity in heaven and earth is named" (Eph. 3:15). But in this way different kinds of authority have between them wonderful resemblances, since whatever there is of government and authority, its origin is derived from one and the same Creator and Lord of the World who is God.[1]

As Pope Pius XI understood, the problem affecting family life, economic life, and political life is the rejection of the Kingship of Christ at every level. "Nor is there any difference between the individual and the family or the state; for all men, whether collectively or individually, are under the dominion of Christ."[2] In the late nineteenth century, Leo XIII concluded that the "long-continued and most bitter war waged against the divine authority" had reached "the culmination to which it was tending, the common danger, namely, of human society."[3]

If this war has reached every level of the commonwealth from the home to the halls of political power, we can see the cause of disintegration at all levels. Yet we need not despair. One age of history always gives way to a new one until it reaches its fulfillment. What form that next age will take depends on the principles on which it rests. The republic of Cicero gave way to the Roman Empire, which spread Roman law throughout the world. Yet that empire had within itself the seeds of its own destruction. It was built not on the eternal law vaguely glimpsed by Cicero but on the human authority of emperors who thought they were gods. That empire eventually began to crumble under the weight of human power seeking to divinize itself. Saint Augustine commented on the transition from the empire to a new society, and he attempted to articulate the principles on which that new order must be built to reflect the City of God rather than the empire of men crumbling around him. The City of God flourished for a period when harmony existed between the soul and the members of the body politic. Yet as Leo XIII noted, a long-fought war was initiated to kill the body politic by separating

1. Leo XIII, *Diuturnum*, no. 11.
2. Pius XI, *Quas Primas*, no. 18.
3. Leo XIII, *Diuturnum*, no. 1.

the body from the soul, the family from its nature, economics from justice, politics from the common good, man from God.

Understanding the principles on which family, economic, and political life must be reconstituted is necessary if our homes, our economy, and our commonwealth are to be reconstituted in the peace of Christ in the Kingdom of Christ. This book has argued for the organic integration of all three societies. The Kingdom of Christ cannot exist solely within the family while the kingdom of unjust debt money, usury, and greed reigns in the economy and unbridled liberty in politics. The consensus on *jus* (law and justice) that Cicero understood as indispensable for a commonwealth must include the source of all law and justice, Christ the King.

Works Cited

Books / Bible Verses / Cases / Laws / Dictionaries

1 Thess. 4: 2–3, 6.

12 U.S.C. §411 (1934).

31 U.S.C. §5103 (1982).

Ambrose. *De officiis ministrorum*. http://www.newadvent.org/fathers/.

Aquinas, Thomas. *Commentary on Aristotle's Politics*. Translated by Richard J. Regan. Indianapolis: Hackett Publishing Company, 2007.

———. *Commentary on the Nichomachean Ethics*. Translated by C.J. Litzinger, OP. South Bend, IN: Dumb Ox Books, 1964.

———. "De Regno." In *Aquinas: Selected Political Writings*. Edited by A.P. d'Entrèves. Translated by J.G. Dawson. 1948. http://dhspriory.org/thomas/DeRegno.htm

———. *Summa Theologica*. 2nd ed. Translated by Fathers of the English Dominican Province. London: Burns, Oates & Washburne, 1920. http://www.newadvent.org/summa/.

———. "Prologue." In "The Two Precepts of Charity." In *Opera Omnia*. Edited by Roberto Busa, SJ. Stuttgart: Frommann-Holzboog, 1980.

Aristotle. "Politics." In *Commentary on Aristotle's Politics*. Translated by Richard J. Regan. Indianapolis: Hackett Publishing Company, 2007.

———. *The Basic Works of Aristotle*. Edited by Richard McKeon. Translated by Benjamin Jowett. New York: Random House, 1941.

Augustine. *City of God*. http://www.newadvent.org/fathers/1201.htm.

Belloc, Hilaire. *Europe and the Faith*. New York: Paulist Press, 1920.

Benedict XIV. *Vix Pervenit*. Vatican City: Libreria Editrice Vaticana, 1745.

Bernard of Clairvaux. *De consideratione*. Translated by George Lewis. Oxford: Oxford University Press, 1908.

Black's Law Dictionary. Edited by Bryan Garner. 8th ed. Eagan, MN: West, 2004.

Brown, Rebecca L. "How Constitutional Theory Found Its Soul: The Contributions of Ronald Dworkin." In *Exploring Law's Empire: The Jurisprudence of Ronald Dworkin*. Edited by Scott Hershovitz. Oxford: Oxford University Press, 2006.

Brown v. Entertainment Merchants Association, 131 S.Ct. 2729 (2011).

Budziszewski, J. *The Line through the Heart.* Chicago: ISI Books, 2009.
Bureau of Labor Statistics. "Labor Force Statistics from the Current Population Survey," Civilian Labor Force Participation Rate.
Catechism of the Council of Trent. Charlotte, NC: TAN Books, 1982.
Cicero, Marcus Tullius. *On the Commonwealth and On the Laws.* Edited by James E.G. Zetzel. Cambridge, MA: Cambridge University Press, 1999.
Coogan, Gertrude M. *Money Creators: Who Creates Money? Who Should Create It?* 1935. http://www.scribd.com/doc/.
De Lorris, Guillaume and Jean de Meun. *The Romance of the Rose.* Translated by Frances Horgan. Oxford: Oxford University Press, 2009.
De Mattei, Roberto. *The Second Vatican Council: An Unwritten Story.* Translated by Michael J. Miller. Fitzwilliam: Loreto Publications, 2012.
Dempsey, Fr. Bernard W. *Interest and Usury.* Washington, DC: American Council on Public Affairs, 1943.
De Roover, Raymond. *San Bernardino of Siena and Sant'Antonino of Florence: The Two Great Economic Thinkers of the Middle Ages.* Boston: Baker Library, 1967.
De Tocqueville, Alexis. *Democracy in America.* http://www.gutenberg.org/files/.
Dickinson, John. *The Statesman's Book of John of Salisbury.* New York: A.A. Knopf, 1927.
Duick v. Toyota Motor Sales, U.S.A., Inc., 131 Cal.Rptr.3d 514 (2011).
Eccles. 26:29.
Eccles. 27:2.
Fahey, Denis. *The Mystical Body of Christ in the Modern World.* 3rd ed. Palmdale, CA: Christian Book Club of America, 1994.
———. *Money Manipulation and Social Order.* Palmdale, CA: Christian Book Club of America, 1944.
Fanfani, Amintore. *Catholicism, Protestantism, and Capitalism.* Norfolk, VA: IHS Press, 2002.
Federal Reserve Act, Pub. L. No. 63–43, 38 Stat. 251 (1913).
Finnis, John. *Natural Law and Natural Rights.* Oxford: Oxford University Press, 2011.
Forman, John. *Making America Work.* Baltimore, MD: The Urban Institute Press, 2006.
Fortescue, John. "De natura legis naturae." In *Medieval Political Ideas.* Translated by Ewart Lewis. Oxford: Routledge, 2012.
Giles of Rome. *De ecclesiastica potestate.* Translated by R.W. Dyson. Suffolk: Boydell and Brewer, Ltd., 1986.
Gratian. "Decretum." In *The Treatise on Laws.* Translated by Augustine

Thompson and James Gordley. Washington, DC: Catholic University Press, 1994.

Gregory IX. "Naviganti." In *Readings in Western Civilization, Vol. 4: Medieval Europe*. Edited by Julius Kirshner and Karl F. Morrison. Chicago: University of Chicago Press, 1986.

Grenier, Henri. *Thomistic Philosophy: Moral Philosophy*. Vol. 4. Charlottetown, Prince Edward Island: St. Dunstan's University, 1950.

Hammond, Colleen. *Dressing with Dignity*. Charlotte, NC: TAN Books, 2005.

Henry of Hesse. "De contractibus." In Gerson, *Opera Omnia*. 4 vols. Cologne, 1483–4.

Hollingsworth v. Perry, 133 S.Ct. 2652 (2013).

Innocent IV. "In Civitate." In *Commentaria apparatus quinque libros decretalium*. Minerva GmbH, 1570.

James 5:1–5.

John Paul II. *Centesimus Annus*. Vatican City: Libreria Editrice Vaticana, 1991.

Justinian. "Code." In *Justinian: The Civil Law*. Translated by S.P. Scott. Cincinnati: The Central Trust Company, 1932.

———. "Digest." In *Justinian: The Civil Law*. Translated by S.P. Scott. Cincinnati: The Central Trust Company, 1932.

Kennedy, John F. Address to the Greater Houston Ministerial Association. September 12, 1960, Houston, TX. http://www.americanrhetoric.com/speeches/jfkhoustonministers.html.

Kozinski, Thaddeus J. *The Political Problem of Religious Pluralism: And Why Philosophers Can't Solve It*. New York: Lexington Books, 2010.

Langholm, Odd. *Economics in the Medieval Schools*. Leiden, The Netherlands: E.J. Brill, 1992.

Leo XIII. *Arcanum*. Vatican City: Libreria Editrice Vaticana, 1880.

———. *Diuturnum*. Vatican City: Libreria Editrice Vaticana, 1880.

———. *Immortale Dei*. Vatican City: Libreria Editrice Vaticana, 1885.

———. *Rerum Novarum*. Vatican City: Libreria Editrice Vaticana, 1891.

Lombard, Peter. "Sententiae." In *IV Libros Distinctae*. 4 vols. Grottaferrata, Italy: Collegium S. Bonaventurae ad Claras Aquas, 1971–1981.

Magna Carta, http://www.constitution.org/eng/magnacar.htm.

Matt. 19:16–24.

McCall, Brian M. *The Church and the Usurers: Unprofitable Lending for the Modern Economy*. Washington, DC: Sapientia Press, 2013.

Merriam-Webster Online Dictionary. http://www.merriam-webster.com/dictionary/endow.

Noonan, Jr., John T. *The Scholastic Analysis of Usury.* Boston: Harvard University Press, 1957.
Pius IX. *Syllabus of Errors.* Vatican City: Libreria Editrice Vaticana, 1864.
Pius XI. *Casti Connubii.* Vatican City: Libreria Editrice Vaticana, 1930.
———. *Divini Illius Magistri.* Vatican City: Libreria Editrice Vaticana, 1929.
———. *Divini Redemptoris.* Vatican City: Liberia Editrice Vaticana, 1937.
———. *Quadragesimo Anno.* Vatican City: Libreria Editrice Vaticana, 1931.
———. *Quas Primas.* Vatican City: Libreria Editrice Vaticana, 1925.
———. *Ubi Arcano.* Vatican City: Libreria Editrice Vaticana, 1922.
"Political Economy." In Catholic Encyclopedia. http://www.newadvent.com/cathen/.
Rao, John. *Black Legends and the Light of the World: War of the Words and the Incarnate Word.* St. Paul, MN: Remnant Press, 2011.
Rziha, John. *Perfecting Human Actions: St. Thomas Aquinas On Human Participation in Eternal Law.* Washington, DC: Catholic University of America Press, 2009.
Shulman, Jeffrey. *The Constitutional Parent: Rights, Responsibilities, and the Enfranchisement of the Child.* New Haven: Yale University Press, 2014.
Suarez, Francisco. *Selection from Three Works.* Vol. 2. Edited by James Brown. Cambridge: Clarendon Press, 1944.
Tawney, R.H. *Religion and the Rise of Capitalism.* Mentor: 1953. First published 1926.
Tierney, Brian. *The Idea of Natural Rights.* Grand Rapids: Wm. B. Eerdmans Publishing Company, 1997.
———. *Medieval Poor Law: A Sketch of Canonical Theory and Its Application in England.* Berkeley: University of California Press, 1959.
Uniform Commercial Code §1–203.
Uniform Commercial Code §9-109(a)(1).
US Dept. of Housing and Urban Development Office of Policy Development Research. "U.S. Housing Market Conditions." *Hud User* (May 2008). http://www.huduser.org/periodicals/ushmc/spring.
US Federal Reserve. Federal Reserve Statistical Release: Money Stock Measures, June 2, 2011. http://www.federalreserve.gov/releases/h.
United States v. Windsor, 570 U.S. 12 (2013). http://www.supremecourt.gov/opinions/.
Wall Street Reform and Consumer Protection Act of 2009—Financial Stability Improvement Act of 2009, Pub. L. No: 111–203.

Weber, Max. *Economy and Sociology: An Outline of Interpretive Sociology.* Berkeley: University of California Press, 1978.

West, Christopher. *Theology of the Body Explained: A Commentary on John Paul II's Man and Woman He Created Them.* Dedham: Pauline Books & Media, 2007.

William of Rennes. "*Glossa* to *peccant* II." In *Summa Sancti Raymundi de Peniafort, Barcinonensis, Ordinis praedicator, De poenitentiaet matrimonio, cum glossis Ioannis de Friburgo.* Farnborough: Gregg Press, 1967.

Wood, Diana. *Medieval Economic Thought.* Cambridge: Cambridge University Press, 2004.

Woods, Jr., Thomas E. *The Church and the Market.* New York: Lexington Books, 2005.

———. *Nullification: How to Resist Federal Tyranny in the 21st Century.* Washington, DC: Regnery Publishing, 2010.

Articles / Letters / Law Reviews / Radio Shows

Anderson, Kerby. "Kerby Anderson's Point of View." Monday, July 19, 2010.

Aroney, Nicholas. "Subsidiarity, Federalism, and the Best Constitution: Aquinas on City, Province, and Empire." *Law and Philosophy* 26 (2007): 161.

Baldwin, John W. "The Medieval Theories of the Just Price: Romanists, Canonists, and Theologians in the Twelfth and Thirteenth Centuries." In *Transactions of the American Philosophical Society* 49, no.4 (1959): 1–92.

Blum, Christopher. "What is the Common Good?" *The Downside Review* 120 (2002): 86.

Engdahl, F. William. "Perhaps 60% of Today's Oil Price is Pure Speculation." *Global Research*, May 2, 2008. http://www.globalresearch.ca/perhaps-.

George, Francis Cardinal. "What are You Going to Give up This Lent." *Catholic New World*, February 26, 2012. http://www.catholicnewworld.com/cnwonline/.

Gordley, James. "Equality in Exchange." *California Law Review* 69 (1981): 1591.

Himmelberg, Charles, Christopher Mayer, and Todd Sinai. "Assessing High House Prices: Bubbles, Fundamentals, and Misperceptions."

Journal of Economic Perspectives 19 (2005): S67, note 4.

Jefferson, Thomas. Thomas Jefferson to Josephus B. Stuart. Letter, May 10, 1817. http://yamaguchy.com/library/jefferson/jeff_.

Jones, Robert P. "After DOMA, the Fading Future of Religious Opposition to Same-Sex Marriage." *Washington Post,* June 27, 2013. http://www.washingtonpost.com/blogs/on-faith/wp/.

Kahn, Ali. "The Evolution of Money: A Story of Constitutional Nullification." *University of Cincinnati Law Review* 67 (1999): 393.

Lawrence-Turner, Jody. "Lack of Emphasis on Cursive has Many Debating." *Spokesman Review,* April 15, 2012.

Lucas, Fred. "Obama Won't Rule Out Value Added Tax." CNS News, April 22, 2010. http://cnsnews.com/news/article/obama-won-t-rule-out-value-added-tax.

Madison, James. James Madison to Mathew Carey. Letter, July 27, 1831. http://memory.loc.gov/cgi-bin/query/r?ammem/mjmtext:@field(DOCID+@lit(jm.

———. James Madison to Nicholas P. Trist. Letter, December 1831. http://memory.loc.gov/cgi-bin/query/D?mjm:

McCall, Brian M. "The Architecture of Law: Building Law on a Solid Foundation: The Eternal and Natural Law." *Vera Lex* 10 (2009): 47.

———. "Consulting the Architect when Problems Arise: The Divine Law." *Georgetown Journal of Law and Public Policy* 9 (2011): 103.

———. "Gambling on Our Future: The Federal Government Fiddles while the Common Law Could Protect Our Future." *Arizona State Law Journal* (forthcoming).

Noonan, Jr., John T. "Authority, Usury, and Contraception." *Dublin Review* 509 (Autumn 1966): 201.

Pennington, Kenneth. "Lex Naturalis and Ius Naturale." *The Jurist* 68 (2008): 569.

Rush Limbaugh Show. "Deciphering the Sad Sack Story of a Classical Studies Scholar." November 1, 2011. http://www.rushlimbaugh.com/daily/.

Sanders, Bernie. "Wall Street Greed Fueling High Gas Prices." *CNN*, February 28, 2012. http://www.cnn.com/.

Siri, Giuseppe Cardinal. "Notification Concerning Men's Dress Worn by Women." Letter, 1960. http://www.olrl.org/virtues/pants.shtml.

Solomon, Lewis D. "Local Currency: A Legal and Policy Analysis." *Kansas Journal of Law & Public Policy* 5 (1996): 59.

Steyn, Mark. "Obama Goes Henry VIII on the Church." *Orange County Register,* February 10, 2012. http://www.ocregister.com/articles/church-.

Strobhar, Thomas. "Holy Porn." *New Oxford Review*, February 2008.
Tatarkiewicz, Wladyslaw, "Paradoxes of Perfection." *Dialectics & Humanism* 1 (1980): 77.
"Usury." *Dublin Review* (Autumn 1873): 323.
"Usury and the Canon Law." *Dublin Review* (Winter 1874): 69.
Von Hildebrand, Alice. "Christopher West's Ideas on Sexuality Ignore 'Tremendous Dangers.'" *Catholic News Agency*, May 12, 2009. http://www.catholicnewsagency.com/news/christopher_wests_ideas_on_sexuality_ignore_tremendous_dangers_alice_von_hildebrand_says/.
Zetter, Kim. "Court Approves Lawsuit Against Toyota over Cyberstalking Ad Stunt." *Wired*, September 12, 2011. http://www.wired.com/threatlevel/.

INDEX

Printed in Great Britain
by Amazon